GAMING UTOPIA

GAMING UTOPIA

Ludic Worlds in Art, Design, and Media

Claudia Costa Pederson

INDIANA UNIVERSITY PRESS

This book is a publication of

Indiana University Press
Office of Scholarly Publishing
Herman B Wells Library 350
1320 East 10th Street
Bloomington, Indiana 47405 USA

iupress.org

Manufactured in the United States of America
First printing 2021

Library of Congress Cataloging-in-Publication Data

Names: Pederson, Claudia Costa, author.
Title: Gaming utopia : ludic worlds in art, design, and media / Claudia
    Costa Pederson.
Description: Bloomington, Indiana : Indiana University Press, [2021] |
    Includes bibliographical references and index.
Identifiers: LCCN 2020026116 (print) | LCCN 2020026117 (ebook) | ISBN
    9780253054494 (paperback) | ISBN 9780253054487 (hardback) | ISBN
    9780253054500 (ebook)
Subjects: LCSH: Video games—Social aspects. | Utopias.
Classification: LCC GV1469.34.S52 P43 2021 (print) | LCC GV1469.34.S52
    (ebook) | DDC 794.8—dc23
LC record available at https://lccn.loc.gov/2020026116
LC ebook record available at https://lccn.loc.gov/2020026117

In memoriam avó, avô

CONTENTS

ACKNOWLEDGMENTS

I AM GRATEFUL TO THE MANY PERSONS THAT supported me in bringing this book into the world. I owe special thanks to Patricia Zimmermann, Professor of Screen Studies in the Roy H. Park School of Communications at Ithaca College. This book would not exist without her intellectual camaraderie, generous guidance, and unwavering encouragement.

I thank the personnel at the Computerspiele Museum, Berlin, Germany, the Center for Social Research, in Amsterdam, and the Gemeentemuseum, in The Hague, the Netherlands, for assistance with research for this project. Funding for this research was partially provided by research grants from the Cornell Institute for European Studies and the Society of the Humanities at Cornell University.

Gonzalo Frasca, Wafaa Bilal, Iván Ochoa Abreu, Porpentine, Roy Ascott, Charles Csuri, Takako Saito, and the Blank Noise community, among others, answered my queries and generously shared materials. Nancy Schröter at the Xul Solar Museum in Buenos Aires, Argentina, kindly provided photographic material. I am grateful to the anonymous readers of the manuscript for helping to make it a better work; to Janice Frisch and Allison Blair Chaplin at Indiana University Press, for their support of this project; to Julia Tulke, for her assistance with images; and to Jane Banks, for her superb editing and for making me laugh. I extend my appreciation to María Fernández, Phoebe Sengers, Timothy Murray, Adriana S. Knouf, and Dale Hudson, for reading drafts of this text at various stages and offering helpful suggestions. All throughout, Ixchel's play enlivened my writing of this book.

I owe much gratitude to my cousin, Teresa Machado Rente, for caring for my grandparents. I dedicate this book to their memory.

GAMING UTOPIA

INTRODUCTION

GAMING UTOPIA: LUDIC WORLDS IN ART, DESIGN, AND Media focuses on games as imaginings of new and better worlds. This book traces the concept of gaming over a hundred-year span from the modernist avant-garde to contemporary video games. It analyzes game designers' critical interventions into video game culture, subverting games as an exclusively white, heterosexual, male, corporatized leisure-time activity. It examines feminist and queer gaming. It includes projects from across the globe, such as projects from India, Latin America, the Middle East, and South Asia, and incorporates the work of Native American and diasporic groups.

This book differs from other books on digital games that situate their practice exclusively in new media theory. Instead, it synthesizes theories and methodologies from art history, Cold War scholarship in cultural studies and science and technology studies, historical and critical game literature, the intersections of these fields with critical digital theory, environmental and media studies, and postcolonial and gender studies. The history uncovered interweaves activist politics, art history, and participatory design from analog arts practices in the early twentieth century, tracing these practices to current digital media games. Analyzing their potential to imagine utopian politics, the book concentrates on open forms across diverse networks and differently situated spaces.

Video games, gaming networks, the internet, and mobile devices are explosive domains. In these spaces, contemporary gaming artists extend and repurpose historical modernist avant-garde strategies through applications, the creation of alternative game platforms, code, in-game environments, networks, and user interfaces. In these projects, activists, artists, and designers collaborate. They place video games in dialogue with critical interrogations of audience, collaboration, ethics, mediation, participation, and representation. These interdisciplinary conceptual lenses help situate and analyze digital games. They counter the scholarly and critical overemphasis on technological differences between digital and analog that effaces the ways in which video games can reimagine how politics might operate, disconnecting these projects from their potent histories in the modernist art avant-garde.

The point, however, is not to establish a resolved lineage to which other historians or artists may add their own reports but to advance the study of games and gaming culture based on interdisciplinary and cross-cultural approaches. Therefore, the book's chronology is based on a series of political milieus across the globe that reflect emerging and changing political conditions and on the use of games as gestures and propositions calibrated to empower critical capacities for perceiving, interpreting, and reimagining the world otherwise.

The concept of utopia constitutes the guiding principle in this book. *Gaming Utopia* understands video games and video game culture as an available, open space for a utopia. Ernst Bloch, who theorized open spatiality as concrete utopia, argues that historical forces shape these spaces but do not constitute them.[1] These spaces are fluid, mutable, and amenable to change. By engaging possibilities in the present, they can always be re-formed. Since the future emerges from shaping the present, concrete utopia represents spaces of anticipation, as envisioning the past and the future to alter the present operationalizes transformative energies. Bloch contrasts concrete utopia with abstract utopia, which is cut off from historical processes and presents idealized, compensatory plans. Bloch identifies this kind of utopia as a fixed utopia of the state. The rule-bound, goal-oriented, commercial industry video games designed for distraction exemplify abstract utopia.

In contrast, games engaging concepts of concrete utopia evoke theorists interested in the spaces of utopian politics. For example, Jürgen Habermas's public sphere as critical arena figures here, as does Gilles Deleuze and Felix Guattari's rhizome, a nomadic, in-between space, allowing for multiple iterations and locations. These ideas shape some of the game projects discussed in this book.

Along with these recognized concepts, the imagining of a concrete utopia reverberates in feminist and queer conceptualizations of utopian spatiality. In her critiques of the masculinist utopianism of Hegel, Heidegger, Kant, and Nietzsche, Luce Irigaray associates androcentric utopias with static, univocal rationalizations of an objectified lost origin projected into the future, premised on absolute transparency and mastery of reality. They present a vision of the future as an idealized version of the present, a problematic proposition for a future that takes the white male body to be the norm against which the other—people of color, queers, other different bodies, and women—are judged. Irigaray's analysis calls for a feminist uto-pian project that rejects mimicry of masculinist and Eurocentric utopias and is defined instead by a critical relation to utopian ideals. Utopia theorist Lucy Sargisson considers Irigaray's call as an example of the open forms and definitions of utopianism.[2] Similarly, literary scholar Tom Moylan uses the term *critical utopias* to identify the feminist utopias of 1970s science-fiction literature.[3] Donna Haraway's cyborg theory builds on this legacy to propose an alliance between women and machines against the forces of colonial-ism, essentialism, naturalism, and patriarchy in technoculture.[4] Artists and activists working with digital networks and technologies often cite Har-away's cyborg manifesto, which extends 1970s feminist utopian thinking. Haraway's cyborg has no single origin: it possesses a multiplicity of origins in fiction, the military, and capitalism. For Haraway, the cyborg utopia is what she calls a "monstrous" fusion of organism and machine intent on reconfiguring feminism into cybernetic codings of resistance.[5] This cyborg world is already center stage in *Sultana's Dream* (1905), a technological feminist utopia created by the Bengali Muslim Begum Rokeya.[6] Published to critique the practice of *purdah*, the confinement of women to enclosed domestic spaces, Rokeya's world, Ladyland, has men confined instead and women free and in charge of science and technologies. This strategy high-lights the misogynist underpinnings of purdah, as Rokeya perceives it. The work also prefigures later calls by feminists in the Global North to use tech-nologies for liberatory ends.

Bloch's concrete utopia informs José Esteban Muñoz's call to engage queerness as a mode of disidentification, forming queer counterpublics to envision queer futurity.[7] Muñoz's intersectional perspective combines auto-biographical, punk, diasporic, and queer utopian sensibilities to articulate queerness as the not-yet-here in Irigaray's and Haraway's terms, a statement that this world is not sufficient. His argument moves beyond univocal iden-tities by articulating a queer utopia fashioned by diverse artists building performative aesthetics. They are performative because their projects nour-ish processes of disidentification that work neither to assimilate nor oppose dominant cultural codes, but instead yield queer/minoritarian counterpub-lics relishing antinormative sharing and belonging. Queer counterpublics sustain communities and relational networks that contest the dominant public sphere. Critical affect and methodology reside at the center of coun-terpublic performances and in contemporary feminist and queer video game design.

These various concepts of utopia highlight the radical potential of world-making: to actuate projects that disidentify with cultural scripts of heteronormativity, capitalism, and whiteness. They create openings for other visions and map different, utopian social relations. Utopia is not in the past. Instead, nourishing alternative, ludic worlds, it projects futurity onto the present and the past. *Gaming Utopia* explores concrete utopian spaces of feminist, queer, and postcolonial futurity, extending this concept to largely ignored playful, performative, and activist practices in virtual spaces.

This book focuses on games that negotiate the abstract masculinist utopia of mainstream video games through strategies of disidentification. These games infiltrate, mobilize, and subvert the infrastructures, spaces, networks, and cultural codes that dominate industry video games. These games recalibrate how we understand ourselves and the world. These games crack open utopian potentials to provoke users to do and experience things that may be impossible in the physical world. Finally, these games mine ludic forms from art history, particularly the modernist avant-garde.

Gaming Utopia analyzes the historical concepts and practices of avant-gardist play, which refute normative art historical narratives about modernism, specifically traditional concepts of the avant-garde and assumptions about the relationships between historical and contemporary avant-gardes.

The practices of avant-garde play call to mind Hal Foster's critiques of prevailing historical accounts of the avant-garde as an aesthetic and political evolution or progression. According to Foster, the avant-garde as an expression of progressive culture does not abide by linear models of cause and effect, before and after, origin and repetition, and therefore always returns from the future. In this way, Foster also discredits narratives of the post-WWII avant-garde representing a devolution and regression or even an end to the utopian ideals of prewar avant-gardism.[8] Here, the avant-garde emerges as a quintessentially utopian cultural tradition. British artist and art historian Stewart Home theorizes the avant-garde in reference to its utopian articulation of cultural and political forms, a focus that also accounts for its interdisciplinary concerns.[9] In effect, utopian thinker Benjamin Olinde Rodrigues coined the term *avant-garde* to give a name to an ethos oriented toward progressive cultural and social change, spanning the arts, sciences, and industry. The complex conjunction of the cultural and the political in the avant-garde tradition is likewise articulated by the

Brazilian cultural historian George Yúdice's argument for a "conjunctural" sense of avant-gardism, which would include all of the different cultures just mentioned within anticolonial struggles. Focusing on Latin American avant-gardism, specifically in Nicaragua and Brazil in the 1930s, Yúdice shows that avant-gardism was often combined with indigenous traditions in order to create national cultures that would contest the deterritorializing forces of imperialism. In many cases, peripheral avant-garde movements were enthusiastic about the forces of modernization, including sciences, industry, and the state, which in these contexts contested the rule of colonial oligarchies. Because of this decolonial focus, the avant-garde form in Latin America was often tied to statist articulations in the early twentieth century and in decolonizing zones, and then to antistate, anti-institutional critique in the West after 1968. Similar to Foster's, Yúdice's conjunctural reading complicates forms of historicism that rely on a linear trajectory, in this case on the narration of avant-gardism based on a Hegelian unfolding of the aesthetic sphere to the point of its terminal moment of crisis, that of full-blown Western capitalist integration. It differs from Foster's, as it also alerts to the relevance of peripheral avant-gardism to calibrate its polarized understandings in the centers. Avant-gardism, in sum, cannot be fully understood as a phenomenon tied primarily to the history and culture of the West, but instead linked to a transnational project of autonomous community building. From this perspective, Yúdice posits that "it is possible, by a postmodern turn, to rethink the avant-gardes as not constituting a particular moment in the history of modernity but, rather, a transformative power that is generated whenever the conjunctural circumstances allow for it."[10] As a utopian ethos, avant-gardism operationalizes conjunctures and feedback between anticipated futures and reconstructed pasts.

Gaming Utopia deploys Foster's and Yúdice's arguments to show that despite its commercialization, the co-optation of avant-garde forms enables the emergence of new spaces of critical play and prompts new models of cultural critique. The contemporary artists, designers, and activists discussed in this book rework avant-gardist aesthetic forms, cultural-political strategies, and social positionings in response to the stultifying logic of global commodification. As a response to this conjunctural circumstance, artists create recoveries that evidence awareness of their predecessors' appropriation by the cultural industry, their connotations of originality, their elitist hermeticism, their Eurocentrism, their ideology of progress, their primitivism, and their sexism. The playful practices of contemporary artists have implications for how we narrate the relationships between historical and contemporary avant-garde. Yet they also complicate framing the modernist avant-garde as a utopian tradition.

This book elaborates on the utopian tradition by placing the following two sectors in dialogue with each other: art historical studies concerned with decentering dominant modernist discourse emphasizing center and periphery, derivation, influence, kitsch, or originality, with a transnational reimagination of modernism ongoing in the contemporary global context of digital art and design.[11] *Gaming Utopia* expands the utopian tradition of modernist art to include African, Asian, Native American, and Latin American artists and artistic networks deploying science- and technology-based concepts and media from the mid-century to the present.

This book contextualizes gaming within debates and practices in art, mass culture, communication theory, emerging technologies, and social activism.[12] These practices and debates about contemporary digital life bear examination in light of early avant-garde movements. In art history, they could provide a bridge between expanding historizations of modernism and growing interest in global contemporarity. The utopian ethos of the avant-garde is not dead. It is propositional, thus transforming and evolving. Borders between high art and popular cultural forms and between technology and design are dissolving as gender, race, sexuality, and increasingly fluid conceptions of periodization recalibrate what is modern and who is avant-garde.

Gaming Utopia offers a concept of utopian ludology, looking at games as places of the radical imagination. This orientation to the study of digital games integrates art historical traditions with political theories of emancipatory social change. It links the avant-garde's century-old interest in the ludic, associated with the spontaneous and the playful, to current artist- and collective-produced alternative video games that imagine a radically different future. Utopian ludology focuses on the study of playfulness as enabling interactions that afford the necessary freedom to generate new kinds of thinking, feeling, and empowerment to concretize a future that dominant culture renders unthinkable. Reshaping avant-garde aesthetics and extending culturally informed practices and politicized recircuiting, these kinds of games crack open the universalizing and exclusionary dimensions of mainstream games.

With their global audience reach, these alternative artist- and collective-produced video games are volatile sites for contestation and emancipatory change. In contrast to games coming out of transnational media corporations, these utopian, politically combustive games are designed to provoke rather than to prescribe, to propose rather than to command. Video games designed to elicit social change differ significantly from mainstream video games. They are not confined to one form. They are not fixed but fluid, not linear but configurational. These radical political projects reject traditional gaming conventions of rules and goals as signifiers of mastery. Instead, they offer more fluid, malleable, and changing interactions. Advancing a more open participatory system, they reconfigure the relationships between high and low culture, artist and audience, and content and context.

This book examines a diverse array of game strategies and interfaces from interactive installations and the internet to locative and mobile technologies, performance, print and visual media, and social media platforms. Many projects combine these formats. These new political games revise traditional forms of social protest, migrating them into digital and virtual realms.

Gaming in Theory

Most books on games fall into two categories: they focus either on technology or on industry. *Gaming Utopia* adopts a different strategy and formulation. It concentrates on the art historical and centers on the image. It addresses the absence of critical analysis of gaming and game culture in art history. It intervenes in art, design, and activist histories by focusing on activist and design practices as they engage art historical trajectories. The book is in conversation with the politicized focus and emerging global orientation of communication and media studies gaming literature and connects this scholarship with concepts of utopia in literary, art historical, and feminist and queer studies.

As one might expect, gaming scholars take up different aspects of the gaming experience when examining and interpreting the politics of specific games. In these differences lies the formation of methodologies for this emerging field. To date, only three books analyze artistic practices in digital games. Andy Clarke and Grethe Mitchell's *Videogames and Art* (2007) offers a broad snapshot of contemporary Western artistic practices in the video game medium. It includes essays, overviews of various artistic game genres, and interviews with renowned artists who use the medium for critique. Mary Flanagan's *Critical Play: Radical Game Design* (2009) examines a broad array of modernist and contemporary artists working with games. However, Flanagan, an artist and designer herself, orients the book as a games-for-change design manual. David Getsy's *From Diversion to Subversion: Games, Play, and Twentieth-Century Art* (2011) features two essays on artistic digital games with the goal of highlighting the role of play and games in Western modernist art practices.

Some scholars have focused primarily on the game as a narrative experience and thus rely on the idioms of literature studies for their analysis of specific games.[13] In communication studies, one often perceives a concern for the rhetorical functions of games.[14] In sum, games are conceived as the sum of older cultural forms, spanning art, literature, theater, cinema, rhetoric, and newer, technological affordances and contexts. In much of this literature, scholars' reliance on humanistic traditions appears to be used primarily to humanize the technology. Recent examinations of video games and video game culture from the perspective of a sociology of science tend to focus on the technical and social processes on which games depend, and which they help construct. In these ways, game scholars situate the politics of gaming in relation to their respective definitions of games, as stories, a set of procedures, or as performance.

In contrast to most scholarship on games, this book situates games primarily as historical and cross-cultural forms and representations of utopia. Like some of this literature, such a focus shifts the concern with technology to elaborate on how artists and designers amplify the utopian affordances of video games. Like some previous scholarship, it focuses on projects that counter the commercial gaming juggernauts by moving their context, forms, function, and meaning in different and new directions. By taking this focus, it highlights cross-cultural trajectories distinct from genealogies that only trace contemporary video games to Cold War military and engineering culture. This view is prevalent in gaming literature and often used to prove how industry video games cannot but reflect the militarist, consumerist, and sexist outlooks of their original cultural context. For example, Patrick Crogan's *Gameplay Mode: War, Simulation and Technoculture* (2011) drives this point by taking as its thesis the view that one should think of video games as "the shadow" of the "military technoscientific legacy" of "the cold war development of simulational technologies."[15] Crogan derides the ahistoricism of gaming literature as a naive attempt at redeeming the military and therefore an a priori oppressive technology.

As Crogan notes, his history shares kindred genealogies, including Roger Stahl's *Militainment, Inc.: War, Media and Popular Culture* (2010) and Nick Dyer-Witherford and Greig de Peuter's *Games of Empire: Global Capitalism and Video Games* (2009). This literature is concerned with the emergence of a control culture and finds echoes in the idea of play as a form of adopting that control, a notion that begins to appear in narratives about games in the 1960s in the United States, most notably as introduced by Buckminster Fuller's writings about his countercultural reworkings of Cold War military games.[16]

This book refutes this view of games not just in consideration of the complex diversity of contemporary gaming culture but in the methodologies employed by these writers. It critiques in particular a bias toward situating the politics of video games within the perspective of a single culture, whether technological or geographical. Such an emphasis on technology and industry, and by extension the cultural and economic contexts of the Global North, results in polarized views and debates about the politics of video games. Examinations of the politics of video games are caught in familiar judgments about digital technologies as either emancipatory or oppressive tools. To avoid these limitations, the study of games requires not just a variety of single disciplinary perspectives but a synthesis of existing approaches in game studies. *Gaming Utopia* brings together historical and contemporary artists' games, broadening the discussion to other parts of the world. Keeping this in mind, it situates the critical analysis of gaming within the debates in art history, environmental studies, postcolonial/diasporic studies, and queer theory, as well as technology and media studies and game studies engaging global gaming culture.

Gaming Utopia

The games and projects investigated in this book do not posit digital art as simply a break from historical practices. Linking art history, social histories, and media studies, this book zeroes in on the politically transformative goals of the games and art projects. Few art historians have focused on artistic interventions in games. Such a focus, addressed in this book, contributes to the growing literature exploring non-Western modernism in art history. Projects included in the book revise modernism, showing that women and artists from the margins were part of the histories of art and technology.

This book also explores the co-optation of avant-garde culture by countercultural ecological activism, a history that video game studies largely ignore. The book restores this history, focusing on how the mobilization of avant-garde ludic forms and concepts is central to the historical emergence of video games as a media form and industry and to contemporary critical interventions into video games and video game culture.

The book analyzes projects from a wide range of geographical areas and cultural contexts, including artists and designers from Asia, Africa, the Caribbean, First Nations, Latin America, the Middle East, and South Asia. It elaborates the global scope of video game culture, aligning with video game scholarly research revising the pervasive focus on North America and Europe, and part and parcel of an emerging concern in science and technology studies with histories of innovation at the "peripheries" of modernity as well as the traditional imperial "centers."[17] *Gaming Utopia* also probes feminist and queer game makers who challenge the hegemony of male heterosexual commercial games, a queer intersectional approach to studies of video games.

Each chapter examines a different nexus between games and utopian impulses in culture. Chapter 1, "The Avant-Garde Plays," examines two early twentieth-century avant-garde movements, Dada and surrealism. International in scope and diverse in artistic output, Dadaists and surrealists expressed an interest in play and games as part of their search for expressive forms invoking new visions of human relations. Against the background of World War I and in parallel with the political avant-garde of their own time, their projects trace back to what British art historian Stewart Home calls the utopian tradition. Home elaborates this tradition as interested in integrating all human activities by confronting politics and culture together to create a new world where specializations and divisions no longer exist. Dada and surrealism's playful works disrupted traditional boundaries and hierarchies in the art world, radicalizing the culture of politics and the politics of culture.

The Dadaists invoked Nietzsche's Dionysian impulse in art, defining Dada as a game.[18] Similarly, playing with Freudian and Marxian perspectives, the surrealists' interest in play mirrored their attempt to integrate the unconscious within a collectivist social order. Both placed art at the service of cultural and social change. These art movements reject homo faber—the person as maker; that is, the individualist bourgeois associated with rationalism—and affirm homo ludens, the playful human described by Johan Huizinga.[19] The early avant-garde assaulted bourgeois (Kantian) definitions of the artist as a specialist individual and genius.[20] Similarly, these movements challenged idealistic notions of beauty and originality because they eventually transformed into commodities controlled by the institutionalized cultural apparatus. In Dada and surrealism, the collective replaces the individual artist. Artistic output assumes the spontaneity, fluidity, improvisation, and chance of play and games. Moreover, kindred avant-garde artists in Latin America, such as Xul Solar, reworked these notions in games that highlighted anticolonial sentiment. This chapter contends that the playful strategies of Dada and surrealism, and in parallel, other international art currents, anticipate the idea common to the diverse cultural contexts examined in this book, namely that the liberation of the ludic impulse and the transformation of collective life are intrinsically interlinked projects.

Chapters 2 and 3 examine the reworking of this idea in art and counterculture during the Cold War period. Chapter 2, "Action, Participation, and the Digital Avant-Garde," investigates how different strands of the digital avant-garde expand on early modernist arts practices by mobilizing games to catalyze spectators' participation in public life. The *digital avant-garde* is British art historian Charlie Gere's term for post–World War II artists whose work reflected the concerns of a world in which information and communications technology and related concepts assumed increasing importance.[21] Geographically and culturally diverse, this category includes the situationists and artists connected with Fluxus networks. Their shared historical context is the utopian age of cybernetics, which combined self-regulation and computer technologies for control and mastery in a complex and polarized world.

This chapter postulates that these practices incorporate cybernetic concepts of information, interactivity, multimedia, networking, and telecommunications in echo of the early avant-garde's political ludicism. In order to critique rationalization and rearticulate cybernetic concepts to formulate alternatives to passive media consumption, these practices transpose the discourses of mastery and control of cybernetic culture into art and counterculture. The games of the digital avant-garde activated audience creativity. As art historian Frank Popper contends, the games represented events designed to incite the spectator's involvement in changing existing environments.[22] This chapter also situates these practices within the cross-cultural context of cybernetic-inspired art, including collectives like

Groupe de Recherche d'Art Visuel (GRAV) (a research art group). However, while interested in networked participation, these games did not engage technology as either a tool or a subject. Artists did not have access to cybernetic machines until the late 1960s.

Chapter 3, "Cybernetic Ecologies of Art and Counterculture," discusses artistic and countercultural experiments with computers and new technologies within the context of late 1960s reconceptualizations of ecology and ends at one of the bequests of this legacy, namely with games no longer understood as countercultural expressions but instead as reflections of control culture. In the 1960s, as cybernetic concepts migrated from the military context into the popular media sphere, ecosystems came to be understood in terms of cybernetic symbiosis between humans, the environment, and machines. To reconfigure the media sphere was to contribute to the creation of a more sustainable, peaceful world. Roy Ascott dubbed this orientation a "telematics of utopia."[23] Likewise, media theorist Gene Youngblood argued that the artist is like an ecologist working within the worldwide network of mass media, cultivating empathy and global interconnection.[24] The projects analyzed in this chapter include artists working with computers in collaboration with other artists, sympathetic engineers, and the public in Australia, Europe, Japan, North America, and Latin America. In opposition to the alienating effects of the top-down media industry and military applications of cybernetic technologies, collaborations between artists and engineers were designed as decentralized and participatory networks. Their games include playful exchanges of images, text, and sound among geographically and culturally diverse artists and audiences. Other games function more like détournements and subversive mobilizations of communication technologies to protest the Vietnam War. In the 1990s, with globalization, these strategies would become foundational to artists using digital technologies and video games. In the late 1960s, the apex of cybernetic art began to wane: ironically, the established art world withheld support of these radical interventions due to the popular culture image of the computer as a tool of the establishment.

The 1960s and 1970s technology-minded counterculture in the United States championed the digital avant-garde's most utopian imagining of digital technology as democratized, decentralized networks. Gere called the entrepreneurial-minded environmentalists in the San Francisco Bay area near Silicon Valley the digital counterculture, which populated the pages of the *Whole Earth Catalogue* (1968–1998), a new Bay-area publication founded by counterculture environmentalist and entrepreneur Stewart Brand.[25] Influenced by systems-thinkers such as Lewis Mumford, Buckminster Fuller, E. F. Schumacher, and Gregory Bateson, the *Catalogue*'s scope was eclectic, spanning environmentalism, media arts, DIY lifestyle interests, and tools ranging from low-tech devices to personal computers and the latest communication technologies. Its diverse readership included commune members, computer engineers, environmentalists, hackers, and radical artists. The *Catalogue* wanted to empower individuals with information and decentralized technologies so they could create alternative, harmonious social and ecological relationships. According to digital historian Steven Levy, other groups' interests in counteracting technocracy shared these ideas. He identifies them as "true hackers," including operations such as the People's Computer Company, which provided people access to computers and published educational books on how to program games.[26]

For Brand and the members of the PCC, the ultimate goal was the creation of appropriate or soft technologies: decentralized, personal, and cheap tools vital for enabling a new, more environmentally and socially sustainable social order.[27] Their position assumed that people connected to a network would work as politicized hackers toward these interests. As self-organized units steering sustainability through design and technological innovation, they would eventually render the state obsolete. To this end, Brand promoted the personal computer, a technological innovation created by *Catalogue* readers Steve Jobs and Steve Wozniak, and helped build a new cybercommunity called Whole Earth Link, which Howard Rheingold eulogized as an electronic utopia in *The Virtual Community* (1993). This signaled a shift in hacker culture. It refashioned the digital avant-garde's utopian ideals of symbiotic interconnectivity and self-realization via cybernetics and computer technology toward capitalist enterprise. Third-generation hackers, the game hackers Levy describes, were more interested in profits than in utopian politics.

Despite its contributions to acceptance of computers and an integrated environmentalism in mainstream culture, the legacy of counterculture environmentalism is not without paradox. One of the most profound ironies of the counterculture technology movement of modernity is that it helped pave the way for the emergence of new industrial behemoths, including the video game industry, post-modernity. Founded by counterculture-inspired entrepreneurs, corporations like Microsoft now dominate the global economy. And from their hacker beginnings, video games rose to become culturally and economically emblematic of the global digital entertainment industry. As many accounts of the period note, play was thus intrinsically linked to structures of social control.

Chapters 4 and 5 examine two decades of artistic and activist interventions into the video game industry's exploitative dynamics and divisive ideologies, including environmental degradation, militarism, sexism, racism, imperialism, labor abuses, and the exploitation of players.[28] The ultimate irony of the spectacular rise of the digital industries to global prominence is their inadvertent enabling of these emergent, similarly global forms of art and activism post-modernity, including interventions in video games.

Chapter 4 examines playful forms of activism associated with tactical media emerging in the mid-1990s with projects by artists and activists working with online games and in urban spaces. Extending contemporaneous alter-globalization movements, tactical media practitioners promote cyberspace as the most suitable environment for social mobilization. However, they diverge from the historical counterculture's vision of cyberspace as a free, self-governed environment. For the Critical Art Ensemble, one of the most prominent tactical media groups, power controls cyberspace. The group promotes an online form of resistance under the banner of electronic civil disobedience. The concept remixes David Thoreau's notion of civil disobedience; Gilles Deleuze and Félix Guattari's concepts of deterritorialization, nomadism, and rhizome; and avant-garde détournement.[29] Elaborating on prior avant-garde's ludic propositions, the group calls for a form of playful resistance based on transnational alliances among like-minded activists, artists, hackers, professionals, and civic society. This examination of electronic civil disobediance focuses on the collaborative exploits of digital games for cultural critique and intervention through game modifications, mobilizations, and reroutings of existing games and networks, as subversive mimicries.

Massive multiplayer online games emerged in the early 2000s, presenting a new form of commercial gaming. Because of their large transnational audiences, ease of modification, and real-time communication capabilities, these games are attractive ready-made environments for art-based interventions. The post–9/11 realist turn of massive multiplayer online games rendered them as inviting spaces for antiwar protests. Emerging with the miniaturization of digital technologies, urban games provide a platform for artists and activists interested in exploiting the connections between virtual and real spaces. The games discussed address the impact of the war on terror that launched safety and surveillance on urban environments, human mobility, and immigrant and Muslim populations.

Chapter 5 examines digital games designed in the utopian tradition of persuasion, an integral characteristic of a robust critical public sphere. Jürgen Habermas's critical publicity and Stephen Duncombe's ethical spectacle ideas resonate with video game theorist Ian Bogost's term for these practices: *persuasive games*.[30] These games operate as rhetorical tools and as propositional statements first emerging from Latin American designers. Many of these games are transnational collaborations between designers from First Nation, feminist, and queer communities. In contrast to the coercive realism and imposition of behavior on players of mainstream games, these projects assume the form of stand-alone games as a simulation, an argument to convince the player about a position on a particular issue, and as a call to re-create gaming as a participatory culture.

Persuasive games, news games, and social games differ from the temporary forms of tactical media interventions and from the subversive fun of the games of the modernist avant-garde. These projects also incorporate avant-garde strategies, however. They extend the 1960s and 1970s counter-culture notion that computers, digital media, and video games can foster decentralized and sustainable forms of democratic deliberation. Many of these projects stress participation, either by invoking and adapting historical avant-garde participatory forms and techniques; by involving video game designers' collaborations with activists, artists, educators, and the public; or by promoting tools that enable the creation of DIY games. In this sense, persuasive games represent a constructive exploration of video games' potential to function as platforms for public involvement in social life in the face of the diminished role of traditional journalistic media, such as newspapers and documentary film. By infusing video game culture with diverse points of view, persuasive game designers use the popularity of digital games as an opportunity to intervene into public discourse. In many cases, their practices share an overarching desire to reshape video games as a cultural form creating space for marginalized perspectives. In short, these persuasive games span advocacy, journalism, participatory forms of education, and storytelling and personal expression.

This chapter analyzes simulations by the Uruguayan game designer Gonzalo Frasca, a former CNN journalist. Frasca's "videogames of the oppressed" draw on Augusto Boal's participatory theater of the oppressed and Bertold Brecht's concept of defamiliarization.[31] They drive political points by making players conscious that they are engaging with a simulation, rather than encouraging identification with characters. Some designers focus on linking education and participation. For instance, Molleindustria's free internet simulations (2006–present) include a project designed to both educate and enable the player to contribute to changing the exploitative dynamics of the digital industries. The chapter also examines alternate reality games based on documentary strategies and critical pedagogies, including video games designed by diasporic communities that engage participants in learning about and sharing perspectives on immigration. It also probes a game created in collaboration with the Iñupiat, an Alaska Native people, titled *Never Alone* (*Kisima Ingitchuna*), which recasts indigenous folklore as a call to restore ecological balance.

The chapter concludes with a discussion of emerging designers working with twine games, an open-source language-based platform. These projects have been associated with GamerGate, an online harassment campaign targeting feminist and transgender game developers and video game critics, beginning in August 2014 onwards. This discussion explores the work of three designers who developed autobiographical games in response to the stereotyping and marginalization of women and queer communities in mainstream video games. The chapter highlights open-source gaming platforms as a significant step toward the realization of video game culture as a bottom-up practice. It chronicles media critics and art institutions' broad support of designers in the wake of intense harassment. The controversies surrounding these designers indicate the cultural narrowness and instrumental orientation of play and the intransigence of competition, gender and racial stereotyping, militarism, and surveillance in video games, and the continued significance of utopian currents in contemporary ludic culture, as exemplified by the projects in this chapter.

Gaming Utopia threads art historical and contemporary political practices together. It explores how digital games have the potential to imagine alternate futures. Marshaling a concept of mutable utopian ludology, the end of the book does not represent an end to this story. Diversity in games and gaming culture continues to emerge in unexpected ways. The once-marginal visions and critical insistence on the possibility of alternatives to the present embedded in these games are increasingly integral to global video game culture as the progressive, evolving dialogue between gaming and utopian politics continues.

Notes

1. Bloch, *Principle of Hope.*
2. Sargisson, *Contemporary Feminist Utopianism.* Sargisson discusses Irigaray to distinguish between closed and open forms and definitions of utopianism.
3. Moylan, *Demand the Impossible.*
4. Haraway, "A Cyborg Manifesto," 149–181.
5. Ibid., 176.
6. Hossain, *Sultana's Dream.*
7. Muñoz, *Cruising Utopia.*
8. Hal Foster, *Return of the Real.*
9. Home, *Assault on Culture.*
10. Yúdice, "Rethinking the Theory of the Avant-Garde from the Periphery," 74.
11. The notions of center, periphery, and originality are central to Rosalind E. Krauss's argument in *The Originality of the Avant-Garde and Other Modernist Myths* (1986); the concepts of influence, kitsch, and derivation are central to Clement Greenberg's ideas about mass culture and art in his essay "Avant-Garde and Kitsch" (1939).
12. For example, in the work of art historians Simone Osthoff, Maria Fernandez, and Ming Tiampo, among many others.
13. For example, in the work of Janet Murray, Espen Aarseth, Nick Monfort, and Noah Wardrip-Fruin.
14. For example, in the work of Gonzalo Frasca, Jesper Juul, Alexander Gallaway, and Ian Bogost.
15. Crogan, *Gameplay Mode,* xiii.
16. Fuller, *The World Game.* The notion of video games as reflections of a culture of control is advanced by other communication and science and technology scholars, including Alexander Galloway, Paul Edwards, and Fred Turner, among others. In media studies, McKenzie Wark's *Gamer Theory* (2007) is a notable exception, as it advances the thesis that video games represent utopian versions of the lived world. In contrast to the experience of real life in a free-market society, games present a level playing field where skill rather than money is the only way to advance. Wark is optimistic about the utopian potential of games. Because they encourage rejection of the status quo, he argues, they are potentially subversive. The idea that video games have utopian potential is also implicit in the work of the game designers Mary Flanagan, Ian Bogost, Gonzalo Frasca, Jane McGonigal, and Celia Pearce, among others.
17. Recent publications include Mark Wolf's *Video Games around the World* (2015) and Phillip Penix-Tadsen's *Cultural Code* (2016). STS scholars contributing to histories of technology from the "margins," include Eden Medina, Anita Say Chan, and Ana Delgado, among others.
18. Ball, *Flight Out of Time,* 134; Wilson, *Escape from the Nineteenth Century,* 160.
19. Huizinga, *Homo Ludens.*
20. The concept of genius is associated with Immanuel Kant's notions of aesthetics in his *Critique of Judgment* (*Kritik der Urteilskraft,* 1790). Kant's notion of genius connects art with originality (a "free play" of forms, or beauty), thus privileging the position of the artist as an exceptional individual innately gifted to channel the transcendent (God, divine inspiration, or the original).

21. Gere, *Digital Culture.*
22. Popper, *Art-Action and Participation.*
23. Shanken, "From Cybernetics to Telematics."
24. Youngblood, *Expanded Cinema.*
25. Gere, *Digital Culture.*
26. Levy, *Hackers: Heroes of the Computer Revolution.*
27. The terms *appropriate* or *soft technologies* hark to the notion of low-cost, small-scale DIY and environmentally friendly technologies managed and controlled by ordinary people, as I will discuss in chapter 3.
28. Lazzarato, "Immaterial Labour," 133–150. The exploitation of players is often connected with the notion of immaterial labor, a concept that the autonomist theorist Maurizio Lazzarato identified.
29. Critical Art Ensemble, *Electronic Disturbance.*
30. Bogost, *Persuasive Games.*
31. Frasca, "Videogames of the Oppressed," 85–94.

1

THE AVANT-GARDE PLAYS

Much game literature contends that play and games are the crux of the artistic and social sensibilities of Dada and surrealism. However, this literature, frequently written by game designers, tends to invoke these movements for the purpose of establishing an artistic lineage for their own work. Avant-gardism is used to signal the countercultural ethos of their work in relation to industry games. In art history, Dada and surrealism are understood as kindred movements, but art historians have generally failed to examine them in light of games and gaming culture. This is surprising, for as this chapter shows, Dadaists defined Dada, among other things, as a game, and the surrealists used concepts about play and created numerous games themselves. Moreover, the Dadaists' and surrealists' ludic sensibilities have been intimately linked historically with a shared utopian ethos, reflected in part in parallel and sometimes allied with political movements organizing contemporaneous social struggles. Modernism, for example, connected with communist, socialist, and anarchist parties and groups. Like these movements, Dadaists and surrealists shared an internationalist, utopian vision of the possibilities of a democratic world and an antipathy to the totalitarian forces emerging in Europe: nationalism, imperialism, and militarism. Dada and surrealism styled themselves as the cultural shock troops to the political vanguard. Their interest in the ludic, although at times a point of connection, would, however, most often be at odds with their social counterparts' emphasis on politics. This concern also differed from prevailing avant-garde views about art and the artist, models of artistic circulation, and their premises on formalism and institutional control.

The avant-garde's shared rejections of common assumptions about art and politics as separate realms invokes British art historian Steward Home's understanding of the concept of the avant-garde as "utopian currents" in culture. These currents, as he theorizes, aim at simultaneously confronting politics and culture by way of integrating all human activities to create a new world in which specialisms no longer exist.[1] For Dadaists and surrealists, this project entails both a rejection of the view of the human as homo economicus, the bourgeois individualist associated with the cultivation of a culture of rationalism, and simultaneously an affirmation of the Dionysian impulse in human nature and the playful human existing and relating through pleasure and desire, homo ludens.[2] From this follows these movements' assault on the ideological role of art under the bourgeois definitions of the artist as a specialist individual and genius, art as creative expression framed within idealist notions of beauty and originality, and art as a commodity operating under the premises of the institutionalized cultural apparatus working to fix and distribute creative production and meaning. Instead, the individual artist was replaced by the collective, and artistic activities took on the character of processes that associated with collaboration and gratuity and aimed to set in motion sociocultural transformation. For the avant-garde, art assumes the characteristics of play and games: spontaneity, passion, fluidity, improvisation, and chance. The shared ludic character of Dada and surrealism relates to the central idea connecting these concepts, namely that the liberation of the creative impulse and the transformation of collective life are one and the same project.

That this idea is not only central to the early European avant-garde is becoming evident through emerging art historical examinations of global avant-gardism. These histories are also part of game studies, and their incorporation and expansion in this field would further contribute to the emerging literature addressing games and game culture from a global perspective. In this spirit, this chapter concludes with an examination of the use of playful approaches and games by Argentinian artist Oscar Agustín Alejandro Schulz Solari, also known as Xul Solar (1887–1963). Like his friend, Argentine writer Jorge Luis Borges, Solar (his adopted name is composed of an anagram, Xul from the Latin Lux, or light, and Solar, Spanish for sun, thus, "the sun light") worked in parallel with the apogee of European surrealism in the 1930s and is connected with the emergence of Latin American avant-gardism. Solar's work shares the utopian impulses behind the Europeans' interest in the ludic and ludic forms and emerges additionally out of concerns with developing a new art and culture independent of European avant-gardist aesthetics and models, in a postcolonial context of Argentina and Latin America. In the end, Solar's games remind the reader of an argument central to both this chapter and the book, namely that games as cross-cultural forms and expressions are embedded in specific historical conditions, though not bound to them.

Dada's Game

In 1916 Zurich, Dadaists invoked games to reposition art as a provocative gesture because it was accomplished through performative and participatory stagings. This strategy undermined the artist's traditional authority as a visionary, someone with privileged access to insights about the human condition. As a result, art could be more communal, since it could be created and accessed by nonspecialists. Reframed as a game, art could become an open and participatory space cultivating democracy and opposition to authority, whether in art or political systems. As Hugo Ball, a central figure in Zurich Dada, put it in his 1927 memoir, Dada was a "farce . . . a play with shabby leftovers," of "expressionism, futurism, and cubism." He described the Dadaist as a "childlike, Don Quixotic being . . . involved in word games and grammatical figures . . . [who] welcomes any kind of mask. Any game of hide-and-seek, with its inherent power to deceive."[3] Zurich Dada emerged from recast themes and aesthetics of modernist art and popular culture. It was an amalgamation of symbolist free verse; expressionism, as conceived by Wassily Kandinski's total art; Marinetti's futurist *Parole in libertà* (words-in-freedom); cubism's simultaneity and its interest in African arts; Yiddish folk theater; cabaret; and the language of propaganda and marketing.[4] As Ball implies, Dada's seizing on the contributions of prewar stylistic movements served to forestall their conventionalization and assert their relevance as a unified platform for propelling art, the artist, and audiences into the present in raucous mockeries of the imperialist culture sweeping Europe amid World War I (1914–1918).

The "total art" of Dada in "pictures, music, dances, poems" is synonymous with the chaotic conditions of its time as addressed by a group of defecting artists and intellectuals coming together in neutral Zurich, Switzerland, in 1914.[5] The group included three Germans: Ball (1886–1927), a playwright and director trained in German literature, history, and philosophy; Emmy Hennings (1885–1948), a dancer, performer, puppeteer, and poet, and Ball's partner; and Richard Huelsenbeck (né Carl Wilhelm Richard Hülsenbeck, 1892–1974), a medical student from Berlin. Jean Arp (né Hans Arp, 1886–1966) was a poet, painter, and sculptor of German and French descent who came from Paris to Zurich. Tristan Tzara (né Samuel Rosenstock, 1886–1963) was a symbolist poet, and the brothers Janco (Jules [1886–1985], Marcel [1885–1984], Georges [1899–?]) were Jewish artists from the kingdom of Romania, which while neutral at the inception of World War I, joined in the conflict in 1916.[6] Other members of the Zurich Dada group included Jewish Romanian painter Arthur Segal (1875–1944), Jewish Polish painter Marcel Slodki (1892–1943) who was later murdered in Auschwitz, and painter and poet Francis Picabia (1879–1953), of French, Spanish, and Cuban descent. Sophie Taeuber-Arp (1889–1943), a painter, sculptor, puppeteer, and trained Laban dancer, was the only native Swiss among the Zurich Dadaists.[7] In fact, with its starting point in Romania among young Jewish artists and intellectuals, Zurich constitutes an intermittent point in Dada's trajectory, driving the modernist art currents emerging in Switzerland, which with the outbreak of the war in 1914 became the focal point of international avant-garde culture in Europe.[8]

In 1916, Ball and Hennings took the initiative to call on exiled artists and audiences to join the Cabaret Voltaire, a nightclub that proved pivotal for the emergence of Dada as Zurich's agent provocateur. Huelsenbeck, who went on later to cofound Berlin Dada, recalls a typical soiree at the Cabaret:

> The Cabaret Voltaire was our experimental stage on which we tried to explore what we had in common. Together we made a beautiful negro music with rattles, wooden drumsticks, and many primitive instruments. I played the precentor, a near mythical figure. Trabaja, Trabaja la mojere—with plenty of schmaltz. . . . We first experimented with our own costumes of coloured cardboard and spangles. Tristan Tzara . . . invented the performance of the simultaneous poem for the stage, a poem recited in various languages, rhythms, intonations, by several people at once. I invented the concert of vowels and the bruitist poem, a mix of poem and bruitist music. . . . Tzara invented the static poem, a kind of optical poem that one looks at as at a forest; for my part, I initiated the dynamic poem, recited with primitive movements.[9]

Among the city's famous residents at this time were "James Joyce, Romain Rolland, Alexander Archipenko, Franz Werfel, Else Lasker-Schüler, Fritz Brupbacher, Otto Flake, Rudolf von Laban, Viking Eggeling."[10] The Russian exile Vladimir Ilyich Ulyanov (1870–1924), soon to become Lenin, lived during this time in the Spiegelgasse 12, a few doors down from the Meierei located on number 1, the restaurant that was to host the first Cabaret Voltaire soirees in Zurich, in 1916.[11] Art and science historian Tom Sandqvist reports that Lenin was a regular at the Meierei and cites Marcel

Janco's remarks that his visits to the cabaret were "to discuss the dadaist ideas, ideas that he was very much opposed to because they could not serve the Communist cause."[12] Tzara later said that he did not know about Lenin at the time.[13] Systematized politics, in general, were of little interest to the members of the Dada group, save as fodder adding to its subversive glee.

The debut of Dada was timed for July 14, 1916, to coincide with France's Bastille Day, which the group mockingly mimicked in their storming of the stage at the Zunfthaus zur Waag in Zurich.[14] According to Richter, who was present at this event, the evening's program consisted of "music . . . dance, theory, manifestos, poems, pictures, costumes and masks" and involved "Arp, Ball, Hennings, the composer Heusser, Huelsenbeck, Janco and Tzara."[15] Huelsenbeck read a "declaration" styled on the *Communist Manifesto*, inviting all to unite under the banner of Dada, which he proclaimed to not mean a thing, except "the best medicine contributing to a happy marriage."[16] Tzara's manifesto "Mr. Antipyrine," whose title comes from an aspirin brand, proclaimed that "Dada is our intensity . . . within the framework of European weaknesses, it's still shit, but from now on we want to shit in different colours so as to adorn the zoo of art with all the flags of all the consulates."[17] Together Tzara and Huelsenbeck recited "Pélamide," a bruitist poem with the following line: "a e ou youyouyou i e ou o . . . you youyouyou . . . drrrrrdrrrrdrrrrgrrr stücke von grüner dauer. . . ."[18] Hennings performed a Dada dance while costumed in a cylindrical outfit and a cubist mask made by Janco. Ball, dressed similarly with a cylinder on his head, recited sound poems, including "Karawane." The evening ended as the lights dimmed and Ball was "carried down off the stage like a magical bishop" amidst general hilarity.[19]

As subversive mimicries of the jingoism of propagandist, commercialist, and moralist discourses reverberated outside of the Cabaret's walls, Zurich Dada's ironic theater invites further social and political contemplation as to its resounding implications. In his memoir, Richter noted that Dada's absurdist stagings represent a strategy of engagement and distancing: "We laughed to our heart's delight. In this way we destroyed, affronted, ridiculed and laughed. We laughed at everything. We laughed at ourselves, as we did at the kaiser, king, and fatherland, beerbellies, and pacifiers. We took our laughter seriously; it was our very laughter that guaranteed the seriousness of our anti-art activities in our efforts to find ourselves."[20] Henry Bergson, who Ball later said influenced the Cabaret Voltaire, captured the irreverent side of laughter as a marker of "a slight revolt on the surface of social life," which in this way "instantly adopts the changing forms of the disturbance."[21] Most significantly, Ball associated Dada with Nietzschean concepts of culture as a domain implicating opposing forces—the Dionysian and Apollonian impulses. In this vein, Ball saw Dada and Nietzschean thought as kindred affronts on metaphysics—thought divorced from "the objects of the real world," underlined by "logic . . . made absolute as an end in itself," citing as examples Kant, Fichte, and Marx.[22] Dada's distaste for a culture of individuation and detachment was reflected by its distancing from a notion of aesthetics associated with contemplation, restraint, and harmony, theorized by Nietzsche as expressions of the Apollonian sensibility. By contrast, the Dionysian impulse, named after the Greek god of festivals, was understood by Nietzsche to function as a catalyst of unbridled passion, or as he put it, "savage natural instincts."[23] Because a passionate state would accompany "the sense of loss of the individual self," it would break down all sense of social barriers and allow community spirit to thrive once more.[24] The Cabaret Voltaire can be seen as such: as a theater conceptualized on the integration of the Apollonian and Dionysian cultures, which in practice would take form as a participatory theater in which the artist and audiences collaborated to re-create art as a collective expression; a notion then associated with popular cultural forms including ludic events, such as festivals and games, rather than high art.

According to anarchist poet Peter Lamborn Wilson, also known as Hakim Bey, the Nietzschean turn was part of a broader romantic revival at the beginning of the twentieth century and connected with anarchist as well as conservative currents.[25] To this point, the focus on the connection of art and life does not only represent the Dadaists' fascination with Nietzschean thought that was influenced by Western art (classical Greek poetry) but also with non-Western art, a broader tendency in art at the time. Art theorist Wilhelm Worringer hailed the abstract character of "primitive art" in *Abstraction and Empathy* in 1907, at the same time that Pablo Picasso was finishing his painting *Les Demoiselles d'Avignon*. Similarly, Ball sets German-Jewish anarchist and art historian Carl Einstein, author of *Negro Art* (1915) and a collaborator of the Berlin Dadaists, in parallel with the "primitivist" resonance of Dada plays.[26] Einstein's anarchism provides the political counterpoint of Dada's "primitivism" expressed in art linked to immediate experience: "Primitive art: that means the rejection of the capitalist art tradition. European mediateness and tradition must be destroyed; there must be an end to formalist fictions. If we explode the ideology of capitalism, we will find beneath it the sole valuable remnant of this shattered continent, the precondition for everything new, the masses of simple people, today still burdened by suffering. It is they who are the artist."[27]

Inasmuch as the term *primitivism* rings offensive to our contemporary ears, it also stands as testimony of the utopian imaginary of the time, notably the association of the ideal society and desires for an alternative order, that is, a more democratic culture, considered to be characteristic of non-Western cultures. Along with non-Western art, the Dadaists drew on ancient ritual, prelinguistic sounds, children's art, unconscious states, and other strategies used to destroy formalism—that is, the separation between politics and culture. In practice, as noted, these models shaped Zurich Dada's performances and environments as assaults on the passivity of audiences, testing in the process, as Nietzsche had suggested, the possibilities for freeing their underlying (transgressive) nature; that is, their participatory or democratic capabilities. This technique failed to find resonance in the materially comfortable, Victorian culture of Zurich, however, instead devolving into indifference or hostility on the part of audiences and internal conflicts among the group.

The end of Dada activity in Zurich, according to Richter, took place at the grand soiree in the Saal zur Kaufleuten on April 9, 1919.[28] The disbanding of the group after three years is attributed to various factors, of which the audiences' habituation to the sensory assaults of Dada and internal political differences appear to have played a considerable role. Following the peace treaty of Versailles on June 28, 1919, Dada's audiences left Zurich, and the group quietly disbanded. Ball and Hennings had already left in 1917 for Bern after a dispute with Tzara about the latter's ambition to systematize Dada as an international art movement.[29] In her account of Zurich Dada's relationship with anarchist thought, Theresa Papanikolas suggests that the conflict was less between Ball and Tzara, both of whom she sees as adhering to an "anarcho individualist" view (filtered through antirationalism and antiauthoritarianism), and more between this view and the "anarcho-communist" line of Dadaists belonging to the Bund Radikaler Künstler (Association of Radical Artists), a splinter group of Zurich Dada that included Richter, Arp, Fritz Baumann, Viking Eggeling, Augusto Giacometti, Hennings, Walter Helbig, Marcel Janco, Otto Morach, and Arthur Segal.[30] According to Papanikolas, this grouping was inspired on the organizational model of Peter Kropotkin's notion of "mutual aid," a communist society free of a central government and based on voluntary associations among members. In contrast, she cites Max Stirner, Nietzsche, Pierre-Joseph Proudhon, Auguste Strindberg, Voltaire, and the Marquis de Sade as major influences for Ball's belief that "real social renewal" ought to be "based on the premise that revolution would inevitably happen at the level of the individual consciousness." In fact, both currents adhered to the notion that the main function of art is to "liberate the individual from 'traditions or laws of any kind.'"[31] The individualist strand of Zurich Dada, as Papanikolas explains, was carried through by Tzara, who followed the brothers Janco to Paris in 1921 as a guest of the group of Dadaists headed by André Breton, soon to form the surrealists.[32] Dadaist tendencies in art developed in parallel to Zurich and Paris at various locations, among them Tokyo, New York, Zagreb, Belgrade, Georgia, Barcelona, Drachten, Groningen, Cologne, Hannover, and Berlin.[33] Upon disbanding in Zurich, Dada moved to Berlin and manifested as a game simultaneously adopting and expanding the performative and participatory forms of its counterparts to mock the internationalist rhetoric of communism post-WWI, or as the Dadaists involved put it, self-styled as a "collective 'brotherhood' of artists" dedicated to working "towards the formation of the new man" by way of serving as cultural leaders of "the people."[34]

Dadas of the World/Cosmos, Unite!

Dada gathered momentum in Berlin around Huelsenbeck, who, upon returning home from Zurich in 1917, sought to establish a club modeled on Cabaret Voltaire. While most Dadaist tendencies concentrated on aesthetic issues, Berlin Dada took on a definite political turn because of the city's explosive social atmosphere post defeat in WWI and on the brink of the November 1918 revolution. Club Dada was to include, among others, Franz Jung (1889–1963), an expressionist poet and play-writer; George Grosz (1893–1959), a painter and caricaturist; John Heartfield (né Helmut Herzfeld, 1891–1968) and his brother Wieland Herzfeld (1896–1988), founders of the Malik-Verlag, a publishing house for left-wing literature; Hannah Höch (1889–1978), who was trained as a graphic designer and briefly worked as a fashion designer; painter Raoul Hausmann (1886–1971); and architect Johannes Baader (1875–1955).[35] These artists were involved with political activism at the time of Huelsenbeck's arrival amidst widespread agitation for radical social change in Berlin during the war. By 1916, the Herzfeld brothers were publishing the *Neue Jugend*, a left-wing literary and political paper. At the same time, Franz Jung and Raoul Hausmann were publishing *Die Freie Strasse*, an anarchist review, with contributions by Baader. Grosz, who was known for his satirical drawings, regularly published in various socialist publications.[36] In effect, many of the expressive techniques and themes of Berlin Dada, such as distortion, juxtaposition, and sociopolitical content, were already appearing in these publications as German expressionism. Similarly, Berlin had highly diverse and engaged artistic and political scenes post–WWI, as Germany began an uncertain path toward democracy during the Weimar Republic (1919–1933).

Like the Zurich Dadaists, the Berlin Dadaists had personal experiences with war as soldiers, objectors, and in the case of Höch, as a volunteer for the Red Cross.[37] Unlike in Zurich, however, their antimilitarist and antinationalist sentiments found political reverberation in anarcho-socialist organizations. This was most notably represented by the Spartacus League, founded in 1916 by Rosa Luxemburg, Clara Zetkin, and Karl Liebknecht, which was to join with the Independent Social Democratic Party of Germany in 1917, and finally take the form of the Kommunistische Partei Deutschlands as a coalition of groups objecting to the support lent by the Social Democratic Party of Germany to the German government's declaration of war. Grosz, who had voluntarily enlisted and was discharged; Heartfield, who was dismissed from the Reichswehr film service because of his support for the strike that followed the assassination of Karl Liebknecht and Rosa Luxemburg in 1919; his brother Herzfeld, who briefly served as a conscript; and Jung, a deserter, all became members of the Kommunistische Partei Deutschlands at its founding in 1918.[38] Dada's political involvement took heart from the news of the Russian Revolution (February 1917), which in Germany led to the eruption of general strikes and the formation of autonomous soldiers' and workers' councils and, finally, to the abdication of Kaiser Wilhelm II in 1918. This highly volatile atmosphere continued with the bloody suppression of the Sparticists in 1919 during the November Revolution and the installation of the Weimar Republic saddled with the legacy of the German Reich's defeat, which resulted in the loss of its military as well as the part of its territories annexed by France. Heavy fines imposed on Germany by the allies (as agreed under the Treaty of Versailles in 1919) compounded the country's state of disarray, and droves of disabled soldiers returned home to swell the ranks of the dispossessed.[39] As a response, Berlin Dada became a set of strategies of dissent, a game positioned between social criticism and propaganda.

Berlin Dada's propaganda included confrontational public performances, incendiary speeches, manifestos, media hoaxes, spontaneous happenings, revolutionary literature, journals, magazines, posters, leaflets,
assemblages, photomontages, and an exhibition, as well as a range of drawings, paintings, and lithographs. These activities were designed to reach
a wide audience, to demoralize the existing order, and lastly to create an
international network of Dadaists by way of correspondence, journals, and
mutual advertising.[40] Dada's campaign differed from communist propaganda in its combination of playful and political elements, though it similarly strove to precipitate the revolutionary process on a global scale.

In 1918, the same year that Rosa Luxemburg composed the Spartacist
Manifesto, the "First Speech of Dada in Germany" was delivered by Huelsenbeck impromptu at a literary reading on January 22. In it he declared that
Dadaism was at the forefront "of major international art movements."[41]
At the Dada Club's official opening event at the Berlin Sezession on April
12, 1918, Huelsenbeck clarified this pronouncement by stressing that Dada
and the Dadaists acknowledged no borders, and from this took its form as
a transcultural attitude: "Dada is a state of mind that can be revealed in
any conversation whatever. So that you are compelled to say: this man is
a DADAIST—that man is not; the Dada Club consequently has members
all over the world, in Honolulu as well as New Orleans and Leseritz. Under
certain circumstances to be a Dadaist may mean to be more a business
man, more a political partisan than an artist—to be an artist means to let
oneself be thrown by things, to oppose all sedimentation."[42] The evening's
uproarious ending, largely provoked by Grosz's illustrative gesture as he
pretended to urinate on nationalist and prowar paintings decorating the
hall, foreshadowed subsequent confrontations between the Dadaists and
authorities for the following two years.[43] In effect, what would transpire
reveals that, unlike in Zurich, opposition to Dada came not so much from
the democratic limitations of audiences but rather from the undemocratic
curtailing of the media sphere under the Weimar Republic. Therefore, the
Dadaist theater in Berlin focused on strategies to democratize art and mass
media in their varied forms, from printed matter to public spaces.

With the exception of the group's first magazine—titled *Club Dada:
Prospekt des Verlags freie Strasse* and published shortly after the April 12
event—publications associated with the Berlin Dadaists were persistently
subject to censorship. The distribution of Huelsenbeck's 1917 *Phantastische
Gebete* (Fantastic Prayers), with drawings by Grosz, was halted by order

of the Reich's Kommandantur.[44] Dada tracts and literature such as news-papers, magazines, and posters were similarly censored. Among these, Baader's manifestos *Dadaisten gegen Weimar* ("Dadaists against Weimar") and *Jedermann sein eigner Fussball* ("Everyman His Own Football") (fig. 1.1), published by Heartfield's Malik-Verlag in protest against the brutal sup-pression of the Sparticist uprisings, were confiscated (the former sarcasti-cally proclaimed Baader as "President of the Earth," while the latter urged counterrevolution). *Jedermann sein eigner Fussball* was seized after 7,600 copies were sold by Dada members marching in the streets of Berlin behind a horse-drawn carriage carrying an orchestra rented for the occasion (the Dadaists were arrested).[45] *Die Pleite* (Bankruptcy), appearing shortly after in March 1919 under the editorship of Heartfield and Grosz, among others, contained drawings and paintings by Grosz alongside communist propa-ganda. The publication was banned during its first year, though it appeared intermittently in print until 1920.[46] The Dada Fair, in which a dummy with a pig's head dressed as a German officer was centrally displayed hanging from the ceiling, took place in 1920. The show was shut down by the authorities, and the artists as well as the gallerist involved were followed and fined for ridiculing the German army.[47] At issue was the directness of Dada's oppo-sitional messages and the Dadaists' alignment with the radical left. In addi-tion, the relentlessness of the Dadaists' public campaigns gave the impression that the group stood for a ubiquitous oppositional force. Between 1919 and 1929, Dada members were involved in the publication of two other periodi-cals, *Der Blutige Ernst* (The Bloody Ernst) and *Der Gegner* (The Opponent), both publishing political satire directed at the authorities and institutions of the Weimar Republic.[48] They also made their opposition visible through twelve official performances; a media campaign consisting of a host of leaf-lets, programs, and posters distributed at these events; and individual pub-lications, which included Huelsenbeck's *Dada Almanac, Dada Triumphs! A Balance-Sheet of Dadaism* and *Germany Must Perish! Remembrances of an Old Dadaist Revolutionary*, all appearing in 1920.[49] In addition, the group published *Der Dada*, which appeared in three issues between 1919 and 1920 and was designed to introduce Dada to a wide scope of readers.[50] The defi-nitions of Dada in these issues as a "club," an "advertising company," and a "savings bank" were underscored by scorn for bourgeois institutions.[51] In the last issue of the periodical, Hausmann's "Dada in Europe" likewise professed scorn for the mass media by framing Dada's activities as "bluff," playing on the "bourgeois" media appetite for sensationalism.[52]

Figure 1.1. John Heartfield, cover of the first edition of the publication *Jedermann sein eigner Fussball* (Everyman His Own Football), February 15, 1919. © The Heartfield Community of Heirs / Artists Rights Society (ARS), New York / VG Bild-Kunst, Bonn 2019. Image courtesy of Akademie der Künste, Berlin, Kunstsammlung, Inv.-Nr.: JH 5278.

The images and layouts of the journals, books, and materials published by Berlin Dadaists attest to the practitioners' artistic goals of sophistication and impact. Among the images accompanying these publications were numerous satirical drawings by Grosz, who focused on developing caricature as a medium through which he conveyed powerful critiques of the classist stratification of Weimar Germany. Grosz's portraits of corpulent businessmen and members of the ruling and religious classes were often juxtaposed with images of exposed prostitutes, mutilated soldiers, jobless workers, and scenes of police brutality. He renders class difference visible via archetypes of greed, hypocrisy, and dejection against fragmented and distorted backgrounds that express the chaos and oppressiveness of social conditions. Deeply influenced by expressionist currents, Grosz's caricatures readily translated into the format of popular print. The fragmentation and jarring characteristics of Grosz's works resonated in Dada photomontage, an innovative technique of which Heartfield's cover for Baader's *Jedermann* is one of the first examples. Though also found in Russian constructivism, it appears that the source of Dada photomontage lies in military photography, as Höch explained in an interview post-Dada:

> We borrowed the idea from a trick of the official photographers of the Prussian army regiments. They used to have elaborate oleolithographed mounts, representing a group of uniformed men with a barracks or a landscape in the background, but with the faces cut out; in these mounts, the photographers then inserted photographic portraits of the faces of their customers, generally colouring them later by hand. But the aesthetic purpose, if any, of this very primitive kind of photomontage was to idealize reality, whereas the Dada photomonteur set out to give to something entirely unreal all the appearances of something real that had actually been photographed . . . our all purpose [sic] was to integrate objects from the world of machines and industry in the world of art.[53]

Among the Dadaists, Heartfield, Höch, and Hausmann were the most active in developing photomontages composed of reassembled images and texts taken from mass media. Whereas Heartfield's works in the medium extoll a propagandist intent similar to Grosz's, Höch and Hausmann focused on producing images that commented on the rhetorical power of mass media in order, as she suggested in the passage cited above, to challenge the media's use of photography's idealized realism to invoke what it promulgated as truth. Dada pioneered photomontage as a modern art form found throughout avant-garde movements and in contemporary media activism in which the mobilization of popular media forms, including video games, became similarly the basis of social commentary and political intervention. These strategies also appeared in mainstream media from the 1920s up to today's history-averse, sanitized, postmodern aesthetics of hyperrealistic remix and simulation, as typified by mainstream video games. In effect, photomontage set the parameters for the ongoing dialogue between art, politics, and truth in motion, for better or for worse.

Heartfield's montages mostly revolved around anticapitalist and anti-fascist themes and his affinity with communist causes. His best-known works originated in his involvement with the Kommunistische Partei Deutschlands as a contributor to various communist publications counter to the rise of national socialism. Two examples from a photomontage series dating from 1932, *The Meaning of the Hitler Salute: Little Man Asks for Big Gifts* and *Adolf, the Superman, Swallows Gold and Spouts Tin*, portray Hitler as a puppet of capital and a demagogue receiving contributions from industrialists while appealing to the masses through working-class rhetoric. A 1934 photomontage titled *Das tausendjährige Reich* (The Thousand Year Empire) (fig. 1.2) puns on the ideologies of domination coalescing within the Third Reich. The image shows a precarious house of cards stacked according to rank. At the top is the king with the face of Fritz Thysen, the owner of the largest steel and coal company in Germany supplying armament to Hitler between the two World Wars. Hitler appears as the lowly drummer boy ("Der Trommler") at the bottom of the pyramid. The implication of this house of cards is that its collapse will follow on the removal of its shaky foundation. In this connection, *The Voice of Freedom in the German Night on Radio Wave 29.8* (1937), a poster designed for a communist radio station broadcasting from Czechoslovakia into fascist Germany, shows Heartfield's belief in how technology can have a democratic impact in the hands of the people, a familiar narrative of classic Marxism and one that continues to resonate in contemporary interventions into the corporate control of media, including video games.

In contrast with Heartfield's photomontages, those of Hausmann and Höch, which date from the Weimar period, are visually overloaded with references to the rise of consumer culture in Germany and the Global North. But as Hausmann and Höch sought to similarly exploit the materials of mass marketing, their works engage with them in different ways, as opportunities to reflect on the cultural context and identity of Berlin Dada. Haussmann's works include Dada and himself in the form of advertisements, as in *Dada siegt!* ("Dada victorious") from 1920, and his self-portrait

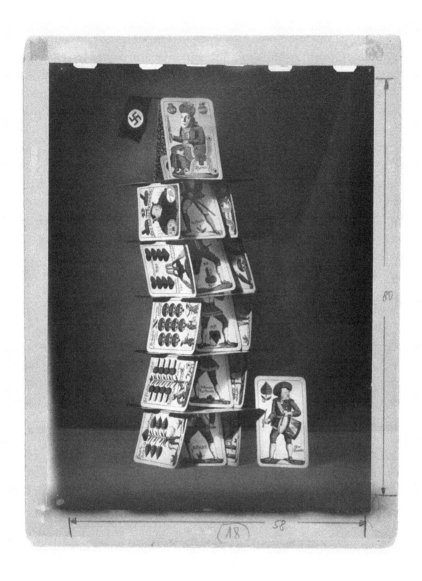

Figure 1.2. John Heartfield, *Das tausendjährige Reich* (The Thousand Year Empire), 1934. © The Heartfield Community of Heirs / Artists Rights Society (ARS), New York / VG Bild-Kunst, Bonn 2019). Image courtesy of Akademie der Künste, Berlin, Kunstsammlung, Inv.-Nr.: JH 2182.

ABCD (1923–24). These montages combine the typographical forms of sound poetry (Hausmann was a sound poet) and visuals to formally convey noise and movement in a mix of self-promotion and irony, as well as to pay homage to Russian constructivism (he collaborated with El Lissitsky on one occasion). Höch also engages self-portraiture in conveying the emergence of media personalities, as in *Cut with the Kitchen Knife Dada through the Last Weimar Beer-Belly Cultural Epoch of Germany* (1919–20), which includes Dada members taken from the group's publications alongside fashion models, revolutionaries, and public figures from the arts, politics, and sciences like Prussian artist Käthe Kollwitz, Lenin, German cabinet ministers, and Albert Einstein. The gendered references of this work, the kitchen knife and a map of European countries granting voting rights to women, abound in Höch's photomontages, with the modern woman a recurring figure. Contrary to Huelsenbeck's self-portrait and advertisement of the "new man," whom he characterized to carry "pandemonium within himself," Höch's portrait of the new woman in *Das schöne Mädchen* (Beautiful Girl, 1920) (fig. 1.3) conveys misgivings about consumerist objectifications of women, salient in the replacement of the woman's face with an oversized light bulb and her encasing amidst overpowering BMW insignias, tires, gears, cogs, and a wrench.[54] A bisexual woman herself, Höch was to later comment on the challenges facing the new woman in both art and mass media framed through masculinist culture, including that of male Dadaists: "The Dadaists were not inclined to abandon the (conventional) male/masculine morality toward woman. . . . Enlightened by Freud, in protest against the older generation they all desired the New Woman. . . . But they firmly rejected the notion that they, too, had to adopt new attitudes."[55]

Alongside print and visual works, Berlin Dada's public performances played into the sensationalist jingoism of mass media in Germany in order to spread agitation. It was Baader who remarked seventy years before Baudrillard on the subject of hyperreality: "World War I was a newspaper war. In reality it never existed."[56] Dadaist media theatrics mocked the militaristic, hierarchical, and submissive attitudes of Germany's mass media to invigorate democratic dissent. This strategy was effective at least for a time at circumventing attempts by authorities to erase dissenting voices from the public sphere. These interventions inspired the development of similar performative interventions into popular media up to the present. Similarly conceived to feed the sensationalist appetite of mass media, Baader and Hausmann founded a number of mock institutions, which informed their

Figure 1.3. Hannah Höch, *Das schöne Mädchen* (Beautiful Girl), 1920. © 2019 Artists Rights Society (ARS), New York / VG Bild-Kunst, Bonn. Image courtesy of Berlinische Galerie.

campaign of public disinformation between 1918 and 1919. These included a political party, the Unabhängigen Sozialdemokratische Partie (Independent Social-Democratic Party), which was dedicated to ending the war and the Protestant-inspired Christus G.m.b.H, a Christian sect that conferred dispensations to army deserters and pacifists in a simultaneous mockery of the religious fervor of the period and an attempt at claiming conscientious objection as Christian martyrdom. The public announcement (a spoof) of the creation of the Dada republic of Nikolasse, a rich neighborhood in Berlin, ironically framed as a push toward a democratic space to be achieved "without violence, bloodshed, or weapons, armed with nothing but a typewriter," met with a disproportionate reaction by the authorities (the mayor deployed two thousand troops in defense of the villa owners), suggesting that Baader's media campaign was highly effective.[57] Baader also sent a series of missives, printed by a number of mainstream Berlin newspapers, which included the "Eight World Sentences," a Nietzsche-inspired "anti-thesis" parodying US president Woodrow Wilson's 1918 speech regarding "fourteen points" to world peace. In another press announcement, Baader postulated his candidacy as a representative of Berlin, District 1, to the German parliament (Reichstag) under the title of "Oberdada," the president of the universe, likely a pun on Nietzsche's notion of the übermensch, and a sarcastic jab at the racial superiority rhetoric extolled in support of the war.[58]

In his cosmic identity as the Oberdada, Baader staged an event in the Berlin cathedral themed Christus ist Euch Wurst (literally, "Christ is sausage to you," roughly meaning "you don't give a damn about Christ"), which took place on November 17, 1918, the first Sunday of the November revolution, and was aimed at church leaders supporting the state's push for war. In response to the pastor shouting "What is Christ to you?" in an attempt to garner support for war, Baader promptly answered the question with "you don't care a hoot." This action provoked a public scandal, and Baader was arrested for blasphemy (he was shortly released on grounds of insanity certified by German army doctors).[59] As Oberdada, he also urged his inauguration as "President of the Earth and the Universe" on the same day as the newly established Weimar parliament was scheduled to meet for the first time, some five days before Friedrich Ebert was elected the first Reichspräsident. On July 16, 1919, he cast a cryptic leaflet titled *The Green Corpse* into the Weimar National Assembly on the day that the assembly introduced an article in the constitution guaranteeing "Every German the right to give free expression to his opinions in word and print or any other form."[60]

Praised by some and scorned by others, Baader's carnivalesque actions caused a stir among the Dadaists themselves. Huelsenbeck, who had left Berlin to practice medicine, was particularly opposed to Baader's role play, which he saw as an attempt at self-aggrandizement.[61] In addition to internal discord among the group, the limits of scandal also became evident during the Dada European tour devised by Huelsenbeck, Hausmann, and Baader in 1920, which was called to a halt because of audiences' hostility.[62] According to Huelsenbeck's account, the provocative antics by the Dadaists drew the ire of Czech audiences incensed because the group was composed of Germans, while the German public saw them as socialists and the socialists deemed them "reactionary voluptuaries."[63] Baader, in turn, cites Huelsenbeck's poor organization as the main reason for his decision to leave the group and return to Berlin.[64] Yet, Baader's subversion of media celebrity and sensationalism were mild-mannered in comparison with Jung's radical political gesture, exemplified by his involvement in a spectacular act of piracy in 1920, which was covered internationally by newspapers.[65] Jung and a shipyard worker, Jan Appel, seized and diverted the German ship *Senator Schröder* to Murmansk in the Soviet Union, where they presented it as a gift to the Soviet revolutionaries on Mayday in an act that extended Dada's artistic subversion to the international political sphere.[66] Jung was received by Lenin as a member of the Kommunistische Arbeiter-Partei Deutschlands and urged to argue for the union of German communist factions upon his return home. He was arrested in Germany on charges of piracy and released in 1921.[67] He eventually left Europe for the United States, disillusioned with the failed revolutions in Germany and Russia.

In Berlin, the Dada Fair in July 1920, the only art exhibition by the group, presaged the imminent dissolution of its activities. The show was organized as an environment composed of assemblages such as Baader's Plasto-Dio-Dada-Drama, a sculptural collage of recycled materials accompanied by prints of odd utopian architectural spaces; photomontages by Haussmann, Heartfield, and Höch (who was included against the wishes of Grosz and Heartfield)[68]; Rudolph Schlichter's dummy titled *Prussian Archangel*, a life-size model of a German officer with a pig's face bearing the legend "Hung by the Revolution"; and typographies and nonsensical poster poems. At the entrance to the show a placard proclaimed: "Die Kunst ist tot Es liebe die neue Maschinenkunst Tatlins" ("Art is dead. Long live the mechanical art of Tatlin"). Both a parody of institutionalized art culture (recalling the *Salon des Refusés*) and a self-mockery, the show attracted the attention of the Reich's lawyers, and the gallery owner as well as four artists received official reprimands for defaming the Reichswehr. Grosz and Wieland Hertzfeld were fined a small amount. The works in the show, which were all for sale, were ultimately either confiscated or discarded after the exhibition, in line with the Dadaist conception of art as a living expression that, once played out, was of no value.[69] The combined activities of the

Berlin Dadaists testify to their profoundly internationalist (and in Baader's case, cosmic) conception in a world tearing apart along nationalist lines. Club Dada self-dissolved as interest in its continuation waned among members, who scattered across the world and across ideological lines. Among them, Jung, Grosz, and Heartfield embarked on a commitment to communism, while denouncing its dogmatization in the Soviet Union. Heartfield escaped the Schutzstaffel (SS, the Nazi's paramilitary organization) by fleeing to Czechoslovakia and subsequently emigrating to Great Britain, where for a time he was interned as an enemy alien. After the war, he repatriated to Germany, settling in East Berlin, where he came under suspicion by the Stasi (East German Secret Police) because of his lengthy stay in Britain. After six years, Heartfield was admitted to the East German Academie Der Kunste (Academy of the Arts), due to the intervention of Bertold Brecht and Stefan Heym. Grosz, Jung, and Richter emigrated to New York, which, along with Los Angeles (where Brecht, Frankfurt school figures, and others took refuge), became meccas for dissident intellectuals and artists as Zurich had been before the war. Under national-socialist rule, Dada and constructivism both became suspect and classified as "degenerate art." Members of the initial group remaining in Germany were forced into hiding, as in the case of Hannah Höch, who in 1926 moved to the Netherlands to join with her then-lover, Dutch writer and linguist Mathilda Brugman. Baader remained in Germany in anonymity, his last mocking gesture as the Oberdada an application to teach at Gropius's Bauhaus in Weimar, which the latter declined. Subsequently, he distanced himself from his former Dada activities, concentrating on utopian architecture.

The two dominant sensibilities of Dada in Europe—Zurich Dada's theatrical experiments and Berlin Dada's media interventions—used participation as a gaming strategy that also emerged in independent avant-gardes in various locations. Even though Dadaist energies took on different expressions within various artistic and countercultural groupings, they all identified with an initial Dadaist axiom: "Art is not an end in itself, we have lost too many of our illusions for that. Art is for us an occasion for social criticism, and for real understanding of the age we live in."[70] This notion would take many participatory forms in practice, including games and interventions in games. As for Nietzsche, the initial Dionysian inspiration for Dada's gaming spirit, he would eventually be mobilized for opposite ends by a rejected painter of mimetic idealizations turned enemy of the avant-garde, Adolf Hitler.

Surrealism's Expanded Consciousness

Surrealism emerged with the rise of Paris as an art node in the 1920s, around a group of artists steeped in Dada's legacy of playful subversion, as older Zurich Dadaists—Tzara, and the brothers Janco—settled in Paris in 1921, and against the backdrop of trauma from the war. The initial group of Parisian Dadaists, soon to become surrealists, included André Breton (1896–1966), Louis Aragon (1897–1982), Benjamin Péret (1899–1959), Paul Éluard (1895–1952), and Philippe Soupault (1897–1990), all of whom had some form of war experience. Oriented by Breton's interests in psychoanalysis (during WWI he had worked in a neurological ward in Nantes), the surrealists likened their efforts to the investigation and the transformation of the psychological dimensions of reality to the role of the analyst.[71] Unlike the analyst, the artist did not use psychoanalysis to cure, that is, to adjust to existing reality; rather psychological pathologies were approached on their own terms as knowledge in line with the surrealists' refusal to make reason the sole criterion for expression and the definition of what it means to be human. Accordingly, art was also removed from aesthetic concerns and devoted to inquiries into the liberatory possibilities of fluid models of subjectivity—a project that Walter Benjamin was to later characterize as a bid "to win the energies of intoxication for the revolution in other words, poetic politics."[72] Breton foregrounded the connection between poetry, play, and politics in surrealism, citing Johan Huizinga's discussion of play as an *action libre*, a spontaneous action, which affirms "the supralogic nature of our situation within the universe" and is akin to poetic expression since both share "beauty, the sacred, magic force."[73] The game of "poetic politics," as implied by Breton, concerns the belief in the subversive power of the "play of imagination."[74] The surrealists' pursuit of the liberation of the imagination developed in a range of activities, including games. According to Breton, the central role of games in surrealism spoke to the group's broader pursuit of knowledge about "the ties that unite us . . . consciousness of our desires, and what they have in common."[75] In this light, the surrealists took to Huizinga's notion of homo ludens (the playful human; as opposed to homo faber, the working man), his definition of play as an equivalent of freedom, and his concern with the repression of the ludic in Western thought because it altogether negates the ascendency of utility and technological efficiency as dominant goals. At the same time, they rejected his notion that the game was sometimes a space distinct from "ordinary" or "real" life, both as to locality and duration.[76] Breton, in his discussion of the game in relation to poetic expression, argues the opposite, contending that play is central to the surrealist project: "The imperious need that we experience to do away with the old antinomies of the type action and dream, past and future, reason and madness, up and down, etc., suggests that we not spare those between the serious and the non-serious (the game), which regulate the domains of work and leisure, of sense and folly, etc."[77]

Surrealism and games are linked by a shared refusal of dichotomies, as evidenced by notions of automatism and paranoic criticism, both playful mobilizations of psychoanalytic language and techniques. Surrealists' experiments in automatism, a technique based on unconscious free association, were appropriated and readapted from Freudian analysis, and thus removed from the authority of the psychoanalyst, to instead facilitate the manifestation of collective and individual imaginations by means of language and images. The game *cadavre exquis* is the best known example.[78] In addition, Breton cites other games such as "school notation (from −20 to +20), analogy (if this was . . .), definitions (what is . . .), conditionals (if . . . when . . .)."[79] These games speak to Breton's definition of surrealism as a "pure psychic automatism," indicative of the investment of the movement in the transformative power of the freed imagination, an expanded consciousness absent of "any control exercised by reason."[80] In the 1930s, Dali formulated "paranoic criticism," a technique based on the simulation of paranoid states used in the study of objects.[81] Dali described the paranoiac-critical method as a "spontaneous method of irrational knowledge based on the critical and systematic objectivity of the associations and interpretations of delirious phenomena."[82] Breton explicitly cites a number of surrealist games belonging to the development of "paranoic criticism" in his discussion, such as "interventions into the irrational (in the knowledge of an object, the embellishment of a city, the extension of a film) . . . which through their focus on pleasure" fold into "processes and techniques" developed within the plastic arts like "frottage, frumage, collage, decalcomania, drawing with candles, etc.," thus accessible to all.[83] These techniques speak to the surrealists' deep mistrust of thought and expression based on the belief that reality exists in itself (as intimated in realism, rationalism, positivism, and objectivism). Surrealism called the "real" into question, arguing that reality is not external to perception but intertwined with the worlds of dreams, fantasy, imagination, and utopia. From this angle, Dali twisted Marx's thesis on false consciousness to argue that consensus reality is a paranoic delusion of the worst kind, given its stultifying effects.[84] Thus, for the surrealists, any effort toward discrediting the world of reality was a revolutionary act set to provoke "a crisis of consciousness" and energize transformation.[85] The surrealists' predilection for games reflects the movement's striving for expanding reality by confronting the real with its opposite, the liberated imagination, as well as the belief that in this process the world would be enriched and transformed. Surrealist games indicate the movement's quest for new ways of perceiving, its intense interest in psychic forces and phenomena, as well as its determination to carry on Dada's vanguard leadership in the quest for freedom in social, moral, and intellectual spheres. These concerns, translated into practices that attempted to fuse the individual and social spheres, are intertwined with the conceptualization of surrealist games as rejections of split notions of consciousness and, conversely, expanding upon Huizinga's magic circle, as spaces to perform and test the potentials of the "ludic function" to bring about the unity in consciousness (synthesis) required to transform the existing reality.[86]

Surrealism's Queer Revolt

The antifacist campaign undertaken between 1940 and 1945 by Claude Cahun (1894–1954) and Marcel Moore (1892–1972) is a compelling application of the surrealist game in antifascist resistance and exemplary of surrealism's striving for this synthesis. The couple had been active in Parisian surrealist circles as performers, poets, and photographers until the late 1930s, when they moved to Jersey in the Channel Islands off the coast of France, where they had been spending summers since childhood. The two artists (whose real names were Lucy Schwob and Suzanne Malherbe, respectively) employed concepts and techniques associated with surrealist games discussed in the previous section. These formed the basis of their relentless counterpropaganda against the Nazis, who invaded Jersey on July 1, 1940, a month after the invasion of France. Schwob and Malherbe (who reverted to their given names upon their arrival in Jersey in 1938) engaged in activities during the occupation that were designed to suggest a widespread, international, and insider-based opposition against Nazism in order to demoralize the occupying forces, in a manner similar to Berlin Dada, a precedent of today's so-called viral campaigns and memes. They were ultimately arrested in July 1944 and sentenced to death, but the sentence was appealed and commuted shortly before France was liberated in

1945, presumably because the Nazi commander was advised not to proceed with the execution of the two women for fear of widespread revolt among the island population.

Since radio was forbidden under the occupation, the campaign included the distribution of transcripts of radio broadcasts, including BBC news broadcasts and Breton's broadcasts for Voice of America, translated by Malherbe, who was fluent in English and German (the couple had a radio, which was later discovered by the Nazis and led to their arrest in 1944).[87] Schwob would subsequently convert the material "to rhyme, conversation, and other literary forms."[88] The notes were typed or handwritten with colored inks on papers and cigarette papers, when available. Each note was accompanied by a request to further distribute and was signed "der Soldat ohne Namen" or "der Soldat ohne Namen und seine Kameraden" ("the soldier without a name" and "the soldier without a name and his comrades"), to suggest the work of an "insider." Dressed up in disguises, the duo set out on regular trips around the island to spread the notes and other materials, targeting places where German soldiers were highly concentrated, such as the café terraces of the island's capital, St. Helier, where they would deposit these items in soldiers' coat pockets, on tables and chairs, and folded inside cigarette packets, magazines, and books. They also spread satirical commentaries via altered comic books, then popular among the soldiers. An example is cited by Schwob in a letter to a friend in which she describes how she had cut out the text balloon above a character facing a German soldier about to leave for Russia so that it produced a window-framing text on the opposite page, which read, "Bonne aventure" ("Have a great time").[89] Their print output also included two issues of a magazine "for the use of the Wehrmacht" with pacifist, antimilitarist, and anti-Nazi articles in various languages (German, French, Italian, Russian, Spanish, Greek, and Czech . . .) and photomontages, which they addressed to the Nazi command stationed in Jersey and left "abandoned" in the streets, beaches (inside Champagne bottles!), and churches.[90] In addition, the slot machines of the island's amusement park frequented by German soldiers were singled out for the dispersion of gambling pieces marked with the slogan "Nieder mit Krieg" ("Down with war").[91] "Ohne Ende," an abbreviation of a Nazi slogan "Schrecken ohne Ende oder Ende mit Schrecken" ("Terror without end or end with terror") taken by Schwob from a Nazi publication, appeared repeatedly on walls throughout the island.[92] Taking advantage of the location of their house, adjacent to the parish church of Brelade and its cemetery, which served as the burial grounds for German soldiers in Jersey, the couple undertook nightly guerrilla excursions undetected. Amid the graves they inserted handmade crosses painted black with red letters reading, "Für Sie ist die Krieg zu Ende" ("For you the war has ended"). Above the church altar, they hung a banner paying homage to Berlin Dada: written in red and black letters the proclamation, "Jesus ist gross–aber Hitler ist grosser. Denn Jesus ist für die Menschen gestorben–Aber die Menschen sterben für Hitler" ("Jesus is great but Hitler is greater, for Jesus died for humankind whereas humans died for Hitler"), modeled after Baader's slogan included in the catalog for the Dada Fair, which read "Allah is great, but the oberdada is greater still."[93] From the house they also dispensed food and supplies to Eastern European war prisoners at the nearby work camp, used as forced labor for the building of the island's defense lines and railway network.

In an interview after their release, in 1945, Schwob said that the couple's actions reflected their positions "against nationalisms, separatisms; that is, against war . . . the most drastic regression from revolution."[94] This position echoes the couple's intellectual activism, notably their participation before the war in the Association des Écrivains et Artistes Revolutionnaires (Association of Revolutionary Writers and Artists), an organization founded in 1932 by artists and intellectuals involved with the French Communist Party. Association des Écrivains et Artistes Revolutionnaires was subsequently repudiated amid disputes with party leaders, and an independent group, Contre Attaque, Union de Lutte dès Intellectuelles Revolutionnaires (1935–1936; Counter-Attack, Union for the Struggle of Revolutionary Intellectuals) was founded. Schwob and Malherbe were among the founding members, along with Georges Bataille, Andrè Breton, and others. Contre Attaque opposed fascism and colonialism (specifically France's colonial wars in Morocco) and was highly critical of the Communist Party's support of the status quo (party leaders favored reforms but stopped short of supporting Moroccan demands for independence from France).

Most significantly, the playfulness of Schwob and Malherbe's activism against Nazi occupation of Jersey in 1940 is concomitant with the overall focus of their artistic collaboration: gender performativity. Their artistic collaboration spanned from 1927 to 1947 and included projects such as a series of photographs of Cahun role-playing a variety of guises (including male, female, gender neutral, and alien personae, as well as human, object, mineral, and animal hybrids). Under their gender-neutral pseudonyms Cahun and Moore, they additionally published *Disavowals* (1930), which was a book of poetry and photomontages focused on themes of love, non-binary and lesbian sexuality, and the modern world's social and economic conditions.[95] Moreover, inasmuch as the totality of their projects challenge normative perceptions of female identity, queer sexuality, love, and beauty, it similarly sheds light on the medium of photography as a documentation of reality through strategies that parallel the couple's employment of simulation and role play for activist ends. Schwob and Malherbe played with gender norms as they had in their artistic collaboration (such as Cahun's photo-portraits), masquerading as different personas to deceive the occupiers whose interrogators found it hard to conceive, even in light of the evidence (as previously mentioned, they found a typewriter and a radio at the couple's residence), that the two women were acting alone. Similarly, their excursions were not regarded with suspicion by the island population accustomed to the women's eccentric public displays (they were notorious for sunbathing naked on their lawn, dressing in outlandish outfits, and promenading their cats on a leash). For their part, Schwob and Malherbe premised the interventions on their conviction that many of the German soldiers stationed on the island would act to overthrow their oppressors given sufficient encouragement.

Taken together, the similarities between the playful tone underlying the antifascist interventions of Schwob and Malherbe, and their artistic projects, including photography, poetry, and surrealist games, are obvious. The composition of their antifascist notes, magazines, and comic books is based on language and visual games developed by the surrealists in conjunction with experiments in automatism, including "translation poems," "found poems," "surrealist collage," photomontage and "inimage" (the reversal of photomontage), and "text montage." Surrealist experiments involving objects with the aim of reinventing the world, including found objects, interpreted objects, as well as objects that function symbolically, figure in the dispersion of altered champagne bottles, gambling tokens, cigarette boxes, and so forth, by the two artists. Their alterations of the walls, church, and cemetery are closely related to surrealist techniques aimed at undercutting abstraction and provoking demoralization, which include the inscription of words on articles, and the examination of certain actions, respectively dealing with the alteration of texts, objects, and environments.[96] In the spirit of surrealist poetic revolt, Schwob and Malherbe also upheld queer love in the face of the "real," the *Realpolitik* of national socialism and its hate of "degenerates" (avant-garde artists, feminists, and queers). Their mixture of activism, gender, and play was preceded by first-wave feminists, including British and American suffragettes, who designed card and board games, dolls, and toys to advocate for women's votes. Taken together, these strategies prefigure subsequent forms of postmodern feminist and queer activism that joined art, gender identity, and playful politics, emerging in force during the 1960s and 1970s, and today spanning video games and gaming culture.

Surrealist Games in the Americas

The recuperation of "poetic politics" (that is, the waning of surrealism's significance as a political force) took impetus in the movement's commodification and, like some of its Dada predecessors, incongruous masculinist posturing. The link between surrealism and art marketing, largely forged by surrealist artists, emerged from the group's desire to contest the prevailing separation between artistic and social spheres against the backdrop of an art market that became increasingly tied to the proliferation of mainstream cultural industries post–World War II, most visibly in the United States. Dali's commercialism and ties to Hollywood earned him Breton's disdainful nickname/anagram, "avida dollars" (a phonetic rendering of the French phrase avide à dollars, meaning "eager for dollars"); Dali worked for Coco Channel, Walt Disney, and Alfred Hitchcock and appeared on television shows like the popular 1950s game show *What's My Line?* as a celebrity panelist. Dali was hardly exceptional given that another surrealist, Luis Buñuel, who professed sympathy for Stalinist politics (as did Paul Éluard), also worked extensively for Hollywood studios, yet Breton was particularly hostile to Dali, presumably because of the latter's "glorification of Hitlerian fascism."[97] For his part, Breton was also involved commercially through his own Gradiva gallery in Paris, selling the work of surrealist artists.[98] His ambivalence became a persistent source of tensions within the movement, as Breton sought to act as the arbiter and leader of the movement, an attitude that earned him the scornful epitaph, the "pope" of surrealism.[99] Yet, in exile in the United States (he fled Vichy France to New York in 1941 and traveled extensively in the United States, Canada, Mexico, and the Caribbean, including Martinique), Breton confronted the merging of surrealism with art commerce in surrealist fashion as attested by his participation in an exhibition dedicated to surrealist games and organized by Marcel Duchamp, who arguably became the avant-garde leader *par excellence* in New York. Duchamp included Breton in "The Imagery of Chess," a show and event at the Julien Levy Gallery in 1944, themed on the game of chess and assembling the work of artists who became fixtures in the modern art canon. Besides Breton, Man Ray, Max Ernst, Alberto Giacometti, Isamu Noguchi, Robert Motherwell, Alexander Calder, Arshile Gorky, John Cage, David Hare, Matta, Dorothea Tanning, Yves Tanguy, Isamu Noguchi, and others contributed chess sets and chess-related drawings, paintings, sculptures, and photographic works.[100] The chess set by Breton and Greek poet and critic Nicolas Calas, titled *Wine Glass Chess Set and Board* (fig. 1.4), included in the exhibit expresses the artists' misgivings about the project.[101] The work consists of a reflective chessboard with ordinary drinking

Figure 1.4. André Breton and Nicolas Calas. *Wine Glass Chess Set and Board*. Original 1944. Drinking glasses, tallest: 8 3/4 in., on a board made of mirrors, 34 in. square, with red and white wine. Replica of lost original authorized by Estate of Andre Breton. ©2019 Artists Rights Society (ARS), New York / ADAGP, Paris. Image ©2019 The Isamu Noguchi Foundation and Garden Museum, New York. Photo by Kevin Noble.

glasses serving as chess pieces, the white filled with white wine, and the black filled with red wine. Above the piece hangs a placard stating the rules (the player who captured a piece was to "drink the symbolic blood of the victim") and a proclamation on chess titled "Profanation," which reads: "The game should be changed, not the pieces."[102] This reference suggests that the work, destroyed after the exhibition, pays posthumous homage to Walter Benjamin (four years after his death while fleeing Nazi Germany) in its paraphrasing of the latter's praise of surrealism, which he characterized as a *profane illumination* (a reference to the Greek word for imagination, "phantasia," meaning light, as for Benjamin, mental images were not only illusions but also a form of illumination).[103]

This intervention into the commercialization of surrealism's playful spirit in New York came on the heels of Jeu de Marseille (1941), a game created at the villa Air Bel in the La Pomme quarter of Marseille, where the soon-to-be exiled surrealists fleeing Nazi-occupied France spent nine months waiting for the dispensation of refugee visas to the United States.[104] The twenty-two cards of Jeu de Marseille, based on an old game of the same name used for play, gambling, and divination, were designed by an international cast of artists, including Jewish Romanian painter Victor Brauner (1903–1966), Spanish artist Oscar Dominguez (1906–1957), German Dadaist Max Ernst (1991–1976), Romanian sculptor and painter Jacques Hèrold (1919–1987), Afro-Cuban artist Wilfredo Lam (1902–1982), and French members of the group: Breton, Jacqueline Lamba (1910–1993) (fig. 1.5), Andrè Masson (1896–1987), and Frèdèric Delanglade (1907–1977), who designed the game's box.

The game was likely inspired by the card decks issued during the French revolution, when the kings and queens on playing cards were replaced with democratic allegories such as "Liberty" and "Equality" (the royal symbolism was reinstated under Napoleon). For Jeu de Marseille, each artist contributed two cards introducing a new symbolism that transformed the original game's military ranks and monarchist hierarchy into a simulation of the group's allegiances to the politics of the imagination and the collectivist ideals of surrealism.[105] Newly arrived in New York, Breton wrote that the game was intended as a rebuttal to the consensus among historians that associated modifications of card decks to military history, which he saw as erroneously endowing objects with fixed meaning.[106] Breton also highlighted the collective character of the project. Commenting on this aspect of surrealism, Alastair Brotchie offers an insight, which also serves

Figure 1.5. Jacqueline Lamba, Baudelaire. *Love Genie Flame*. Card design for Jeu de Marseille, 1941. Chinese ink, gauche, 27.9cm x 18cm. C 03.05.03. Photo by Jean Bernard. © 2019 Artists Rights Society (ARS), New York / ADAGP, Paris. Image © RMN-Grand Palais / Art Resource, NY.

Figure 1.6. Xul Solar, *Panajadrez* (Panchess), ca. 1945, 62 chess pieces. Transportable box-board and 2 container boxes; wood, handle and metal locks; wood carved and oil painted, 43 x 41 x 2.7 cm. Rights reserved Pan Klub Foundation–Xul Solar Museum.

to illuminate Breton and Calas's message behind *Wine Glass Chess Set and Board*: "To some extent the surrealist project can be seen as a search for, and intervention in, the new myths underlying contemporary history, the unconscious current beneath everyday events . . . part of Breton's rejection of the position of the 'artist' was his belief that personal creativity produced only a personal mythology, the task and importance of collective activities being the creation of collective myths."[107]

In this regard, the *panajadrez* or *panjuego* (panchess or universal chess, ca. 1945) (fig. 1.6) invented by Xul Solar stands similarly as a counterpoint to Duchamp's more solipsistic engagement with chess and Breton's notoriously contradictory attitude toward the collectivist politics of surrealism. Solar straddled various artistic currents, integrating futurist, expressionist, and surrealist currents, with which he was well acquainted through his travels in Europe between 1912 and 1924. Additionally, Solar's work, including games, paintings, works on paper, and toys, reflects wide ranging interests in literature, mathematics, astrology, divinatory models including the I Ching, music, architecture, theater, marionettes, and pre-Colombian aesthetics and cosmologies. Upon his return to Argentina, he joined a loose network of artists and writers, the Florida or *Martín Fierro* group. Among them was Jorge Luis Borges, who would become his regular panchess partner. Understood to represent the syncretic sensibility of the Latin American avant-garde, Solar, as Borges observed, "lived convinced that reality could be unceasingly modified, thus believing his mission to be [tantamount to] a continuous revolution."[108] In this light, Solar's ludic outlook appears akin to the central belief of utopian currents in culture and in particular surrealism, namely, that the creation of a new world changes our divided perceptions of the spaces of reality and fantasy. For Solar and other members of the modernist avant-garde in Argentina, however, this project was primarily concerned with decolonization. At stake was the take-down of gaucho (cowboy) paintings glorifying settler culture (and masculinist ideals) and their replacement with a new aesthetic and artistic culture independent of European models, a goal shared by similar groups across Latin America post–European colonization. In fact, Solar, in an essay about Argentine painter Emilio Pettoruti on the occasion of his first exhibition in Buenos Aires, writes the following: "Let us admit, in any case, that among us now—if mostly still hidden—are many or all of the seeds of our future art, and not in museums overseas, and not in the homes of famous foreign dealers. Let us honor the rare ones, our rebellious spirits who, like this artist, before denying others, find affirmation in themselves; that instead of destroying, seek to build. Let us honor those who struggle so that the soul of our country can be more beautiful. . . . Because the wars of independence for our America are not yet over."[109]

The *panajadrez* encapsulates Solar's utopian visions of a culturally renewed Latin America and world and his belief in the power of the play to call it into being. Hence, contrary to Duchamp, Solar rejected the original military conception of the game of chess, its binary logic and competitive frame: "This game [*ajedrez creollo*] has the advantage that no one loses and that all win in the end."[110] The board, originally a representation of the battlefield, was modified to stand for a universe: a grid of thirteen rows by thirteen columns. With the first and last columns interconnecting, it represented an open space. Without beginning or end, the grid stands for the infinite possibilities for creation. Similarly, unlike chess pieces, which represent the monarchical order, the pieces of panchess stand for consonants, musical notes, and worlds. Each player receives thirty pieces, which are placed on the board as the game progresses, similar to the Chinese game Go. In order to increase the complexity of creative discovery, up to three pieces could be stacked on one square. The pieces included conventional chess pieces but also oneiric versions of them, including the counter-tower, the bi-tower, the tri-tower, and a piece that could be used by both players: chance. Reflecting its material fluidity, the rules of panchess were not fixed but continually evolving, as Borges recalls in his memoirs of Solar.[111] Solar wrote that the game was a dictionary of a new language, *Pan Lingua*, that combined duodecimal mathematics, astrology, experimental music (*musica libre*), and abstract art. Solar also invented *pancreolo* (pancreolle), a mixture of Spanish and Portuguese, designed to function as the lingua franca of postcolonial Latin America, thus underpinning his Pan-American vision of the postcolonial continent. These foci reflect concerns with syncretism, as well as Solar's position as an artist moving in both local and global avant-garde networks. Much like other linguistic experiments like the Zurich Dadaists' simultaneous and bruitist poetry and the Russian futurists' *Zaum*, Pan Lingua and pancreolo were meant to help re-create the world into a civilization "more perfected intellectually, scientifically, and aesthetically," and to play the game was to help articulate this new world.[112] In "Tlön, Uqbar, Orbis Tertius," his quasi-science-fiction protest against totalitarianism, Borges imagined this utopian cosmos as a juxtaposition of real and fictional places, citing Solar: "There is no word corresponding to the word 'moon,' but there is a verb which in English would be 'to moonate' or 'to enmoon.' 'The moon rose above the river' is 'hlor u fang axaxaxas mlo,' or as Xul Solar succinctly translates 'Upward, behind the onstreaming, it mooned.'"[113] As an appropriation of a tool with imperial (military) origins used for opposite ends, on behalf of syncretic processes, Solar's panchess has significance with the legacies of the Latin American and European avant-garde. As it parallels Breton and Calas's *Wine Glass Chess Set and Board* and like experiments in surrealism, the game anticipates the intermedial chess sets produced by the Fluxus network of the 1960s, the games of electronic literature emerging with net art and cyberfeminism in the 1990s, and the present forms of queer games, which similarly focus on language, games, and alternate realities. Solar would not return to Europe until 1962, on the occasion of his exhibition at Musée National d'Art Moderne in Paris, where his games were shown for the first time in postwar Europe.

As WWII drew to conclusion, exiled European surrealists returned from the Americas to a fast-changing Europe set on rebuilding and in thrall of modernization. In this technocratic context, embraced widely by the art and academic establishments, the returning surrealists failed to find their subversive footing, dragging on to reiterate distaste for reason and its products, the new consumer technologies. The 1965 exhibition titled Absolute Deviation is a case in point. Organized in Paris by Breton and a number of surrealists as an attempt to denounce the blandness of retrospective exhibitions of surrealism by curators unconnected with the movement, the exhibition became instead the epitome of revolutionary chic. The cultural caché of the 1965 exhibition stood in stark contrast with the media scandal provoked by the first surrealist exhibition in 1938, in which the gallery was transformed into a precarious cavernous labyrinth enveloped in soot. Yet, both surrealist exhibitions were meant as wry denouncements of the sinister cultural purging of totalitarian politics and the alienating impact of contemporaneous technocracy—the 1938 exhibition in response to the Nazi's Degenerate Art Exhibition (*Die Ausstellung Entartete Kunst*) in Munich and the International Exhibition of Arts and Technology Applied to Modern Life in Paris, both held in 1937; and the 1965 exhibition satirizing the dulling effects of American technology and France's imitation of it.

As the focus shifted from an industrial to a cybernetic or information society, the Dada and surrealist projects were taken up and transformed in various ways by a number of key intellectual figures later grouped under the canon of poststructuralist and postmodern thought emerging after the 1968 uprisings in France.[114] For example, postmodern notions of the self and reality as fragmented, decentered, and fluid processes, a popular topic of debate among left-leaning academics until recently, resonate with the avant-garde's utopian visions of the ludic human and its world. On the streets of Paris, Dada and surrealism were acknowledged by the 1968 slogan scribbled on the walls by university students: "All power to the imagination." In the United States, Dada and surrealism were echoed in the literary works of the 1950s Beat generation and the 1960s counterculture movements' concerns with the liberation of sexuality and the unconscious. The scope of Dada and surrealism extended through the transnational networks of artists and intellectuals in exile and in transit, to exhibitions and publications spanning Latin America, the Caribbean, Japan, and Africa, where it found fertile ground in ongoing anticolonial struggles in which native artists played a crucial role. The idea also found sympathy among younger artists emerging in the late 1950s and early 1960s, who sought to revive the political dimensions of Dada and surrealism by synchronizing these movements' legacies, such as their focus on games and play to empower and expand on participatory processes, notions of consciousness, and utopian perspectives, with their respective historical conditions: the emergence of digital culture. Among these, the digital avant-garde, spanning groups and networks of artists in Europe, the Americas, and Asia, proved influential for carrying forward Dada's and surrealism's project in their own time and beyond, further merging it with historical native currents and readapting it to the specificity of present conditions in various locations. In the last two decades these currents were themselves brought into the limelight of cross-cultural mobilization, appearing in parallel in the idealized spaces of industry games and as open-ended, contemporary feminist, queer, postcolonial/diasporic, and transnational games.

Notes

1. Home, *Assault on Culture.*

2. Huizinga, *Homo Ludens*, 9–13 (translations mine). The term *homo ludens*, or human player as used here, relates to the writings of Dutch cultural theorist Johan Huizinga, who argued that play is an element that both predates and defines human culture.

3. Ball, *Flight Out of Time*, 105.

4. Haftmann, "Postscript," 217–218.

5. Ball, *Flight Out of Time*, 104.

6. Sandqvist, *Dada East*, 78.

7. Waldberg, *Surrealism*, 105–111.

8. The Victorian atmosphere of Zurich in 1916 is exemplified, for instance, by a night-curfew implemented by Zurich legislators to "strengthe[n] . . . old Swiss liberty" and oppose the "foreign" vices flooding Niederdorf, Zurich's amusement quarter, home to the cabaret and assembly point for international refugees. Lewer, "From the Cabaret to the Kaufleutensaal," 45–49. Huelsenbeck recalls that women were rarely seen in the cabaret, while undercover agents of the Sittenpolizei (vice squad) were often spotted in the audience, prompting the actors to redouble provocation. Huelsenbeck, *Reise bis ans Ende der Freiheit*, 118.

9. Huelsenbeck and Green, *Dada Almanac*, 111–112.

10. Sandqvist, *Dada East*, 30.

11. Ibid., 34; Codrescu, *Posthuman Dada Guide*, 18; Ball, *Flight Out of Time*, 117.

12. Sandqvist, *Dada East*, 34.

13. Livezeanu, "'From Dada to Gaga,'" 248.

14. In addition to Dada events, the group produced one magazine, *Cabaret Voltaire*, which was published on June 15, 1916, and featured collages, drawings, and poetry contributed by Tauber, Ball, Marcel Janco, Arp, Hennings, Slodki, Max Oppenheimer, Otto van Rees, Filippo Tommaso Marinetti, Pablo Picasso, Amedeo Modigliani, and Guillaume Apollinaire, among others. The *Dada* magazine, which totaled eight issues published from July 1917 to September 1921, shows the surrealist turn of Zurich Dada under the direction of Janco, Arp, and Tzara, with increasing contributions by Paris-based surrealists, such as André Breton, Paul Dermée, Paul Éluard, and Louis Aragon. Raabe, "German Literary Expressionism Online," 2008.

15. Richter, *Dada: Art and Anti-Art*, 41–42.

16. Sandqvist, *Dada East*, 37.
17. Ibid., 39; also reprinted in Ades, *Dada Reader*, 191–192.
18. Sandqvist, *Dada East*, 39.
19. Ball, *Flight Out of Time*, 71.
20. Richter, *DADA- KUNST UND ANTIKUNST*, 66f.
21. Ball, *Flight Out of Time*, 134; Bergson, *Laughter*, 200.
22. Ball, *Flight Out of Time*, 12, 145. Ball wrote his dissertation on Nietzsche.
23. Nietzsche, *Birth of Tragedy*, 147.
24. Sedgewick, *Nietzsche*, 60.
25. Wilson, *Escape from the Nineteenth Century*, 160.
26. Ball, *Flight Out of Time*, 10. Ball mentions Carl Einstein's *Dilettanten des Wunders* [Dilettantes of the Miracle] as pointing the way for a Kunstlertheater, a model for the Cabaret Voltaire.
27. Einstein, "On Primitive Art," 124.
28. Richter, *Dada: Art and Anti-Art*, 77.
29. Hockensmith, "Hugo Ball," 462–463.
30. Papanikolas, *Anarchism and the Advent of Paris Dada*, 105.
31. Ibid., 89.
32. Tzara's efforts to spread Dada internationally included a letter campaign to French, Italian, and American artists. Sandqvist, *Dada East*, 40–41.
33. Richter, *Dada: Art and Anti-Art*, 198–200.
34. Papanikolas, *Anarchism and the Advent of Paris Dada*, 105. Excerpt from the manifesto of the Bund Radikaler Künstler.
35. Heartfield is the anglicized version of Herzfeld—in a gesture of repudiation of German nationalism.
36. Richter, *Dada: Art and Anti-Art*, 101–102.
37. Biro, *Dada Cyborg*, 200.
38. Taylor, *Left-Wing Nietzscheans*, 200.
39. Broue, *German Revolution*, 266–283.
40. Ades, *Dada Reader*, 12.
41. Huelsenbeck, "First Dada Speech in Germany (1918)," 111–112; see also Biro, *Dada Cyborg*, 37.
42. Richter, *Dada 1916–1966*, 35.
43. Biro, *Dada Cyborg*, 37.
44. Available at the University of Iowa Libraries (website), International Dada Archive, accessed April 6, 2020, http://sdrc.lib.uiowa.edu/dada/Phantastische/index.htm.
45. Taylor, *Left-Wing Nietzscheans*, 200.
46. Biro, *Dada Cyborg*, 33–34.
47. Foster and Benguis, *History of Dada*, 272–282.
48. Biro, *Dada Cyborg*, 48.
49. Ibid., 48–49.
50. Ibid., 38–48.
51. Ibid., 39–48.
52. Ades, *Dada Reader*, 92–93.
53. Roditi, "Hanna Höch Interview with Edouard Roditi," in *Dada*, 232. Höch's account of the roots of photomontage is corroborated by Raoul Hausmann. Hausmann, "Dadaism and Today's Avant-Garde [1964]," 280.

54. Huelsenbeck, "Der Neue Mensch," 2–3.

55. Hannah Höch, 1966, quoted in Scheub, *Verrückt nach Leben*, 159 (translation mine).

56. Huelsenbeck and Green, *Dada Almanac*, 95.

57. Sudhalter, "Johannes Baader," 215–220; Huelsenbeck and Green, *Dada Almanac*, ix.

58. Stephen C. Foster, "The Mortality of Roles," 190.

59. Huelsenbeck and Green, *Dada Almanac*, 39.

60. Ibid.

61. See a letter addressed to Baader by Huelsenbeck titled "A Personal Dada Matter," with Baader's reply reprinted in Huelsenbeck and Green, *Dada Almanac*, 37–43.

62. Huelsenbeck gives an account of this tour through the German Reich in Huelsenbeck, "Avant Dada," 45–47.

63. Ibid., 46–47.

64. Huelsenbeck and Green, *Dada Almanac*, 42.

65. *New York Times*, "Why German Reds Seized The Ship."

66. Michaels, *Franz Jung*, 48.

67. Ibid.

68. Höch was included after Haussmann threatened to boycott the show. Gammel, *Baroness Elsa*, 332.

69. Huelsenbeck and Green, *Dada Almanac*, 134–135.

70. Tzara et al., "Dadaist Manifest (Berlin 1920)," 22.

71. The group's interest in the unconscious is also indicative of the influence of the emphasis on individual expression found in the writings of anarcho-individualist thinkers such as Pierre Janet (*L'Automatisme pshychologique*, 1910), whose work, known to the surrealists, broke with the prevailing assumption that the individual's unconscious and "rational external persona" were split and the unconscious was not real. For Janet, the unconscious was precisely what informed the individual's uniqueness. Papanikolas, *Anarchism and the Advent of Paris Dada*, 156–157.

72. Benjamin, "Surrealism," 215.

73. Johan Huizinga cited in Breton, *L'un Dans L'autre*, 8–9 (translation mine).

74. Ibid., 9 (translation mine).

75. Ibid., 7–9 (translation mine).

76. Huizinga, *Homo Ludens*, 9–13.

77. Breton, *L'un Dans L'autre*, 8 (translation mine).

78. The *cadavre exquis* game consists of passing around a single piece of paper to several people. Each person writes or draws something, then folds the paper, so as hide the contribution, and passes it on to the next person; at the end of the game the paper is unfolded to reveal the collective result.

79. Breton, *L'un Dans L'autre*, 8 (translation mine).

80. Breton, "Manifesto of Surrealism (1924)," 26.

81. Dali, "Object as Revealed," 87–97; Dali, "Stinking Ass," 97–100; Dali, *Collected Writings*, 212–272.

82. Lippard, "Abridged Dictionary of Surrealism," 210.

83. Breton, *L'un Dans L'autre*, 8 (translation mine).

84. Dali, "Object as Revealed," 90.

85. Dali, "Stinking Ass," 100.

86. Huizinga, *Homo Ludens*, 57.

87. Leperlier, *Claude Cahun*, 275 (translation mine).

88. Downie, *Don't Kiss Me*, 84.

89. Ibid., 278.

90. Leperlier, *Claude Cahun*, 275. The Wehrmacht[o] was the name of the unified armed forces of Nazi Germany from 1935 to 1945, including the army, navy, and air force.

91. Ibid.

92. Ibid., 272–273.

93. Cited in Benson, "Mysticism, Materialism," 52.

94. Downie, *Don't Kiss Me*, 83.

95. Cahun, *Disavowals*.

96. See descriptions of these games in Brotchie and Gooding, *A Book of Surrealist Games*, which is an abbreviated selection from the French; and Garrigues, *Archives du Surrealisme*. Brotchie and Gooding's book includes the following surrealist games relevant to Schwob and Moore's activist actions: translation poems: "For any number of players. This game can also be played by post. . . . A poem is sent by the first player to the next, who translates it into another language, sending this version on to the next player, and so on. At the conclusion, each poem is regarded as an original work in its own right, created collectively by the processes of inadvertent transformation" (32); found poems: same as "To make a Dadaist Poem" by Tristan Tzara and "To make a surrealist story: Take a newspaper, magazine or book: cut and paste at will" (36–39); visual techniques: surrealist collage: "Max Ernst invented this method of pasting together fragments of given or found pictures. By using images that already had a similar 'look' (principally engravings illustrating novels, magazines, and technical or commercial publications) he was able to create 'illusionist' new pictures—bizarre, fantastic, dream-like, ironic, or grotesque" (60); photomontage: "A variation of collage using photographs" (64); inimage: "In this reversal of the two collage techniques . . . sections are cut away from an already existing image in order to create a new one" (64); text montage: "printed texts from different sources and combined for different purposes" (65); experiments with objects: found objects: "objects which simply have a particular presence, or which seem destined to be found, and whose function must be discovered by the finder" (110); interpreted objects: "objects given a new meaning by juxtaposition with other objects, or by negation of their function" (107), e.g., gambling coins with antiwar slogans; objects to function symbolically: "Objects . . . which symbolize the state of mind . . . of both the maker and the spectator" (110); and the irrational embellishment of a city: "For any number of players. The players are asked whether they would conserve, displace, modify, transform, or suppress certain aspects of a city" (120).

97. Breton, "To the Light House," in *Drunken Boat*, 159–161.

98. Pfeiffer and Hollein, *Surreal Objects*, 22.

99. Lewis, *The Politics of Surrealism*, 64; Rosemont, *Surrealist Women*, xxxv.

100. List, *The Imagery of Chess Revisited*, 181–186.

101. Ibid., 72–76.

102. Ibid., 74–75.

103. The notion of profane illumination falls in line with the "energies of intoxication" salient in the poetic legacy of the symbolists and Romantics, and expressionist currents in Northern Europe (i.e., their emphasis on the body and the everyday world as sites to investigate the conditions for "revolution"). Accordingly, Benjamin repudiated the detachment of religious moralism and contemplation as the basis for a politicized artistic praxis. Benjamin, "Surrealism," 209–216.

104. Giraudy, *Le jeu de Marseille*; Breton, "Le Jeux de Marseille," 89–90 (translations mine).

105. The mirrored division of a traditional playing card is retained in reference to the surrealists' fascination with reversed and double images relating to the occult and the imaginary, along with "associations . . . the omnipotence of dream . . . the disinterested play of thought." Breton, "Manifesto of Surrealism (1924)," 26. The cheap and nonuniform materials used for the cards (some of the cards were drawn on cover pages taken from books) reflect the circumstances of war and scarcity and suggest emphasis on the relationship between art and life. The game is divided into a red suit and a black suit, respectively representing love (a red flame) and revolution (a red wheel) and dream (a black star) and knowledge (a black keyhole). The monarchical order is replaced with the categories of genius (Hegel, Baudelaire, Lautreamont, and de Sade), siren (Helene Smith, the Portuguese Nun, Alice, and Lamiel), and magus (Paracelsus, Novalis, Freud, and Pancho Villa). The joker is Pere Ubu, a figure from Alfred Jarry's play of the same name (first produced in 1896 as a puppet show), a reference to subversive sensibility qualified by Breton as "black humor." Breton, *Anthology of Black Humor.* Breton's anthology of black humor includes a list of literary and fictional figures, playwrights, philosophers, etc., considered to be precursors of surrealism (a kind of surrealist pantheon). Breton's term *black humor* refers to "intelligent humor" ("fine and elevating," xviii) in contrast to "satiric and moralizing" humor (xvi); the term is also connected to Breton's friend, reluctant soldier, and dandy poet Jacques Vaché's conception of "umor," which stands for cultivated indifference. Sanquillet, *Dada in Paris*, 57–58. Many of the figures represented by the cards, including Alfred Jarry, D.A.F. de Sade, Baudelaire, and Ducasse (Comte de Lautreamont), are introduced in the anthology, which also includes Vaché and Jarry. The latter was a contemporary and friend of Polish playwright, poet, pornographer, and later war supporter, Guillaume Apollinaire (1888–1918), who is credited with inventing the term *surrealism* (used in the program notes for Cocteau's ballet Parade performed in France in May, 1917).

106. Breton, "Le Jeux de Marseille," 89. The drawings for Jeu de Marseille were shown at the Museum of Modern Art in New York in the first surrealist exhibition in the United States, First Papers of Surrealism, in 1942, and were published for the first time in Revue VVV, edited by Marcel Duchamp, Max Ernst, David Hare, and Breton in New York, in 1943. The complete designs for the card set were finally published in 1983 by Andre Dimanche, the editor of *Cahiers du Sud*, and are now available as an art collector's item, rather than as originally intended as a game that could be both played as a traditional card deck and as a model for inventing new games.

107. Brotchie and Gooding, *Book of Surrealist Games*, 161.

108. Borges quoted in Olea, "Xul's Innermost Experience," 63.

109. Artundo, *Alexandro Xul Solar*, 111 (translation mine).

110. Xul Solar quoted in Artundo, *Alexandro Xul Solar*, 193 (translation mine).

111. Borges and Kodama, *Atlas*, 77–81.

112. Solar, "Pan-Ajedrez o Pan-Juego," 194.

113. Borges, *Collected Fictions*, 73.

114. Among them is Jacques Lacan, a surrealist and later psychoanalyst known for his notion of hyperreality: a representation, or a sign, without an original referent, which typifies the postmodern condition akin to schizophrenia, the inability to distinguish the "real" from the symbolic (and the preference for the simulacrum). Fredric Jameson speaks to the simulacrum in his critique of the history-averse cultural forms of postmodernism, which he

likens to a "surrealism without the unconscious." Jameson, *Postmodernism*, 174. Previously, Guy Debord characterized this condition as the triumph of the "spectacle." Debord, *The Society of the Spectacle*. Similarly linking schizophrenia with postmodern capitalism, Gilles Deleuze and Félix Guattari (the latter, a former disciple of Lacan) also addressed it more favorably as *becoming*, a fluid notion of being central to "schizoanalysis." Deleuze and Guattari, *Anti-Oedipus*; Guattari, *Chaosmosis*, 61.

2

ACTION, PARTICIPATION, AND THE
DIGITAL AVANT-GARDE

THE *DIGITAL AVANT-GARDE* IS BRITISH ART HISTORIAN CHARLIE Gere's term for the post–World War II artists whose work reflected a world in which information, communications technology, and related concepts took on increasing importance.[1] Stewart Home identifies it as a strand of the utopian currents in art, including groups like the situationists in Europe and Fluxus in the United States. Both the games of situationism and Fluxus parallel the emergence and development of *cybernetics* (1945–1980), a term used in this instance to include not only the theory of Norbert Wiener but also related notions of cybernetics as a culture of control, as often found in communication, science and technology studies, and some gaming literature drawing on these disciplines. Largely ignored in art history until recently, the legacies of situationism and Fluxus have been resurrected in game studies by contemporary artists and designers but have often re-emerged decontextualized and given disproportionate prominence. This chapter positions the utopian impulses of situationism and Fluxus in relation to their shared roots in Dada and surrealism and as part of the many cross-cultural groups straddling art and counterculture in the 1960s. The apogee of cybernetics as an influential organizational framework, tracing in part to the militarized science context of WWII and the Cold War, was then impacting culture and redefining Western views of the world. Concepts central to the games of the situationists and Fluxus artists testify to both the prestige and the ambivalence accorded to cybernetics at this time, and include interactivity, multimedia, networking, telecommunications, and information.

As part of the digital avant-garde, situationist and Fluxus members mobilized these science-inspired concepts against the passivity demanded

by mass entertainment and the depoliticized formalism of contemporaneous tendencies in art, including machine-inspired modernist architecture,
the protopop of nouveaux realisme, and abstract expressionism. Extending
the interrelated concerns with cultural and political change that underpinned the early avant-garde's use of play and games, situationists and
Fluxists similarly refuted the authority of the artist and the valorization of
the object.[2] Instead, their collective working processes focused on designing playful interactions, which they deemed games, and games themselves,
conceived to activate audiences' creative capabilities. As Czech art historian
Frank Popper, one of the earliest art theorists of this current suggests, the
focus on participation, a chief concern of art in the 1960s, reflects the artists'
desire to incite the spectator's involvement in changing existing environments.[3] In practice, both situationists and Fluxists did this by mobilizing,
reflecting on, and testing the possibilities and limitations of participation
as a concept interrelated to art, counterculture, and cybernetic and related
discourses in Europe and North America. As a result, they took different
approaches to the conception of games as participatory spaces designed to
free and channel collective creativity toward effecting cultural and social
change at the dawn of digital culture. Like some of the broader cultural
currents in their time, the situationists conceived games as participatory,
decentralized frameworks answering the changing spatial politics of urban
areas of Europe after WWII. In North America, the Fluxists represented
another approach to games as cultural forms articulated in response to the
circumscribed art and media spheres of the 1960s and the mobilization of
games themselves, as exemplified by chess, as emblematic stand-ins for
cybernetic control in the context of the Cold War.

The Situation

Within situationism, games were associated with events designated as situations, a concept defined by the group as "a moment in life concretely and
deliberately constructed by the collective organization of a unitary ambiance and a game of events."[4] In this context, the notion of a unitary ambiance refers to the integration of play and function, art and technology, such
that the resulting spaces and environments, while satisfying basic human
needs, would as well account for leisure and ludic impulses. Accordingly,
at the founding event of situationism (SI, 1957–1972) at Cosio d'Arroscia
in northern Italy in 1957, this syncretic focus brought together two groups

related by shared affinities: the Lettrist International (LI, Paris 1952–1957), a neosurrealist-Dada movement represented by Guy Debord (1931–1994) and Gil Wolman (1929–1995), and the International Movement for an Imaginist Bauhaus (IMIB, 1954–1957), a neosurrealist group that consisted of Danish artist Asger Jorn (1914–1973) and Italian painter Giuseppe Pinot-Gallizio (1904–1964), among others.[5] Situationism developed out of the recognition of the "devaluation" of the political dimension of Dada and surrealism, which as Guy Debord suggested, paralleled the failure of the "proletarian revolutionary movement's last great offensive; and the halting of that movement, which left them trapped within the very artistic sphere that they had declared dead and buried."[6] In absence of political adherences, situationism foreshadowed the decentralized orientations of the countercultural currents emerging in the 1960s. This position was likewise articulated by fellow situationist Raoul Vaneigem's call for "the suppression and realization of art" in favor of a re-creation of everyday life—in essence, the realization of the situation through "playful affirmation."[7]

Key to the creation of situations is *détournement*, a term referring to forms of intervention designed to infiltrate and mobilize the tools and ideologies used to uphold the dominant order for ends diametrically opposed to this purpose.[8] Echoing the Zurich Dadaists, who defined Dada similarly as a game based on the integration of past and contemporaneous art movements, Debord and Wolman defined détournement as the main goal of situationism, namely "the integration of present or past artistic production into a superior construction of a milieu." Debord and Wolman added in a mocking stab at communism, that, "in this sense there can be no situationist painting or music, but only a situationist use of these means" (the reclaiming of Dada and surrealist projects is a case in point). The aim of détournement is likewise in line with Dadaist and surrealist notions of art; as Vaneigem indicates, it ideally functions as "the reversal of perspective . . . a kind of anti-conditioning . . . a new game and its tactics," when applied within the space and time of "everyday life."[9] In sum, situationists saw creative subversion as a two-fold project: a means toward "the victory of a system of human relationships grounded in three indivisible principles: participation, communication and self-realisation" and as a contemporaneous oppositional force against the technocratic forces underlying "cultural conditioning, specialization of every kind, and imposed world-views" at the inception of the information society of today.[10]

The Great Game to Come

The initial focus of the development of situationist détournement as a distinct ludic aesthetic (or ethic) centered on researching "unitary urbanism," defined as "the theory of the combined use of arts and techniques for the integral construction of a milieu in dynamic relation with experiments in behavior."[11] In short, the idea was to conceive of urbanism as a practice concerned with dynamic environments proper to ludic life. In its historical context, unitary urbanism was a critique of the idealized rationalist staticity of modern urbanist schemes. As such, the ludic character of the techniques and practices associated with unitary urbanism responded to the application of architecture and urban planning for purposes of control or determent, or to paraphrase Le Corbusier, to prevent revolution. Situationist critiques were, in particular, directed toward the rationalized urban design schemes by post–World War II architects, which they saw as desituated, decontextualized, or abstract spaces reflecting the exigencies of efficiency and speed; in sum, urbanism in the image of capitalist production. In fact, the notion of unitary urbanism found its way into situationism via CoBrA (1948–1951), an international network of artists, architects, ethnologists, and theorists from ten different countries in Europe and Africa (including future situationists Asger Jorn and Constant), all sharing a commitment to art and socialism in the tradition of surrealism.[12] CoBrA's members' ire was especially reserved for Le Corbusier's Fordist-inspired machine architecture. As CoBrA member Michel Colle wrote in the first issue of the group's magazine, "Buildings must not be squalid or anonymous, neither should they be show pieces from a museum; rather they must commune with each other, integrate with the environment to create synthesized 'cities' for a new socialist world."[13] In the context of situationism, unitary urbanism stood against the reigning rationalism of urban renewal blueprints in postreconstruction Europe, as symbolized by the alienating *Habitation à Loyer Modéré* towns in France (rent-controlled housing, or state-sponsored housing that rapidly turned into dreary planned communities in the suburbs of Paris). In contrast to the vision of the human as homo faber (worker/consumer bourgeois) implied in these schemes, the development of new forms of urban design concerned environments chiefly aimed at satisfying the playful impulses of homo ludens. To this end, the dérive or drift became central to situationist psychogeographic research in urban spaces. Psychogeography was defined by the situationists as "the study of the specific effects of the geographical environment (whether consciously organized or not) on the emotions and behavior of individuals," in short, the environment's sensorial effects on humans.[14] As initially conceptualized by Russian French poet and theorist Ivan Chtcheglov, the dérive is akin to "the flow of words" to which the psychoanalyst listens "until the moment when he challenges or modifies a word, an expression, or a definition."[15] Debord in turn defines the dérive as "a technique of rapid passage through varied ambiences that involve playful-constructive behavior and awareness of psychogeographical effects."[16] The dérive constitutes an act of refusal of the commodified city, instead relating to urban space through play and pleasure.[17]

As elements of the situation, the concepts and practices of unitary urbanism, psychogeography, and the dérive were likened by some situationists to Bakhtin's articulation of the medieval carnival as freed time and space: "the utopian realm of community, freedom, equality, and abundance," as opposed to what he called the "spectacle" of artistic forms that relate to the audience through a construction of the viewer as passive (e.g., theater based on the separation between spectators and participants).[18] Some situationist tracts draw extensively on Bakhtin's work in their critique of the "spectacle" of commodity culture. In an unattributed tract titled "The Use of Free Time" (1960), the piece chastises "leftist sociologists" (i.e., Marxists) for situating the "problem of free time" within "passive consumption."[19] Rather than a critique of consumption—the understanding of leisure as "empty time"—for the SI the question of "free time" calls forth the possibility of a time and space of "free creation and consumption," a direct paraphrasing of Bakhtin that also frames this position as a refusal of "classic forms of culture" (i.e., formalized cultural and social interaction such as "tragic theater, or bourgeois politeness"), "degraded spectacular representations . . . televised sports, virtually all films and novels, advertising, the automobile as status symbol, [and] the spectacle of refusal" of sanitized forms of "avant-gardism."[20] In practice, the construction of situations meant the creation of "experimental revolutionary art" or culture, which Vaneigem, for example, associated with the "unitary" energies of free play.[21] In effect, psychogeographic research is largely an extension of surrealist games, which were first extensively taken up within the LI and sometimes updated by integrating them with popular games at the time. For instance, LI members, among them Debord, devised a concept for a game based on locations in Paris gathered during urban dérives and a pinball machine; the play of the lights and the more or less predictable trajectories of the balls would represent the "thermal sensations and desires of people passing by the gates of the Cluny Museum around an hour after sunset in November."[22] Other LI game concepts included the surrealist-inspired "Proposals for Rationally Improving the City of Paris," a tract that urged the abolition of museums and the exhibition of art in bars; keeping the Metro open all night; opening the roofs of Paris to pedestrians in conjunction with the placement of escalators for access; the installation of streetlamps with on and off switches; and the replacing of streets named after saints with new names.[23] Debord's interest in games is exemplified by the Game of War or Kriegsspiel, which emerged in a collaboration with his second wife, Alice Becker-Ho, in the 1960s, though it was first conceptualized in 1955 when he was involved with LI (the game was patented in 1965). Based in part on the Chinese game of Go as a form, the object of Kriegsspiel is the exploration of possible movements of the player in relation to those of the enemy within the constraints of the game board. The rules are based on an interpretation of von Clausewitz's treatise on military strategy *On War* (1832, compiled and edited posthumously by von Clausewitz's widow, Marie von Clausewitz, née Countess von Brühl).[24] Debord attempted to release the game commercially in partnership with Gerard Lebovici, one of his publishers and patrons. The company was named Société des Jeux Strategiques et Historiques (Society of Historical and Strategic Games). However, this project came to a halt when Lebovici was found shot and Debord withdrew his works, including his films, in protest against insinuations that he was involved in the murder. The game was forgotten until its reappearance thirty years later as a digital adaptation by Alexander Galloway.

Also among the initial projects undertaken by situationists as preliminary research on unitary urbanism are psychogeographic reports realized in Paris, Copenhagen, Amsterdam, and Venice. Abdelhafid Kathib's report on the popular Des Halles market in Paris, recommending demolition because of the commercialization of the market, was delayed by his two arrests for breaking the police curfew imposed on Algerian residents at dark.[25] In 1959, Dutch situationist groups conducted similar investigations in Amsterdam during dérives, using walkie-talkies to survey the possibilities of transforming the central neighborhood around the stock exchange building in Amsterdam into a ludic space. At the same time, they planned an ultimately unrealized project involving the construction of a labyrinth connecting the Stedelijk Museum with the city via an aperture in the museum's wall.[26] By breaking through the museum wall to allow the passage of urban drifters, this project was intended to open up the institutionalized barriers between art and life. British SI member Ralph Rumney developed a psychogeographic guide to the city of Venice based on photos and short typewriter texts but was expelled from the SI for failing to deliver it on time to be included in the first issue of SI's journal, *Internationale Situationniste.*[27] Finally, Debord and Jorn collaborated on a number of psychogeographic projects in Paris and Copenhagen. *The Naked City* (screenprint, 1957) is one of the few images of situationist art, representing nineteen Parisian neighborhoods as a collage made up of pieces taken from official maps and connected through arrows. The arrows suggest flows and connections between the neighborhoods that stand for the complex web of social, political, and historical forces shaping these spaces as understood or experienced by the mapmakers. (The title of the piece refers to *Naked City* [Jules Dassin, 1948], a semidocumentary employing the language of film noir to convey a portrait of New York and its people at a moment of fragmentation prompted by large scale urban renewal.) The map counterpoints reconfigurations of the Parisian urban fabric, which were, in effect, modeled after modernist urbanist schemas tested in French Algeria and meant to reinforce social and racial divisions.[28] In the context of Paris, this meant the construction of satellite cities or suburbs for the working classes, often immigrants from Southern Europe and French colonies in Africa, which were connected to the city center, the seat of work and commerce, and thus of the managerial classes, by newly built highways. In *Fin de Copenhage* (1957), Debord and Jorn further illustrate this dynamic by imbricating France's consumer culture, rationalist Corbusier-inspired urbanism, and French colonial ideologies in reference to images and texts taken from advertisements and comics, two important areas of popular culture at the time. The resulting collage is split in two. On the left, two French businessmen appear above a bottle of wine with the text "black and white" printed on it. The right side references this text in relation to racial categories and negates them with another text: "there's no whiteness" (likely a reference to the *pieds-noirs*, French settlers in Algeria), which appears above an image of French soldiers attacking a native Muslim man. A proclamation of support for ongoing anticolonial insurrections, this image is underlined with another text reading "Long live free Algeria." Similarly, *Memoires of 1959* includes reassembled maps of Paris, London, and Copenhagen and images and writings cut out of magazines against backgrounds of colored ink blotches and drips suggesting a tribute to the avant-gardist strategy of playful media subversions tracing to Dada and surrealism, of which the dérive, détournement, and unitary urbanism are extensions. Together these works stand for the situationists' radical refusal of dehistoricized space as exemplified by the frozen models and the logic of centralized control of conventional mapping, urbanism, museums, and colonies; and conversely, the articulation of modes of spatial representation that speak of the liberatory and decentralist ethos of unitary urban dwelling: participation, communication, and self-realization.

The creation of unitary urbanism began with the environments constructed by Giuseppe Pinot-Gallizio and his son, Giors Melanotte, in 1959 under the term *pittura industriale* or industrial painting, which they developed with collaborators, among them Dutch SI member Jaqueline de Jong, at the plein-air laboratory in Alba, Italy. The project was set to appropriate the tools and applications of industrial production for artistic experiments, in this instance creating rolls of canvas up to 145 meters in length by hand and working with painting machines and spray guns with special resins devised by Pinot-Gallizio, who was trained as a chemist.[29] Pinot-Gallizio's paintings are aesthetically similar to abstract expressionist works. He created surfaces combining painterly substances concocted from pigments augmented by cigarette ash, mud, and gunpowder, with particles of dust and materials from the outdoor environment. Pinot-Gallizio diverged from the abstract expressionists in that his work was intended as a critique of the two main currents in art at the time: abstraction in high art and functionalism in industrial arts. In reference to Pinot-Gallizio's project, British art historian Frances Stracey notes that industrial painting differs from "other productivist artwork precedents . . . such as the Bauhaus or Russian Constructivism, whose geometric forms tended to resemble the machines they so admired."[30] Pinot-Gallizio's "machine aesthetics based on accident and randomness . . . deliberately aimed to rupture notions of the systematic, the orderly, or the symmetrical."[31] Pinot-Gallizio also mocked the democratizing rhetoric of these art and design movements by declaring his plans to sell the rolls of paintings by the meter in streets, markets, and department stores, and claiming that their applications were universal, ranging from fashion to the creation of whole environments. Similarly, in echo of the Berlin Dadaists' mockeries of Russian constructivism, he facetiously alluded to the utopian aspirations of constructivist art, declaring that the ultimate goal of the project was the development of a "unitary applicable art" intended to engulf all cities and ultimately transform the planet into "a luna-park without borders, arousing new emotions and passions."[32] A more modest demonstration of applied industrial painting took place at the prestigious Renè Drouin Gallery in Paris in 1959, where Pinot-Gallizio constructed the *Anti-Material Cave*, an environment that vaguely recalls the cave created for the 1938 surrealist exhibition in Paris.[33] The *Anti-Material Cave* was presented as a blueprint of a unitary environment with large canvas rolls covering the walls and windows of the gallery where female models dressed in cuts of the canvas wandered.[34] The installation also included a "terminofono," a motion-detection device (developed by Italian composers Walter Olmo and Cocito de Torino) that emitted notes of variable pitches in response to the movements of gallery visitors.[35] The whole setting related a labyrinthine playground propitious to the sensibility of the ludic human. Yet just like their predecessors, the conventional adherence to gender categories among male SI artists stood in direct contradiction with the "unitary" rhetoric behind their practice: in an interview, Jong characterized Pinot-Gallizio and his son as Italian "machos," commenting on the fact that she collaborated with them on realizing pittura industriale, yet was neither acknowledged nor remunerated for the work. She sees this as symptomatic of the widespread masculinist attitude of the 1960s and Pinot-Gallizio's overall "bourgeois" attitude, which ultimately lead to his expulsion from the SI.[36]

It was also at the Alba estate that Pinot-Gallizio's friend, Dutch artist Constant Nieuwenhuis (1920–2005) began developing his famous urban design titled *New Babylon* (1949–1970) (fig. 2.1) partly in homage to the nomadic lifestyle of the groups of Roma who regularly camped in the premises.[37] Constant employed nomadism as a model for his sketches, paintings, and three-dimensional structures to convey a vision of unitary urbanism set as a situation, or "the terrain of a game in which one participates."[38]

The New Babylon project consists of a global network of environments integrating a wide variety of media (sound, smoke, color, etc.) that were designed to be reorganized by dwellers at their pleasure. People would permanently drift within these spaces if they so choose. In time, Constant framed his project within a utopian vision of a universal technonomadic society:

New Babylon ends nowhere (since the earth is round); it knows no frontiers (since there are no more national economies) or collectivities (since humanity is fluctuating). Every place is accessible to one and all. The whole earth becomes home to its owners. Life is an endless journey across a world which is changing so rapidly that it seems forever other. . . . A renewed, reinvented

Figure 2.1. Constant [1920–2005], Yellow Sector, 1958. Iron, aluminium, copper, perspex, ink and oil paint on wood. Height 21.2 cm, width 82.3 cm, depth 78.2 cm. Collection of the Gemeentemuseum Den Haag. © Fondation Constant, Artists Rights Society (ARS), New York / c/o Pictoright Amsterdam 2019. © Photo: Tom Haartsen.

audiovisual media is an indispensable aid. In a fluctuating community, without a fixed base, contacts can only be maintained by intensive telecommunications. Each sector will be provided with the latest equipment, accessible to everyone, whose use, we should note, is never strictly functional. In New Babylon air conditioning does not only serve to re-create, as in utilitarian society, an "ideal" climate, but to vary ambiance to the greatest possible degree. As for telecommunications, it does not only, or principally, serve interests of a practical kind. It is at the service of ludic activity, it is a form of play.[39]

A statement against the functionalism of modern architecture, the project also constituted a synthesis of Constant's entire artistic trajectory of collaborations with others interested in the interrelations of art, technology, politics, and space. Constant's collaborative practice spanned CoBrA, a group with a socialist vision of architecture, and the Dutch version of the International Style, the Liga Nieuwe Beelden (the league for new representation), which included Gerrit Rietveld and favored "spatial colorism." It also included his joint works with Dutch architect Aldo van Eyck, whose notion of "structuralist architecture" developing from Eyck's interest in vernacular architecture (African architecture) built on adaptable structures, interstitial spaces, nonhierarchical compositions, and participative planning, echoed in *New Babylon*. Finally, the project also incorporated his collaborations with Hungarian sculptor Nicholas Schöffer, with whom Constant, along with former CoBrA member Stephen Gilbert, formed the group Néovision in 1954, to explore cybernetic sculpture.[40]

Confronted with questions about the practicalities of maintaining such a complex structure, Constant echoed Pinot-Gallizio's luna-park idea, proposing that the automated spaces of *New Babylon* would be serviced "by teams of specialized creators who, hence, will be professional situationists."[41] He also suggested that the funds needed for maintenance would be provided by tourism. Both suggestions met with disapproval from the Parisians, and Constant resigned from SI in 1960. In hindsight, the conflict concerned divergent views within the group on the political implications of cybernetics, either as a tool of control or freedom. For Constant, automation (cybernetic technology) meant the latter. He believed that cybernetic automation would bring about "new conditions in the field of economy," because, as he saw it, automation meant the erasure of human labor and ultimately the increase of leisure. Constant dedicated *New Babylon* to homo ludens, the playful human whom he lauded as a product of the advent of cybernetics. Moreover, in his view, cybernetic automation meant the simultaneous obsolescence of rationalist architecture and its implied vision of the worker/consumer. Freed from labor, the new human, homo ludens, thus required a new architecture.[42] *New Babylon* was Constant's response to these developments. Again, in his collected writings published in 1969 Constant would cite in this respect Norbert Wiener's view of the human worker as "a wasteful producer" in comparison with the efficiency of cybernetic machines applied to industrial production.[43] Though Wiener never intended for machines to replace humans (rather, he saw cybernetics as the integration of humans and machines), Constant still argued that "the replacement of humans by machines, even in regulatory or control functions, cybernetics, does not entail the degradation of the human, but rather its liberation"; a chance to experience utopia, to be "life artists."[44]

In fact, the articulation of *New Babylon* as a cybernetic utopia reflected Gil C. Wolman's definition of *unitary urbanism* in 1956 as "the synthesis of art and technology that we call for—[which] must be constructed according to certain new values of life, values which now need to be distinguished and disseminated."[45] Subsequent references to the term included a declaration by Debord and Constant, who jointly framed it as "the complex, ongoing activity which consciously recreates man's environment according to the most advanced conceptions in every domain . . . the fruit of an entirely new type of collective creativity . . . [and] the creation of ambiances favorable to this development."[46] In the broader contemporaneous cultural context, *New Babylon* testified to a transnational tendency in art in industrialized countries, including Europe, the United States, Latin America, Japan, and the Soviet Union, during the 1960s and 1970s. This current was sometimes identified as Neo-Dadaism; however, as art historian Frank Popper theorized at the time, this trend can also be a reflection of a broader democratizing sentiment in art, which Popper understood as being motivated in part by the difficulty of showing time-based work in art institutions, then dominated by abstract painting, as well as artists' concerns with involving the spectator's participation in artistic activity. Accordingly, as he summed up, artists working in this fashion defined the environment as "the particular meeting-ground of the physical and psychological factors which govern our universe," and used public participation toward "the incitement of the public to participate effectively in transforming the existing environment, in incorporating artistic activity into the construction of new cities, and in bringing art into the street."[47]

Additionally, alongside artists associated with SI were artists focusing on exploring new scientific concepts and technologies as sources for aesthetic, and sometimes social, transformation. In France, for example, artists working in relation to participation and cybernetics included the Groupe de Recherche d'Art Visuel (GRAV, 1960–1968), a collective of Latin American, French, and Hungarian artists, whose work consisted of designing interactive labyrinths and temporal "playgrounds" for passersby on the streets of Paris.[48] GRAV came to public attention during the third Paris Biennial in 1963, when it published the *Assez des Mystification* (Enough Mystification) manifesto alongside an elaborate twenty-room labyrinth consisting of kinetic game-like objects and environments produced for the Biennial. The accompanying manifesto stressed collaboration and participation against the cult of individualism and originality pervading the Biennial. The group's uptake of cybernetics dovetailed with its members' twofold goals: the development of an objective or anonymous aesthetic and a critique of technocratic rationalism.[49] On a more grandiose scale, Hungarian-born French artist and one-time Constant collaborator, Nicolas Schöffer, was well known for his fanciful, cybernetically inspired proposals to transform Paris into a gigantic interactive art-machine. In the United States, cybernetics (and information-related concepts) provided a model for artists and countercultural figures, including Buckminster Fuller, artists associated with Fluxus, Experiments in Art and Technology, and a plethora of media collectives including USCO ("The Company of Us") and Ant Farm. Similarly, Gutai, in Japan, and groups in the Soviet Union took these models to create environments designed to elicit playful interactions with the participation of the public. Gutai's engagement of cybernetics is emblematic; in the context of postwar Japan, as Ming Tiampo puts it, the group's playful spirit sought to foster "a radical individualism that could resist the mass psychology of fascism."[50] In turn, Popper theorized these developments in relation to Umberto Eco's notion of "open work," or work whose meaning emerges from the audience's interactions with it.[51] *New Babylon* was conceived likewise, including its central focus on leveraging cybernetics' utopian possibilities to instigate concrete or tangible participation in creatively and playfully reconfiguring the global environment. In sum, like the aforementioned cross-cultural currents in art and counterculture of its time, Constant's project negated the association of cybernetics with a culture of control, using it instead to rearticulate the world in the image of freedom.

By contrast, members of SI saw this incorporation of cybernetic automation and cybernetics as naive because it failed to account for the imbrication of cybernetics with technocratic control. In other words, such artistic expressions merely reflected, and (sometimes unwittingly) supported, the technocratic development of capitalism enabled by cybernetics. This implication underlines the notion of the *cybernetic state*, Vaneigem's term for the contemporaneous paradigm of capitalist organization.[52] In an interview, Vaneigem addressed Constant's project as follows: "New Babylon's flaw is that it privileges technology over the formation of an individual and collective way of life, the necessary basis of any architectural concept."[53] Vaneigem's misgivings were shared by Debord, who in a letter to Constant, objected to his friend's privileging of an intellectual class as the bearers of a new order.[54] Debord's aversion to technocrats and their attendant scientific discourses (in this instance, cybernetics) likely issued from the reorientation of political participation under Cold War technocracy toward capitalist accumulation. For instance, in France, President Charles de Gaulle's 1967 ordinance instigating "the participation of salaried workers in the expansion of enterprise" put it in rather stark terms, as it defined "participation" in terms of profit sharing (usually restricted to the managerial class).[55] It is in this sense that Debord decried the emergence of participation in contemporaneous art as an uncritical phenomenon. Debord's critique was not solely reserved for Constant but extended to the groups discussed earlier, including GRAV, which he discussed in his essay "L'avant-garde de la présence."[56] In it, Debord contrasts two contemporaneous cultural currents: the avant-garde of absence, which represents the impossibility of developing society, and the avant-garde of presence, which seeks to attend to renewal through attentiveness to the present moment (situationism belongs to the latter). Debord praised GRAV for its commitment to encourage presence through the integration of materials of everyday life and the spectator's participation but admonished the group for holding on to the object (meaning art as defined by objecthood and, by implication, the logic of commodity). Debord argued that the issue of participation concerned life, not art. Participatory art, as he viewed it, risked merely reflecting technocratic programming (a semblance of participation) because audiences compelled by artists to manipulate preset rules of engagement were not actually participants but still merely spectators.[57] The more relevant task would be to appropriate technology (once sufficiently developed) for antiauthoritarian ends, as Vaneigem intimates. He contends that "by laying the basis for a perfect power structure, the cyberneticians will only stimulate the perfection of its refusal. Their programming of new techniques will be shattered by the same techniques turned to its own use by another kind of organization, a revolutionary organization."[58] Similarly, Constant would later speak of *New Babylon* as a conceptual project, an archive for future generations, "I am very much aware of the fact that New Babylon cannot be realized now, that . . . [it] . . . depends on new conditions in the field of economy. Automation now does not mean freedom from slavery and toiling, but poverty and boredom for the workers."[59] The break with Constant, signaling a schism in SI roughly corresponding to the LI/IMIB–CoBrA divide in 1961, did not mean a rejection of art on the part of the Parisian Lettrists as much as it did their awareness of technocracy's mobilization of participation. Subsequently, until its dissolution in 1972, the Parisian Situationists would dedicate their efforts to reinstitute participation to its earlier meaning, the political struggle for freedom; in this instance pitting the forces of play, exemplified by the spontaneous 1968 student uprisings in Paris, against control, personified by the academic technocrats of the cybernetic state.

Dispersing Situationism

Not until 1966, the year of Breton's death, did the Parisian situationists come to public attention through media reports about student activism involving the Tunisian situationist member Mustapha Khayati. Khayati's tract "De la Misère en milieu Ëtudiant" ("On the Poverty of Student Life," 1966), written in collaboration with student protesters at the University of Strasbourg and urging students to resist political isolation by linking their struggles with "working class militants," stressed collectivism and participation, concerns that corresponded with the central role of play in situationist politics. In a brief essay titled "Contribution to a Situationist Definition of Play" (1957), the SI echoed Huizinga by associating the marginal position of play and its link with competition to the broader "idealization" and development of "the forces of production."[60] At the crux of the group's engagement with play was the negation of these conditions. Opposed to the competitive element and the separation of play and everyday life, SI affirmed a "collective concept of play: the common creation of selected ludic ambiances," or the creation of "conditions favorable to direct living."[61] In light of this, the involvement of the group with student protests and its urging of collaboration with workers indicates its investment in politics pitting play ("direct participation") against the forces of technocratic management of economic, social, and cultural relations, then gaining authoritative momentum in academia.

Media reports following the Strasbourg protests focused on the diversion of funds from a student union to subsidize the printing of ten thousand copies of " On the Poverty of Student Life" that were distributed among students during the official ceremony marking the beginning of the academic year.[62] The situationists' rebuttal foregrounded, once again, the group's perception of cybernetics as a discursive extension of authoritarian power, in this case as relating to the spheres of intellectual and artistic production.[63] Stating that the focus ought to be on the broader grievances against authoritarianism, especially in academia, the text noted the background that preceded the scandal was a series of protests targeting Abraham Moles, then an assistant professor of social psychology at the University of Strasbourg.[64] Moles was the focus of protest at a conference held in conjunction with an exhibition of kinetic sculptures by Hungarian artist Nicolas Schöffer in 1965 at the University of Strasbourg, and also six months prior, during a lecture at the Musèe des Arts Dècoratifs in Paris (Moles was one of the first to discuss and promote the connection between aesthetics and information theory, and as earlier noted, Schöffer was a former collaborator of Constant).[65] The involvement of SI in the student protests was preceded by an exchange between Moles and the group in 1963, when he sent an open letter to SI in regard to the concept of *situation*.[66] In the letter Moles, citing his friendship with Henri Lefebvre, offered a series of suggestions on the development of the "situation." The crux of the letter argues for the combination of "novel situations" with "novel assemblages" as a way to counteract what Moles calls "the society of control." To this end, he suggested body modifications meant to create "variations" that would function to counteract the constraints of tradition and morality. These variations would include adaptations of the human body to foreign environments ("gravity-less environments," "underwater living," "walking on the ceiling"), gender deviations (the creation of an infinite number of genders), and sensorial mutations leading to the development of new art forms, which he considered "the dream of 'Total Art.'"[67] (Moles's proposal can be seen as an aesthetic readaptation of the *cyborg*, a term coined by Manfred E. Clynes and Nathan S. Kline in 1960 to describe induced biological adaptations of humans to extraterrestrial environments, which they advanced in relation to space travel).[68] Moles's letter accompanied by Debord's riposte, which described Moles's propositions as "pornographic reveries" and cited his harassment of a student involved with SI, was distributed during the student protest at the 1965 conference.[69] On the whole, the affair speaks of SI's contempt for technocracy as personified by Moles's "Kantian ethic," that is, the belief that democracy is best arrived at through rationalist means, in this case through cybernetics-aided design. As SI saw it, far from indicating democratic promise, this belief was in itself but a reflection of the dominant ideology, the technocratic turn of capitalism.[70]

In 1963, *Destruktion RSG-6* (June 22–July 7), a situationist art show further illustrated the Parisian group's upholding of the situation as a subversive gesture, a détournement, or play as direct action.[71] Obliquely jabbing at Sartre's concept of the situation in theater as existentialist angst, the show was held at Galerie Exi in Odense, housed in the cellar of the first commune in Denmark, Huset (the House). With the backdrop of the Cuban missile crisis of 1962, the exhibition's announcement lauded a covert action by British activists who called themselves Spies for Peace and made public the secret location of six of the British government's nuclear shelters, the "Regional Shelters of Government-6."[72] The exhibition space was divided into three sections: The first section, which was untitled, was designed as a bomb shelter, with cans, water, and plank beds with dummies in body bags on them. The room was unlit and attended by men in protective suits offering visitors "the last pill."[73] The second section, titled "Revolt," was designed as a shooting range where visitors provided with rifles could shoot at pictures

Figure 2.2. Visitors at "Destruction RSG-6," 1963. Image courtesy of Mikkel Bolt Rasmussen.

of political, military, and religious leaders, including President Kennedy, Khrushchev, De Gaulle, Danish foreign minister Per Haekkerup, and the pope (fig. 2.2). Debord's *Directives*, canvases with slogans like "Réalisations de la philosophie" (Realization of Philosophy) and "Abolition du travail Aliéné" (Abolition of Alienated Labour) painted on them, hung alongside the targets.[74] The third section, "Exhibition," showed Michele Bernstein's three-dimensional tableaux titled *Victories du prolétariat* (Victories of the Proletariat), which consisted of plaster casts with toy soldiers and plastic tanks representing "reconstructions" of past popular revolts, and J. V. Martin's *Thermonuclear Cartographs*, olfactory maps made of soft cream cheese (fig. 2.3) representing the meltdown of the world after a nuclear attack.

Upon entering, visitors met with the nihilistic underside of cybernetic culture, as literally represented by the suicide pill and the militarized architecture of the nuclear shelter. Next, they were provided the opportunity to symbolically destroy contemporaneous political, military, and religious authorities on the backdrop of Debord's *Directives*, one of which paraphrased the Marxist call to the masses: "The philosophers have only interpreted the world, the point is to change it" (the other one, painted on a pittura industriale canvas by Pinot-Gallizio, conveyed misgivings about art as commodity). Besides presenting visitors with the choices at hand—revolt or die—the exhibition was intended as a critique of the depoliticized realm of contemporaneous art. Bernstein's revisionist détournement of boys' toys (miniature plastic soldiers and tanks) commented on the detached use of consumer products in pop art movements like the Nouveaux Réalistes,

Figure 2.3. J. V. Martin, "Thermonuclear Cartographs" titled *4 Hours and 30 Minutes After the Third World War*, 1963. © 2019 Artists Rights Society (ARS), New York / VISDA.

celebrating realism via "poetic recycling of urban, industrial and advertising reality," while J. V. Martin's *Thermonuclear Cartographs* sarcastically addressed the Nouvelle Figuration group's call to reintroduce figurative painting with social and political themes.[75] In the catalog essay, Debord, in reference to Michele Bernstein's tableaux, remarks that "each new attempt to transform the world is forced to start out with the appearance of a new unrealism," and Bernstein humorously cites J. V. Martin's series of paintings as "nouvel irrealisme." Debord's comment on his détourned *Directives* sums up the overall effect as a "simultaneous ridicule and reversal of that pompous academicism currently in fashion which is trying to base itself on the painting of incommunicable 'pure signs.'"[76] At the same time, the controversial closure of the exhibit by the gallery owner demonstrated the difficulties of sustaining a position of radical critique from within the art world, even in the structures of countercultural spaces, in this case a commune (the gallerist, presumably a committed pacifist, cited his disapproval of "the shooting tent," only allowing audiences to visit "Exhibition," leaving the situationists no choice but to retract the event). As Martin explained, *Destruction RSG-6* was not an art show, but "an attack on a society that allowed its ruling powers to expose humankind to deadly dangers through the threat of nuclear war and nuclear tests."[77] In effect, Martin's position echoed the early avant-garde's dictum: for the situationists, art was similarly nothing if not a call to action.

Incongruently, in spite of their decentralist vision of urbanity and public upholding of "direct participation," the Parisian situationists structured themselves on a centralist model. After a long series of resignations and purges, the isolated Parisian group declared its official dissolution in 1972. The previous year, Debord acknowledged that SI was successful in its agitational aims but failed to address the "deficiencies" of its own organizational structure.[78] In the last document addressing the dissolution of the group (drafted with Italian situationist Gianfranco Sanguinetti), Debord concluded that the problem of organization was no longer the purview of a single group (i.e., the political/cultural avant-garde) but was at the heart of "the vast and formless protest movement currently at work."[79] Outflanked, yet boldly defiant, he presciently concluded: "Henceforth, situationists are everywhere, and their task is everywhere."[80]

Fluxus Networks

Instead of the centralist organization of SI, Fluxus's loose conceptualization and structure as a conglomeration of geographically dispersed artists was to become the favored form of later groups emerging postmodernism in conjunction with the mainstreaming of the internet in the early 1990s. Similarly, Fluxus members were, contrary to the situationists, uninterested in defining either art or game, focusing instead on questioning the impulse to categorize. Accordingly, Fluxus games involved audiences' participation in both questioning their assumptions about art and articulating alternative structures and networks to institutionalized art and media in their time.

The group itself coalesced around the term *Fluxus*, a Latin word meaning to "flow."[81] Like situationism, Fluxus emerged in the ferment of the 1960s, with footings in the avant-gardist currents tracing back to Dada and in contemporaneous counterculture. The group formed on the initiative of Lithuanian artist George Maciunas (1931–1978), around John Cage's and Richard Maxfield's classes at the New School, and through the series of feasts held at Yoko Ono's loft on Chambers Street in New York, for the purpose of promoting exchange between like-minded artists in Europe, North America, and Asia, as well as to bring their work to a broad audience paralleling the existing art venues where abstract expressionism and pop art were the rule.[82] Initially, Maciunas sought to position Fluxus as a neo-Dadaist group in the spirit of Berlin Dada, writing to former Dadaist Raoul Hausmann to outline his ideas. Allegedly, Hausmann advised against the term "'neodadaism' because neo means nothing and . . . ism is old-fashioned," offering that the term Fluxus seemed more appropriate to the spirit of its time.[83] Fluxus's focus on networking and exploits of communication systems emerged in response to the abstraction (abstract expressionism) favored by the high-art world, in part under the influence of Marcel Duchamp's notion of antiretinal art and against the backdrop of countercultural utopian visions premised on self-organizing communitarian networks. Similarly, in an increasingly mass-media-saturated environment, Fluxists were contrary to the Parisian situationists in that they were not averse to mass media but rather sought to mobilize it to their own ends.

From its inception as a media-aware group, Fluxus's initial three years (1961–1964), which centered on neo-Dada (or noise) music and poetry performances held in New York and Europe, introduced Fluxus to a wider public via televised performances (streamed live in Germany). Initial members included Cage's and Maxfield's students, Americans George Brecht (1925–2008), Dick Higgins (1938–), Allan Kaprow (1927–2006), La Monte Young (1935–), and Japanese composer and Yoko Ono's first husband Toshi Ichijanagi (1933–), as well as the African American composer Ben Patterson (1934) and Maciunas, among others. Their Europe-based counterparts included Korean composer Nam June Paik (1932–2006), German Swiss sculptor Dieter Rot (1930–1998), American poet Emmett Williams (1925–2007), and French artist Robert Filliou (1926–1987).[84] Fluxus collaborators included Daniel Spoerri, Christo, Ray Johnson, and a host of other artists. In addition to being highly interdisciplinary in practice, the group itself was fluid in membership, with exception of the constant presence of Maciunas. The distinctive character of Fluxus art, which, while vastly heterogeneous, was uniform in its conception as self-consciously positioned in and between systems of classification. These characteristics also reflected Fluxus members' concern for the interrelation between the aesthetic and political dimensions of their work. The political dimension of Fluxus was contested by critics, among them Higgins and Knowles's daughter and art historian Hannah Higgins, who implied the ambiguous political nature of Fluxus by noting that the group was above all defined by its "gaming spirit."[85] By contrast, artists associated with Fluxus have tended to situate the movement as an anti-institutional response to existing cultural, social, and political structures of technocratic society, or a society of control emerging alongside 1960s countercultural and political movements seeking enfranchisement and equal rights.[86] In this light, Fluxus's "gaming spirit" and collectivist ethos need not be indicative of a depoliticized stance. Assessments to the contrary speak, in my estimation, of a particular concept about what constitutes the political (i.e., a hierarchical, separate organization), a view that was consistently refuted in Fluxus's engagement with play as a conceptual and formal fold for interrogating existing and developing new notions of what antiauthoritarian culture and politics could be. In this light, notions such as intermedia, the eternal festival (or network), and later attempts at forming Fluxus communities, testify to the group's conceptions of games as spaces associated with decentralized culture and politics.

Intermedia and the Eternal Network

In a 1965 essay titled "intermedia," Dick Higgins discussed the ideas underlying the intermedial arts to which Fluxus was devoted as a conceptual and practice-based nexus of genres, forms, and media.[87] According to Higgins, intermedia arts respond to the rise of "a classless society" and "populism" in the East and the West.[88] Making this point, he contrasts the democratizing impulse of mainstream media and culture with the hierarchical organization of art-historical frameworks. As an update of Duchamp's historical "intermedial" practice, for Higgins *intermedia* stood as a term denoting the rejection of the art commodity to which a purist approach to the medium and the categorization of art into genres and styles was inherent.[89]

Higgins's notion of intermedia likewise reflected the influence of Duchamp's friend, Cage, on Fluxus. It echoes Cage's conception of music, which in a 1957 lecture on experimental music he described as "a purposeless play" that is "an affirmation of life—not an attempt to bring order out of chaos nor to suggest improvements in creation, but simply a way of waking up to the very life we're living."[90] Like any form of intermedia, Cage's music was not limited to musical instruments; he used radios, magnetic tape, prepared pianos, everyday objects, fluids, plants, computers, slides and film, and the I-Ching, among other "instruments." His musical explorations would lead to the first "happening," a chance event with no plot and of indeterminate duration, in 1952 at Black Mountain College (his student, Allan Kaprow, would later define the term). Rejecting conventional musical notation or structure, Cage's experimental music lauded the aleatoric: chance, indeterminacy, randomness, failure, accident, "dissonance and noise," and all aspects of play.[91] He attributed this focus to several of his interests, including his grounding in avant-garde art and its veering away from the artist's control (authorship), his research on non-Western music and philosophies, including Zen Buddhism, his anarchist sympathies, and not least to the influence of his father, an engineer and inventor who worked on problems of radar detection during WWII. Cage worked with his father before and during the war, which exempted him from the draft and presumably brought him into contact with the ideas of Wiener, Shannon, and others.[92] In "Experimental Music," he obliquely references *information theory* to contrast his notion of music as noise with the concept of noise in engineering. In Claude Shannon's information theory, noise is repressed; it represents the elements extraneous to the message being transmitted (Shannon's concern was with achieving a noiseless environment, that is, to minimize "entropy," so as to most efficiently transmit a signal). [93] In contrast, Cage refuted the separation of silence and noise. To this point, he references his experiment in Harvard's anechoic chamber, listening to his nervous system and blood circulation (an oblique reference to cybernetics' research origins at Harvard and its basis in biology).[94] For Cage there is only noise (or embodiment), as noiselessness stands for the privileging of structure and abstraction (disembodiment). Cage's notion of noise embraces the open-endedness of play to, as he believed, focus attention on the act of listening. In other words, on the role of the observer (the spectator) in the construction of meaning (or music, or reality). As Gene Youngblood would later write in relation to intermedia forms, Cage's music aims at creating the conditions for "expanding consciousness" and, by proxy (in echo of Constant), turns people into artists themselves.[95] Cage's ideas reflected the shift theorized by N. Katherine Hayles as characteristic of the second order of cybernetics (1960–1980), one of *reflexivity*, essentially, a focus on the role of the observer in constructing the meaning of a particular system (a notion elaborated by researchers such as Chilean cyberneticists and fellow Buddhists, Humberto Maturana and Francisco Varela).[96] A queer man, Cage's focus on materiality and the body was additionally shared most significantly by women artists associated with Fluxus whose intermedial games stood in negation of dichotomies between matter/spirit and/or mind/body (as will become evident in the next section).

Maciunas picked the threads of Higgins's and Cage' ideas when defining Fluxus art in terms of gratuitous gestures or as cheap mass-produced products; a combination of art and entertainment: "Fluxus art-amusement." Its main characteristics are playfulness and interactivity. "Therefore," he writes, "[the work] must be simple, amusing, unpretentious, concerned with insignificances, require no skill or countless rehearsals, [and] have no commodity or institutional value."[97] In this vein, Maciunas characterizes Fluxus in terms of "the monostructural and nontheatrical qualities of the simple natural event, a game . . . the fusion of Spike Jones, Vaudeville, gag, children's games and Duchamp."[98] Thus, the art object is bypassed in favor of focusing on creating interactions. Maciunas clarified the types of interactions he had in mind by pointing to the subversive potential of Fluxus's practices based on (mis)appropriation of mainstream communication and distribution systems. In this respect, intermedia referred to "noisy" interventions or "exploits" of mass media and communication networks for the purposes of simultaneously disrupting "the spectacle" and control logic of media/commodity culture and, conversely, enabling democratic participation in creative and global exchanges and networks outside the control of art institutions and media channels.

Similarly, the concept of *fête permanente*, in literal translation, "eternal festival" but translated in English as "eternal network," applied the ideas underlying intermedia to communication networks. The term *eternal network* originated with American artist George Brecht and French artist Robert Filliou, who used it in 1968 on a poster mailed to friends announcing the closing of La Cerille Qui Sourit, a Fluxus shop managed by the duo in the south of France.[99] Today, the eternal network is mostly cited in connection to mail art and correspondence networks in which the goal is gifting or exchanging art as a gesture against commodity art, but originally Filliou had sabotage in mind when he called on artists to appropriate public spaces, communication and media channels, postal and transportation systems, and even electoral processes, to foment "(subversive) nuisance" globally.[100] In addition, the eternal network offered solutions to pragmatic concerns with projecting Fluxus's ideas externally, as access to media and communication technologies became increasingly cheap and widespread in response to the needs of military and government institutions and transnational business in the 1960s. For example, Maciunas's appropriation of the subsidized postal system—intended to keep up the morale of US military personnel stationed overseas—to promote Fluxus (through Flux mailings) is a forerunner of Filliou's eternal network. In 1961, Maciunas's undertakings during his tenure as a graphic designer working for the US Air Force in Wiesbaden, Germany, prompted his dismissal. In 1963, back in New York City, Maciunas penned a set of suggestions to broaden the scope of Fluxus via "propaganda through sabotage and disruption."[101] These included disrupting the New York transportation system by means of strategically situated breakdowns on city roads; spreading misinformation (Maciunas did not specify how); sabotaging communication networks; overloading the postal system with thousands of unstamped pieces of mail in the form of packaged bricks and other materials addressed to newspapers, galleries, artists, and museums; interrupting cultural events at museums and other art venues using stink and sneeze bombs, fake announcements, and telephone calls to direct emergency and delivery services. In this light, Fluxus would function solely as the noise within communication systems, evoking kindred interventions such as Brazilian Cildo Meireles's *Insertions into Ideological Circuits* in the 1970s. Additionally, Maciunas's conceptualization of Fluxus's intermedia as a subversive gesture would reemerge in hacker culture in the 1970s and find its full expression in art with the advent of widespread public access to the internet in the early 1990s.

Insofar as Maciunas's proposals recall earlier activities by Dada, surrealist, and situationist members, Fluxus member Henry Flynt said that Maciunas envisioned them as a historically situated response to international media corporations and networks emerging as new forms of power in the 1960s. In this sense, Fluxus was a wry parody modeled along the lines of "international corporatization" and "alluding to utopian communalism."[102] This echoes Maciunas's provocative characterization of Fluxus in relation to Russian constructivism on various occasions and his attempts to steer the movement into a collectivist enterprise incorporating Fluxus workers, a collective newspaper, a Flux housing cooperative, and a Flux mail-order catalog styled on the then-popular Sears Roebuck catalog, but in this case offering Fluxus products available for purchase at low cost. A network of Flux shops and warehouses located in New York, the Netherlands, France, and Japan also carried such items, among them Fluxus games.

Fluxus Games for One Player

Speaking on the role of "jokes, games, puzzles and gags" in Fluxus, member Ken Friedman noted the various dimensions of play significant to the movement: "Play comprehends far more than humor. There is the play of ideas, the playfulness of free experimentation, the playfulness of free association and the play of paradigm shifting that are as common to scientific experiment as to pranks."[103] The meaning of Fluxus games resides in their concept and form as intermedial, in their indeterminate and cross-cultural works in between genres and fields, with open-ended meaning as vehicles of audience participation and their embeddedness across distribution systems, including artist-run, educational, public, and art spaces.[104] In short, Fluxus games reflect the indeterminate definition of Fluxus as a network, and in so doing, they highlight context, in this case, the larger circuits of exchange and meaning in which art and media commodities, play, and the player are embedded. Fluxus games offer players a tool and a metaphor for understanding that contexts (their sense of social reality) are not fixed but emerge within a network of power relations in which they participate, and thus produce, on a daily basis, be it wittingly or unwittingly.

For instance, the Flux kit Flux Paper Games: Rolls and Folds (1969–1976) plays on the performative dimension of intermedia, showing that its coming into being depends on the player's actions.[105] The kit contains many games: two by Paul Sharits, respectively Sound Fold, a piece of crumpled paper that produces sound when unfolded, and Unrolling Screen Piece, a film fragment with instructions that read, "Pull down roll, fold into pad, wipe until clean, drop into toilet, flush away paper"; three games by Gregg Sharits, including Bag Trick, a corn-filled bag in a paper roll; Roll Fold, a paper rolled and folded once; and Roll Trick, a folded paper with matchsticks sticking out with the instructions "Ignite here"; David Thompson's Un Roll, a piece of wallpaper and a paper with a printed letter game showing the word "roll"; and Bob Grimes's Pull Fold, a perforated paper with an inserted loop with a printed instruction: "Pull."[106] Ridiculing the ocular-centrism of Western art, the kit reflects Fluxus's concern with the intermedial as a nexus for engaging a range of human senses: sound, smell, touch, and vision. Moreover, it prompts the player to consider their own actions and articulate their position, for to follow the rules of this game is to ultimately be willing to participate in destroying it (as an art object, a game, and a commodity).

Playing Fluxus games did not always involve destruction, and in some cases, Fluxus artists denied this possibility to call attention to ways in which our interactions with objects are often conditioned, or can be used for deconditioning. An example is Maciunas's Flux Snow Game (1966), which consists of a transparent plastic box containing styrofoam bits with a label showing a diagram of snowflakes.[107] This game involves a visual pun on the networked nature of Fluxus in reference to the physical structure of snowflakes that similarly results from self-organization processes. The game obliquely refers to emergence, a concept associated with general systems theory (related to cybernetics, systems theory is an interdisciplinary study of the organization of systems, whether they are biological, technological, or social entities).[108] It suggests that Fluxus-like games are created out of the interactions or relationships among the players and that these interactions ultimately determine their overall structure (as is the case with snowflakes). George Brecht, a chemist by profession, likewise produced games exploring the links between structure, signs, and interactivity and included recycled instructions in the form of experimental music scores, like some of the scores produced by Cage and other Fluxus musicians.[109] Brecht's puzzle games, such as the Puzzle Series (fig. 2.4), combined found materials with scores typed on cards in the form of instructions.[110] These instructions, which followed the free association principles of Fluxus music, were designed to induce a sense of puzzlement. A card included in Bead Puzzles reads, for instance: "Bead Puzzle, arrange the beads so that they are the same. Arrange the beads so that they are different."[111] The Swim Puzzles (1965, 1983) contain shells and a directive printed on a card urging the player to "Arrange the shells in such a way that the word CUAL never appears."[112] The Inclined Plane Puzzle series (1965) contains a stainless steel ball and instructions printed on a card: "Inclined Plane Puzzle/Place ball on inclined surface/Observe the ball rolling uphill."[113] As playful explorations of the word *puzzle* these games draw attention to the deductive process of puzzle-solving to suggest that the expected approach to play (i.e., to solve the puzzle) is not applicable. Both in anticipation of poststructuralist and deconstructionist notions of the sign, and as an extension of the legacy of playful subversions of language in the early avant-gardes, Brecht's games point to the arbitrary nature of rules, signs, and structures and their power to affect behavior and shape the material world. These concerns are evoked in the artist's other games, which are similarly rendered unplayable. An example is Closed on Mondays (1969), a Flux game that consists of a black plastic box containing adhesive materials sealing it permanently; the label, designed by Maciunas, shows five children playing in front of a set of double doors bearing the title of the game spelled out in graffiti.[114] Does the title refer to museum hours? Similarly, Direction (1965) by George Brecht, is a

Figure 2.4. George Brecht (1925–2008), Games & Puzzles/Ball Puzzle, 1983. Plastic box with offset label, containing offset card and wood ball; overall (closed): 3¹⁵⁄₁₆ × 4¹¹⁄₁₆ × ⅝″ (10 × 11.9 × 1.6 cm). © 2019 Artists Rights Society (ARS), New York / VG Bild-Kunst, Bonn. Publisher ReFlux Editions. The Gilbert and Lila Silverman Fluxus Collection Gift. The Museum of Modern Art, New York, NY, U.S.A. Digital Image © The Museum of Modern Art/Licensed by SCALA/Art Resource, NY.

simple white box with a label affixed on top and the image of a hand on the bottom with the index finger ending in the title of the game and pointing upward.[115] The game's visual prompt, upward, is equivocal, dependent on the player's interpretation: does upward mean to move the box according to direction? Or to look up? Or to do both? Designed to puzzle the player, Fluxus games simultaneously call attention to and are contrary to the normative conception of games, in which to play is to submit to the designer's imposed rules and constraints. Fluxus games ask the player to decide how to play, that is, to invent the rules of participation.

Fluxus Games for Multiple Players

If these games reflect concern for the conditioning effects of a burgeoning informational culture on the individual, other Fluxus games foreground the utopian vein underpinning Fluxus's belief in the transformative impact of the freed imagination and the power of collective play for creating a cooperative and international community. For instance, the Leeds game (1976), a card game by French American Robert Filliou, a trained economist, admirer of the utopian socialist Charles Fourier, fighter in the communist resistance during the Nazi occupation of France, and George Brecht's collaborator, can be considered an homage to surrealism's engagement of games as a metaphor of poetics, or a creative space intent on suspending individual alienation and dedicated to the exploration of the utopian possibilities of playful community. The game involves drinking and is played blindfolded and using the Obvious Deck (1967), a deck containing fifty-four cards with the same image on both sides so that audience members can shout instructions to the players, who must trust to be directed by the people watching over them.[116] The game fits Filliou's notion of the *un-school*, a term connected to a broader project he deemed "Principles of Poetic Economy" (1966) and elaborated in the form of art-based pedagogy in *Teaching and Learning as Performing Arts* (1967–1970). The overarching principle was that "a great deal of artists' work has to do with un-learning, with anti-brainwashing."[117]

Trust is similarly a central theme in Play It by Trust (1966) (fig. 2.5) by hippie icon, lifelong pacifist, and Fluxus associate Yoko Ono. The game reflects Duchamp's influence as well as the activist edge of Fluxus.[118] Play It by Trust consists of an all-white chess set that is part of a larger installation consisting of two white chairs and table with an inscription that reads: "Chess Set For Playing As Long As You Can Remember Where All Your Pieces Are."[119] In contrast to Duchamp's cerebral engagement of chess, Ono's is unequivocally activist. It is an antiwar statement. The installation alludes to chess as a simulacrum of war and the Cold War era military conflict, of which the Fischer-Spassky world championship chess match in 1972 would become an emblem. At the age of twelve, Ono experienced firsthand the firebombing of Tokyo by the US Air Force in 1945. At the height of the Vietnam War, Ono's act of painting all the chess pieces white stands as a gesture that erases the binary logic of war, as simulated by the chess board in black and white. Instead, Ono transforms the board into a space for negotiation with the color white standing as a symbol of pacifism.

Similarly, the games of Japanese Fluxus member Takako Saito overlap concerns related to activism, pedagogy, and embodiment. They are rooted in the activism in Japan and the United States after WWII.[120] As in the

Figure 2.5. Yoko Ono, *Play It by Trust*, 1966. Wooden chess set, table, chairs. Photo by Iain Macmillan. © Yoko Ono / Courtesy Galerie Lelong & Co., New York.

United States at the time, Japanese universities were important nodes of dissent involving a wide range of groups, some with specific political leanings like the anarchist-communist league Zengakuren, of whom the situationists were fond, and others adhering to cultural currents such as Sozo Biiku Undo, the Creative Art Education movement, in which Saito participated as a psychology student at the University of Tokyo.[121] This movement emerged out of theories developed after WWII by Japanese pedagogue and art collector, Teijiro Kubo, reflecting his critique of the colonial ideologies underlying the transformation of Japanese art education in imitation of Western models. The movement responded by using art and play to stimulate students' and teachers' creativity and free will.[122] Saito's friendship with members of the group living in and between Japan and the United States, such as Japanese artist Ayo, led to her association with New York Fluxus, where she continued to develop her concerns with play and pedagogy.

From 1964 forward, Saito began developing a series of wooden chess sets crafted in high-quality materials, an unusual trait in Fluxus works though the interest in fine crafts would become salient among feminist artists in the 1970s. Saito's chess series includes sets that, like Ono's, are conceived as intermedial disruptions of chess as a highly formalized simulation of militarist space. Similarly, Saito's use of chess differed from Duchamp's, as her sets have a distinctive focus on sensuality, articulating chess as a space for engaging the gamut of the senses though play. The series includes Sound Chess (1965 and later), which "contains six different sound-making objects in identical wooden boxes," so that the pieces are only identifiable by the aural cues; Weight Chess (1965 and later), the pieces of which are only recognizable by their difference in weight; Spice Chess, in which a series of test tubes containing different spices are used and values are determined by the smell, color, and texture of the contents; Smell Chess (1965 and later) (fig 2.6), in which "thirty-two glass containers with liquids of various odors have to be sniffed and identified"; and Wine Chess (late 1970s and later) and Liquor Chess where the pieces are glasses of wine and liquor that players must drink, perhaps in an oblique homage to surrealism.[123] As noted by art historian Midori Yoshimoto, Saito's chess sets do not adhere to the binary logic of chess play as "winning was no longer as important as one's physical interaction with the game pieces."[124] Rather, "by involving the senses that were normally unrelated to the traditional game, Saito transformed the ultimate conceptual game into a play of sensuous interactions."[125] Saito's holistic approach to sensual experience reflects similar concerns of other artists, such as John Cage, though because this is her practice's main focus, Saito's attention to the body is more consonant with parallel countercultural currents in art and culture at the time, including feminist, queer, civil rights and anti-colonial movements.

Saito also developed games involving simple forms like paper cubes and other modified game props for Fluxus events, or Fluxfests, held at

Figure 2.6. Takako Saito (b. 1929) © 2019 Artists Rights Society (ARS), New York / VG Bild-Kunst, Bonn. *Smell Chess, Liquids*. Ca. 1965. Wood chessboard with thirty vial pieces (two missing), originally containing various liquids, and lid. Overall 2 9/16 × 5 7/8 × 5 7/8″ (6.5 × 15 × 15 cm). Publisher: Fluxus. The Gilbert and Lila Silberman Fluxus Collection Gift. The Museum of Modern Art, New York, NY, U.S.A. Digital Image © The Museum of Modern Art/Licensed by SCALA/Art Resource, NY.

various venues, including colleges. Saito's game, Kicking Boxes Billiard, was played with the participants' feet, using the boxes in lieu of balls, at the Flux Olympiad in Stony Brook, New York, on August 18, 1969, in conjunction with other disrupted games. There was a version of Ping-Pong played with altered rackets: "Convex, corrugated rackets, rackets with water containers, rackets with a hole in the center, inflated or soft rackets," tennis and badminton played on the floor with balloons, and other games with modified equipment.[126] In February 1970, another Fluxfest held at Douglass College in New Brunswick, New Jersey, included "soccer played on stilts, a javelin event that substituted a balloon for a javelin, and table tennis played with paddles with holes in the center or corrugated metal cans glued onto the paddle."[127] Given the pedagogical basis of Saito's work, it was apropos that these fests took place at educational institutions, where Fluxus events coincided with a period of intense student agitation against war and demands for educational and broader social change. Within this context, the games reflect Saito's cultivation of sensuality and pleasure as a political position against the rigid rationalism and masculinism at the height of the Cold War.

The nurturing of politicized forms of sensuality and pleasure were not a given in Fluxus, however, as another member, Carolee Schneemann, discovered. Maciunas's disapproval of her live performance, Meat Joy in 1964, because of its explicitly erotic themes, led to her estrangement from the group. Far from ambiguously political or apolitical, Saito's games best exemplify Fluxus's alternative formulation of the political, understood to broadly include any creative act and expression antithetical to the logic of control in the forms of imperialism, militarism, and sexism in art, education, and games.

Fluxus Ludic Environments

As products, Fluxus games, along with the Flux shops and warehouse ventures, were not particularly successful at attracting a mainstream audience. Like Saito's, many of the games were mainly intended to be played at Flux events held at institutions. From 1966 on, Fluxus activities were mostly devoted to the realization of artist-run communes, as was the case of the Flux-House project, which Maciunas envisioned as living, working, and exhibition environments under the management of Fluxus.[128] In one iteration, Fluxus took on the form of a nonprofit organization presided over by Maciunas and Robert Watts that purchased warehouse buildings in an area in New York City known today as SoHo, at the time transforming as a locus of housing speculation. An update on Dadaist appropriations of institutional authority, this project involved the creation of a Flux amusement center managed by the Greene Street Precinct, Inc., a Fluxus company meant to operate "a unique entertainment and game environment" that combined a shopping mall and arcade format, as well as coordinated "the development, distribution, and sale of a new product line utilizing the talents of new and well-known artists and designers."[129] Fluxus members Dick Higgins, Claes Oldenburg, and Wolf Vostell were also active in thinking about what they termed *Fluxarchitecture*. Vostell's introduction to *Fantastic Architecture* (1966), a volume that included contributions by R. Buckminster Fuller, the former Berlin Dadaist Raoul Haussman, and John Cage, delineated its aims as follows: "A new life. . . . Our projects—our environments are meant to free men—only the realization of utopias will make man happy and release him from his frustrations! Use your imagination! Join in . . . share the power! Share property!"[130] Though initially successful, the realization of Flux-Housing projects, according to Schneemann, was generally limited to squatting, prevented from a more official existence by opposition from the mafia and legal action by New York City officials.[131] The confrontation between the city and Maciunas was transformed by the latter into a Flux-event titled "Flux Combat with New York State Attorney General (& Police)" (1966). Archival documentation of the project includes Maciunas's satirical letters of petition to city officials, photos of Maciunas in various disguises as a gorilla ingesting the letters sent by the attorney general's office, other materials used as disguises to elude the police, postcards mailed by friends in Europe and Asia to city offices in order to make it appear as if Maciunas was traveling abroad, and plans for and photographic documentation of the "Flux-fortress," a transformation of Maciunas's living space into an elaborate labyrinth devised to frustrate the city's law enforcement.

Unlike situationism, whose concepts such as unitary urbanism, psychogeography, the dérive, and détournement would not become fashionable again until the 1990s, during its time Fluxus was acknowledged as a force for shaping nascent practices involving art and technology. Though some Fluxus artists worked extensively with mass-media technology, including photocopy machines, video, television, and computers, in hindsight, Fluxus's notions of intermedial arts and eternal network were the group's most significant legacies to both artistic and countercultural currents at a key moment in the emergence of the information society and its technological structures, including digital networks and media. The influence of Fluxus was acknowledged by art critic Thomas Albright's two-part series published under the title "Correspondence Art" in Rolling Stone in 1972.[132] In this series, Albright argued for Fluxus's influence beyond art, citing its impact on the digital counterculture, noting the similarities between the "correspondence network" (this allusion referenced mail art, including Filliou's eternal network and Fluxus's mail-order catalogs) and Stewart Brand's *Whole Earth Catalogue* (the precursor to virtual communities like the Well and the Whole Earth 'Lectronic Link, at the inception of the internet), even though, as he notes, the latter was framed within "a survivalist model" and was commercially driven.[133] Similarly, in 1970, media theorist Gene Youngblood would take up the notion of intermedia as a framework for theorizing the playful merging of art, counterculture, and environment, through then-emerging cybernetic technologies.

Notes

1. Gere, *Digital Culture*, 75.
2. Art historian Lucy Lippard characterized this period (1966–1972) as one marked by dematerialization in art. Lippard, *Six Years*. Otherwise worded, dematerialization in art reflects the impact of cybernetics and other information-related concepts on art at this time.
3. Popper, *Art-Action and Participation*, 7.
4. Andreotti and Internationale Situationniste, *Theory of the Dérive*, 68. Another definition would reprise Sartre's notion of the situation: "Up till now philosophers and artists have only interpreted situations; the point now is to transform them. Since human beings are molded by the situations they go through, it is essential to create human situations. Since individuals are defined by their situation, they need the power to create situations worthy of their desires." Internationale Situationniste, "Questionnaire," 178; Gilman, "Asger Jorn's Avant-Garde Archives," 201. A Dadaist-inflected definition of the concept was explained by the SI in reference to Bakhtin's carnivalesque, a concept underlying the latter's attack on Soviet social realism mandated by Stalin: "Similar to Marx, who deduced a revolution based on science, we deduce a revolution based on the festival . . . a revolution without a festival is not a revolution. . . . We demand the most serious of games." Berréby, *Documents Relatifs à la Fondation de l'Internationale Situationniste: 1948-1957*, 39 (translation mine). Bakhtin's "carnivalesque spirit" provides a counter to "the Enlighteners' reason" in its *profane illumination* of the transgressive politics of folk laughter—its power to invade, dismantle, and turn serious culture against itself. Bakhtin, *Rabelais and His World*, 118.
5. Debord and Wolman were previously part of the Lettrists (LI, 1946–), a neo-Dada group led by Jewish Romanian poet and filmmaker Isidore Isou. Following disputes with Isou, the dissident offshoot of Lettrism, the Lettrist International (LI, Paris 1952–1957) was founded by Debord, Wolman, Jean-Louis Brau, and Serge Berna; see "Finis les Pieds Plats," originally published in *Internationale Lettriste* 1 (December 1952), reprinted in Berréby, *Documents Relatifs à la Fondation de l'Internationale Situationniste, 1948-1957*, 147. Hadj Mohamed Dahou, Cheik Ben Dhine, and Ait Diafer were among others members of the Lettrist International group in Algeria and Tunisia but little is known about the group. However, the "Manifesto of the Algerian Group of the Lettrist International," first published in *Internationale Lettriste* 3, August 1953, and other tracts such as "The Most Unshakable of Colonies," unattributed, published in *Potlatch* 12, September 28, 1954, suggests that agitation against French colonialism was high on the group's agenda. Asger Jorn was, at one point, a pupil of Le Corbousier and a cofounder of the CoBrA group (1948–1951). Whereas the LI favored Dadaist provocation, the IMIB privileged the surrealists' interest in the unconscious, which they sought to apply in inquiries into environments. IMIB artists were highly critical of the Bauhaus's project development into functionalism under the leadership of Max Bill (who had invited Jorn to join the Ul- based Bauhaus), a development that Jorn attributed to the employment of a pedagogical model based on imitation and utilitarianism; see Jorn, "Notes on the Formation of an Imaginist Bauhaus," 23–24.
6. Debord, *Society of the Spectacle*, 136.
7. Vaneigem, *Revolution of Everyday Life*; Internationale Situationniste, "Questionnaire," 178.
8. Debord and Wolman, "A User's Guide to Détournement," 14–21.
9. Vaneigem, *Revolution of Everyday Life*, 188.

10. Ibid.

11. Internationale Situationist, "Definitions," 2.

12. CoBrA stands for Copenhagen, Brussels, and Amsterdam, the three cities where member artists resided.

13. Cited in Home, *Assault on Culture*, 11.

14. Ibid.

15. Ivan Chtcheglov, excerpt from a 1963 letter to Michele Bernstein and Guy Debord reprinted in *Internationale Situationniste 1958–69*, 38–40; partially translated in *Situationist International Anthology*, 481, note 64.

16. Debord, "Theory of the Dérive," in *Situationist International Anthology*, 62.

17. See McDonough, "Situationist Space," 75.

18. Bakhtin, *Rabelais and His World*, 7–9.

19. Unattributed, "The Use of Free Time," in *Situationist International Anthology*, 74–75.

20. Ibid.

21. Ibid.; Vaneigem, *Revolution of Everyday Life*, 188. The influence of these views extended to sociological currents emerging in parallel with the SI's concept of "unitary urbanism," converging in a common privileging of everyday life as the central site of analysis concerning the dialectical relationship between the production of space and the reproduction of social relations. The work of French sociologist Henri Lefebvre (1901–1991) was well known among situationists (Debord and Vaneigem, along with the theorist Jean Baudrillard, attended Lefebvre's sociology course during the academic year 1957–58). Lefebvre argued that the transformation of everyday life within the city into a specifically urban experience (and the complete urbanization of society) was influenced by and influenced the dynamics of social relations. Control over the production of space was therefore linked to social control and inversely the transformation of social relations necessitated new ways of conceptualizing and organizing space.

22. Sadler, *Situationist City*, 90–91.

23. Lettrist International, "Proposals for Rationally Improving the City of Paris" (1955), in *Situationist International Anthology*, 12–14.

24. Becker-Ho and Debord, *Game of War*.

25. Khatib's report was published in *Internationale Situationniste 1958–69*, 13–17; Khatib, "Attempt at a Psychogeographical Description of Les Halles" (1958), reprinted in Andreotti and Internationale Situationniste, *Theory of the Dérive and Other Situationist Writings on the City*, 72.

26. Home, *What Is Situationism*, 10; Sadler, *Situationist City*, 115–116.

27. Rumney, *Consul*, 54–55.

28. Feldman, "National Negotiations," 101–141.

29. Stracey, "Pinot-Gallizio's 'Industrial Painting,'" 396.

30. Ibid., 397.

31. Ibid.

32. Ibid., 403.

33. Home, *Assault on Culture*, 33–35. The first show of industrial painting was realized at the Notizie Gallery in Turin in 1958, however. For a discussion of the 1938 surrealist exhibition, see Mahon, *Surrealism and the Politics of Eros, 1938–1968*, 23–63. Like the 1938 surrealist exhibition, the *Anti-Material Cave* consisted of a cavernous environment designed to encourage playful interactions, except that Pinot-Gallizio replaced the mannequins and female performers included in the surrealist exhibition with female models.

34. Frances Stracey suggests that Pinot-Gallizio intended the models to be seen as a celebration of the emergence of a new subjectivity that was associated with the feminine emerging from the "uterine cavern." Stracey, "The Caves of Gallizio and Hirschorn," 92–93. I am reluctant to interpret the models in such a positive light given the overall masculinist tone of the situationist circles, in which few women were active participants (Bernstein was married to Debord, and Dutch artist Jaqueline de Jong, the editor of *Situationist Times* [1962–1967], was Jorn's partner for ten years). Bernstein has yet to comment on the issue, but Jong has recently talked about the masculinist posture of SI men. In an interview during the 1989 ICA exhibition, Ralph Rumney commented on the gendered labor division among the group as follows: "[Bernstein] typed all the Potlatchs, all the SI journals and so on. . . . Women were there to type, cook supper, and so on. . . . A lot of the theory, particularly the political theory, I think originated with Michele rather than Debord, he just took it over and put his name to it." Rumney, "About the Historification of the Situationist International."

35. Stracey, "The Caves of Gallizio and Hirschorn," 90.

36. Kurczynski, "A Maximum of Openness," 187–188.

37. Art historian Alyce Mahon points out that the title "New Babylon" refers to Grigory Kozinstev and Leonid Trauberg's 1929 silent film of the same name, which was a celebration of the Paris commune of 1871. She also cites Charles Fourier's vision of the *Phalanx* and the work of Chilean painter Roberto Matta as influential to Constant's vision for New Babylon. Mahon, *Surrealism and the Politics of Eros, 1938–1968*, 196.

38. Situationist International Online, "Unitary Urbanism at the End of the 1950s."

39. Constant, "New Babylon" (1974), cited in Andreotti and Internationale Situationniste, *Theory of the Dérive and Other Situationist Writings on the City*, 150–151.

40. Oudenampsen, "Aldo van Eyck," 25–39.

41. Constant Nieuwenhuis, "Another City for Another Life."

42. Schaik and Máčel, *Exit Utopia*, 10.

43. Constant, *Opstand van de Homo Ludens*, 131 (translation mine).

44. Ibid., 62–63.

45. Wolman, "Address by the Lettrist International Delegate to the Alba Conference of September 1956."

46. Constant and Debord, "La déclaration d'Amsterdam."

47. Frank Popper, *Art and Participation*, 7–8.

48. GRAV consisted of François Morellet, Julio Le Parc, Francisco Sobrino, Horacio Garcia Rossi, Yvaral, Joël Stein and Vera Molnár.

49. Woodruff, "Groupe de Reserche d' Art Visuel."

50. Tiampo, *Gutai*, 42.

51. Umberto Eco's notion echoes his involvement with the New Tendencies movement in the 1960s and 1970s, a network of artists interested in the synthesis of art and technology, which centered in Zagreb, Croatia, in former Yugoslavia, and included group Zero from Germany, the groups N and T from Italy, Equipo 57 from Spain, and Paris-based Group de Recherche d'Art Visuel (GRAV), among others. Medosch, *New Tendencies*.

52. Vaneigem, *Revolution of Everyday Life*, 73.

53. Obrist, "Hans Ulrich Obrist In Conversation."

54. Debord, *Correspondence: The Foundation of the Situationist International (June 1957–August 1960)*, 231–235.

55. Woodruff, "Groupe de Reserche d' Art Visuel," 26.

56. Debord, "L'avant-garde de la presence," 20.

57. As one of the GRAV members, Joël Stein, later acknowledged, interactions with the interactive playgrounds of the group could become "entertainment" or "a spectacle." Cited in Bishop, *Artificial Hells*, 90–91.

58. Vaneigem, *Revolution of Everyday Life*, 85.

59. Constant to Sean Wellesley-Miller, August 8, 1966, 1–2, "Correspondence 1966–1969" file, Constant archive, Rijksbureau voor Kunsthistorische Documentatie, The Hague (translation mine).

60. Debord, "Contribution to a Situationist Definition of Play."

61. Ibid.

62. Khayati, "On the Poverty of Student Life," in *Situationist International Anthology*, 408–429. The student union was immediately closed by court order.

63. Ibid., 363–373.

64. Ibid.

65. Ibid., 265–266; Moles, *Information Theory and Esthetic Perception*.

66. Debord, "Correspondance avec un Cyberneticien," 4 (translation mine).

67. Ibid.

68. Ibid.; Clynes and Kline, "Cyborgs and Space".

69. Debord, "Correspondance avec un Cyberneticien."

70. Khayati, "On the Poverty of Student Life," 408.

71. The exhibition's name was 'Destruktion Af RSG-6: En Kollektiv Manifestation Af Situationistisk Internationale' (In English, Destruction RSG-6: A Collective Manifestation of the Situationist International').

72. Sartre, "For a Theater of Situations," 185–186. For a discussion of the exhibition, see Stracey, "Destruktion RSG-6," 311–329, and Rasmussen, "To Act in Culture," 75–113. This show was followed by a second one titled "Operation Playtime," realized by J. V. Martin in 1967, in Denmark, which included works by Michèle Bernstein (The Victory of the Spanish Republicans), J. V. Martin (the Golden Ships series), and five *Nothing Boxes* by René Viénet. Debord, "Situationists and the New Action Forms," 402–407; Rasmussen, "To Act in Culture," 75.

73. Rasmussen, 95.

74. Ibid., 75.

75. Restany, *60/90:Trente ans de Nouveau Réalisme*, 76; Mahon, *Surrealism and the Politics of Eros*, 174.

76. Martin et al., "Response to a Questionnaire," 188; Debord, "Situationists and the New Action," 407.

77. Quoted in Rasmussen, "To Act in Culture," 198.

78. Debord, "Untitled Text," 478.

79. Debord, Sanguinetti, and Internationale Situationniste, *Real Split in the International*, 71.

80. Ibid., 67. The gist of this document testifies to Debord's penchant for mystique; as Ken Knabb remarked: "The SI was exemplary not only for what it said, but above all for all that it did not say." Knabb, "The Society of Situationism." Some of these groups—including the Angry Brigades in Britain, Kommune 1 in Germany, and the "Metropolitan Indians," a group of anonymous political pranksters emerging in Italy in 1977—were familiar with situationist ideas. Sadie Plant, philosopher and founder of the now-defunct Cybernetic Culture Research Unit, discussed the connections between SI and these groups in a Guattarian vein, in relation to the "molecular" arrangements of these movements as "configurations of desires rather than solidarities between people or social groups." Plant, *Most Radical Gesture*, 124.

81. Maciunas et al., *Mr. Fluxus*, 40–41; Philpot, "Fluxus," 10.
82. Friedman, "Early Days of Mail Art," 5–6.
83. Raoul Hausmann, quoted in Maciunas, *Mr. Fluxus*, 40.
84. Home, *Assault on Culture*, 50–51.
85. Hannah Higgins, "Fluxus Fortuna," 31.
86. Hendricks, *Fluxus Codex*, 21.
87. Dick Higgins, *Poetics and Theory of the Intermedia*, 18–23.
88. Ibid., 18.
89. Ibid., 18–19.
90. Cage, "Experimental Music," 12.
91. Ibid., 11.
92. Gere, *Digital Culture*, 78.
93. Information theory was proposed by electrical engineer Claude Shannon, leading to wartime research in cryptography, the scrambling of radio signals, and antiaircraft missile control systems. He expanded on it in collaboration with mathematician Warren Weaver in their 1949 paper "A Mathematical Theory of Communication." In this canonical work, Shannon distilled the communication process to a linear model that consists of these elements: the source of the message, the device that encodes the message, the channel that transmits the message, and the message's destination. Known popularly as SMCR (sender, message, channel, receiver), the basis of this model, separating semantic meaning from technical problems of delivery, enabled engineers to concentrate on the system of delivery itself. Additionally, Shannon adopted the term *entropy* from thermodynamics to refer to the measure of a communication system's efficiency in transmitting a signal, which consisted of the statistical properties of the message source.
94. The reference here is to Mexican doctor and physiologist Arturo Rosenblueth, then working at Harvard, who collaborated with Norbert Wiener and Julian Bigelow to formulate cybernetics, leading to the joint publication of "Behavior, Purpose and Teleology" in 1943, a groundbreaking paper of the discipline. Interestingly, at Harvard he also taught courses in musicology.
95. Youngblood, *Expanded Cinema*, 348.
96. N. Katherine Hayles distinguishes between first order and second order cybernetics. First order cybernetics covers the period from 1945 to 1960. Established by mathematician Norbert Wiener, who coined the term, and engineer Claude Shannon, among others, this is the foundational era of cybernetics. As Hayles notes, both Wiener and Shannon theorized information as something devoid of meaning; meaning decontextualized and disembodied. Embodiment becomes a central theme in second order cybernetics, as researchers such as Chileans Humberto Maturana and Francisco Varela reintroduce the notion of the observer as a locus of meaning. Hayles, *How We Became Posthuman.*
97. Maciunas et al., *Mr. Fluxus*, 88. By contrast, Maciunas characterizes art commodity as "complex, pretentious, profound, serious, intellectual, inspired, skillful, significant, theatrical," in order to "appear rare, limited in quantity, and therefore obtainable and accessible only to the social elite and institutions."
98. Ibid.
99. Filliou, "La Cedille Qui Sourit," 198–204; Perkins, "Utopian Networks and Correspondence Identities."
100. Filliou, "La Cedille Qui Sourit," 204. Home, *Assault on Culture*, 51–54.

101. Home, *The Assault on Culture*, 53–54.

102. Maciunas et al., *Mr. Fluxus*, 114.

103. Friedman, "Forty Years of Fluxus".

104. Fluxus games are intermedia forms made of recombined art forms like sculpture, graphic design, photographic works, film, musical scores, and mass-produced materials packaged in kits. The intention was to issue these kits in serial form like other commodities, though this scheme remained unrealized, leaving Maciunas in charge as the principal solicitor and assembler of such products. On the other hand, his editorial function ensured a degree of uniformity.

105. Conzen, *Art Games*, 105; Hendricks, *Fluxus Codex*, 82–83.

106. Conzen, *Art Games*, 105.

107. Ibid., 108.

108. Austrian biologist Karl Ludwig von Bertalanffy developed general system theory and ascribed its applications to the fields of biology, information theory, and cybernetics in the early 1950s. *Emergence* is now a concept encompassing a wide variety of fields, including art history. See Fern'andez, "'Life-Like': Historicizing Process and Responsiveness in Digital Art," 471.

109. Brecht was also a student of composer John Cage from 1958 to 1959, along with Alan Kaprow, Jackson Maclow, Higgins, Claes Oldenberg, and other key figures of American modernism. Brecht's musical scores consist of written instructions much like those included in his puzzles. See Robinson, "Scoring the Event," 28–33.

110. Hendricks, *Fluxus Codex*, 197–201; Conzen, *Art Games*, 53–56; Tzara, *Seven Dada Manifestos and Lampisteries*, 39.

111. Conzen, *Art Games*, 24.

112. Ibid., 50.

113. Ibid, 58–59.

114. Ibid., 59.

115. Ibid.

116. Ibid., 66.

117. Quoted in Léger, "A Filliou for the Game," 68.

118. Yoshimoto, *Into Performance*, 128.

119. Ibid.

120. Ibid., 115–137.

121. Post–WWII Japanese culture involved a regressive turn to authoritarian politics, the rise of the nation's economic and technological power, and the discontentment of a generation of artist-activists who experienced the hardships of World War II and were coming of age in the volatile sociopolitical sphere of the 1960s, peaking in Japan on the occasion of the renewal of the Japan-US Security Treaty in 1963. Yoshimoto, *Into Performance*, 148.

122. Yoshimoto, *Into Performance*, 118.

123. Ibid., 125–127.

124. Ibid., 126.

125. Ibid.

126. Hendricks, *Fluxus Codex*, 54, 328, 365.

127. McDowel, "Fluxus Games," 70–71.

128. Maciunas et al., *Mr. Fluxus*, 169–214; Higgins, Vostell, and Oldenburg, *Fantastic Architecture*, no page number.

129. Maciunas and Watts, "Proposal for the Greene Street Precinct, Inc. (ca. December 1967)" in *Fluxus Codex*, 44.

130. Higgins, Vostell, and Oldenburg, *Fantastic Architecture*, no page number.

131. Personal conversation with Carolee Schneemann.

132. Albright, "New School: Correspondence Art," 32; Albright, "Correspondance Art," 28–29.

133. Albright, "New School: Correspondence Art," 32. Incidentally, Albright's articles appeared in *Rolling Stone* eight months prior to Stewart Brand's article "Spacewar" in the December 1972 issue, in which he called for "computers to the people." I will return to this in chapter 3.

3

CYBERNETIC ECOLOGIES OF ART AND COUNTERCULTURE

N OT ONLY DID THE GAMES OF THE DIGITAL avant-garde reflect a concern with participatory forms of urbanism and art, together with the counterculture they were exemplary reconceptualizations of ecology in the late 1960s. Though embedded in different contexts, these communities shared similar notions of ecosystems modeled on cybernetics as a systems ecology based on a symbiosis between human, machine, and their environment, Earth.[1] From this expanded perspective, media theorist Gene Youngblood argued that the role of the artist was akin to that of the ecologist, as "one who deals with environmental relationships."[2] Similar ideas underpinned R. Buckminster Fuller's notions of humans as "whole systems" thinkers and Steven Levy's retrospective typifying of 1960s engineers as hackers (the pioneers of contemporary hacker culture). As Youngblood summed up, in the cybernetic age, the shared task of the artist, the human, and the engineer was to engage the utopian potentials of "the global intermedia network" of mass media. In a related vein, artist and art historian Jack Burnham's notion of *system esthetics* summarizes the main concerns of systems ecologists. According to Burnham, system esthetics denotes a shift in focus from formalist concerns with objecthood, or "products" in "art and life," to "the biological liveability of the earth, producing more accurate models of social interaction, understanding the growing symbiosis in man-machine relationships, establishing priorities for the usage and conservation of natural resources, and defining alternative patterns of education, productivity and leisure."[3] To these ends, a wide range of creative practices in a plethora of media and media forms, including cybernetics-inspired games created with computers, would articulate and educate about alternative relationships between the human and their increasingly mediated environments.

Games conceived on behalf of systems ecology were also mobilizations of game theory, a field concerned with the study of mathematical models of strategic interaction between rational decision makers, then undergoing a revival. Game theory provided the framework for computer simulations used by military strategists and based on so-called zero-sum games, or win/lose scenarios pitting the United States and Soviet Russia in a closed loop of moves and countermoves aimed at nuclear deterrence. The games of the digital avant-garde and the counterculture rejected the binary logic of game theory and the use of cybernetic technologies (computers) for commercial and military applications, to instead invoke the interdependence of human, mechanical, and biological environments. In practice, games modeled on systems ecology stood counter to zero-sum control underpinning centralized media and frameworks, instead operating in light of alternative models of decentralized and individualized media conceived as a framework for participatory and reciprocal interactions echoing utopian notions of games as open and cross-cultural forms developed in previous avant-garde currents.

At this time, such games often took the forms of educational simulations designed to involve citizens and institutional representatives in ecological and peaceful sustainability and in playful exchanges of images, text, and sound among geographically and culturally diverse artists and audiences via cybernetic media and media networks. As forms of transnational play, such games were meant to foster a sense of the interconnectedness of all things and, in this utopian spirit, catalyze global empathy and involvement. Born out of a historical moment of extraordinary synergy between the arts, sciences, and counterculture, these games reflected the utopian vision driving their shared goal: to interconnect the global community so as to empower their capability to reshape the world into more peaceful and ecologically sustainable environments. Additionally, the promises and pitfalls of this project continue to play out in contemporary culture, including in the media and cultural forms made possible by digital technology and networks such as video games. Contemporary gaming culture is both a tribute to the continued significance of the utopian vision driving the games of the digital avant-garde and the counterculture, as well as to the reformulation of this vision as a mainstream, corporate ideal.

From this perspective, the historical notion of video games as media forms associated with the adoption of control culture in the 1960s, often assumed in communication studies and science and technology studies, appears as a one-sided narrative focused mainly on the military applications of games as exemplified in game theory. But as this chapter shows, contemporary video games have multiple historical origins, including one that is rarely acknowledged in game studies, in the field of ecology. As a shared concern of utopian currents in the arts, engineering, and counterculture of the 1960s and 1970s, systems ecology yields visions of computer games (simulations) and computer networks as tools of planetary survival. From this perspective, their rejection of media models conceived in the image of centralized and hierarchical military and corporate structures, including gaming simulations, seems inevitable. Similarly, their rearticulation of game theory as a tool of systems ecology meant that games designed for change—for instance, to restore ecological balance—required interlinking the biological, technological, social, and political dimensions of ecology, as well as governance based on decentralized principles, that is, on global mutualistic, participatory, and democratic feedback.

The *World Game* and the *Ecogame*

Admired by leading figures in the digital avant-garde and counterculture in the 1960s, such as Youngblood and editor of the *Whole Earth Catalogue* Stewart Brand, Richard Buckminster Fuller (1895–1983), conversant with both art and science, was considered to be the ideal of the artist as ecologist. A former navy engineer turned designer, Fuller was well acquainted with the artists associated with Fluxus and their notions of intermedial arts. As an invited artist, he taught alongside John Cage at the now iconic Black Mountain College in North Carolina during the summers of 1948 and 1949, serving as its Summer Institute director in 1949. Although short-lived (1933–1957), the college's interdisciplinary and experimental foci proved to be significant breeding grounds for the American digital avant-garde. It was there that Cage first staged the happening (later developed by his student, Allan Kaprow); there that Cage's life partner, dancer Merce Cunningham, would form his influential dance company; and there that Fuller, in collaboration with students and other faculty, would reinvent the geodesic dome.[4] The construction would become an icon of *hippie modernism*, a term coined by curator and graphic designer Andrew Blauvelt to describe counterculture design practices influenced by the hybrid practices of the digital avant-garde, including, as he notes, "expanded cinema, intermedia, installation art, performance."[5] As a symbol of counterculture, the geodesic dome was the epitome of cybernetic-inspired environmental design, especially among *Whole Earth Catalogue*'s target readership, members of hippie communes.[6] However, the construction was also attractive to the US government, which commissioned Fuller's firm, Geodesics, to make small domes for the marines. As proposed by Fuller, a geodesic dome would similarly house the *World Game* at Expo 67 in Montreal, Canada. Because US government officials rejected the game in favor of an eclectic display of Americana, only the geodesic dome was built at the US pavilion. Befitting Fuller's vision of *World Game* as a form of mass-participation pedagogical tool, the dome functions today as an environmental museum housing exhibits designed to educate the public about climate change, ecotechnologies, and issues related to sustainable development.[7]

Originally conceived in 1964, Fuller defined *World Game* as "an organization of computer capability to deal prognosticatingly with world problems."[8] The goal was to build a giant simulation of Earth (the size of a football field) that could be controlled electronically by remote individuals or teams playing collaboratively.[9] This system echoed the Fluxists' notion of the intermedia network, though in this case it was not art that was exchanged but environmental information provided in part, as Fuller proposed, by Russian and American spy satellites. (Fuller claimed that the satellites' optical sensors and thermographic scanners extended human vision such that the electromagnetic spectrum could now be detected in any form of energy, from seeds, water, and metal, to livestock and humans). Though the game was never fully implemented in the form that Fuller proposed, it was played, as were many Fluxus games, in more abbreviated forms at various educational institutions during the 1970s (the game was first played at the New York Studio for Drawing, Painting and Sculpture in 1969). Guiding the play was comprehensive data including statistics about Earth's resources and trends, together with knowledge of "generalized principles operative in the physical universe," gathered by the team at the Southern Illinois University Edwardsville campus, the headquarters housing Fuller's then newly minted design science division.[10] As a playful expression of what Fuller called "whole systems thinking," the ultimate goal of the game was advancing the "means of making five billion humans a total economic and physical success at the earliest possible moment without anyone being advantaged at the expense of another."[11] In practice, the idea was to use the game to simulate world trends and then, based on the information gleaned, propose alternative scenarios toward increasing wealth for the entire world population without human exploitation and negative environmental impact.

Fuller described the project conceptually as "world peace gaming science," the inverse of "world war gaming science," the latter a reference to game theory, a cybernetics-related war science proposed by Princeton mathematician John Von Neumann in 1928.[12] The mathematics of game theory, as Fuller explained, were premised on "drop dead" or "zero-sum" scenarios of Cold War simulations of nuclear war between the United States and the Soviet Union.[13] According to Fuller, who was familiar with game theory through his military career, the underlying assumption of these simulations was Malthusian (based on Thomas Malthus's notion that an increase of wealth did not result in a sustainable higher standard of living and a utopian society but instead spurred population growth, which led to famine and disease). This underlying assumption, that the planet lacked resources to sustain an increasing human population, inevitably led political and military leadership to always choose a winner-loser situation.[14] In contrast, *World Game* worked from the assumption that the path to utopia pivoted on better management of the world's resources. To this end, Fuller rearticulated game theory's goal to focus on overcoming energy scarcity. He predicted that the redistribution of global resources would also erase territorial politics, creating lasting peace, a task that would be aided through collective play in the form of *World Game.*

In this context, Fuller's conception of *World Game* as a pedagogical, planning, and managerial tool was also part of his broader vision to transform education according to cybernetic principles, or as he put it, cybernetic's "practical utopianism." In this light, he rejected specialization, a focus that he saw as no longer appropriate to the conditions of a complex informational world. Only an educational system consonant with cybernetics and system theory would prepare the global public to manipulate comprehensive simulations like *World Game*, thereby empowering them to apprehend the whole system and address all its facets. Like technocrats leading Cold War research into "real-time" computing, such as J. C. R. Licklider, Fuller argued that the computer could be leveraged symbiotically or, in other words, used to augment the human's innate "generalist" capacities to rationally apprehend and intervene into the whole system.[15] The difference was that instead of war and ecocide, computers would be put in service of peace and ecological sustainability.

As an ecologically responsive simulation, however, *World Game* was not unique, nor in the end was it realized as originally conceived, as a computer-driven system. A game that better fulfilled these ends, titled

Ecogame (1969), was actually created in Britain by a team of art-inspired engineers within the interdisciplinary context of the Computer Arts Society, an art and engineering collaborative founded in Britain during the same year (still ongoing).[16] British computer scientist George Mallen, who programmed it, discussed it as the world's first interactive, multimedia, computer-controlled game. *Ecogame* consisted of a simulation of an economic system shown on interactive graphics screens driven by a minicomputer that could be controlled using a light pen. The computers were linked to slide projectors through which the decisions that players made about allocating resources were projected on the walls of the room in which the game was installed. Like Fuller's vision of *World Game*, *Ecogame* was originally arranged as a multimedia environment or theater in a small geodesic dome. Designed four years prior to the first oil crisis of 1973, the goal of *Ecogame* was to encourage participants to reflect on their behavior in the system. The pedagogical function of the game was influenced by British cybernetician and media-arts pioneer Gordon Pask, with whom Mallen worked at System Research Ltd., a nonprofit research organization founded by Pask and dedicated to developing computer simulations and other models for learning and problem-solving processes (System Research Ltd. was largely funded by the US Army and Air Force).[17] Like Fuller, Pask was interested in issues concerning learning and evolution. Additionally, Pask was deeply interested in theater. He combined these interests in what he called *cybernetic theater*, his term for a theater that would take shape through the audience's participation. This notion of the theater echoed also in Pask's concept of learning and evolution (as well as art) as self-organizing, mutual, participatory processes, a notion similar to Fuller's pedagogical outlook. As a pedagogical simulation designed to engage participants in considering adaptive behavior in relation to environmental sustainability, *Ecogame* was the embodiment (Pask's term) of cybernetic theater. (Moreover, its multimedia conception testifies to Pask's notion of intuitive interfaces, which would be familiar to the user and thus did not necessitate instructions.)

Ecogame was first played at the offices of System Research Ltd. by a team of journalists from the main Sunday newspapers in Britain, who gave the game favorable reviews. It was subsequently shown at Computer '70 trade show held at Olympia, London, in September 1970, where it similarly met with a positive reception. Enthusiastic press reviews and the successful demonstration of *Ecogame* at Computer '70 caught the attention of a team at the Centre d'Etudes Industrielle in Geneva, then developing the program for the First European Management Forum, the forerunner to the World Economic Forum, scheduled for Davos in February 1971. On their invitation, the game was installed at Davos (without the geodesic dome) as part of the educational support for the main conference. There it was played by businesspeople and politicians. The team was subsequently approached by British government officials of the Treasury and the Department of Environment about a possible version for the 1974 Stockholm United Nations Environment Conference; however, these initiatives were never realized. A version of the game was later sold to IBM for use in its management education center in Blaricum in Belgium. Interestingly, a component of the multimedia theater of *Ecogame*, the slide projection technology, was incorporated by British cybernetician Stafford Beer, a close friend of Pask, then working on Salvador Allende's Cybersyn project in Chile (1971–1973).[18] Fittingly, Cybersyn was conceived by Allende's socialist government as a decentralized decision support system, which incorporated an economic simulator, custom software to monitor factory performance, an operations room, and a national network of telex machines linked to one mainframe computer. (The name of the project in English, Cybersyn, combined the words *cybernetics* and *synergy*, per Beer's notions of organizational cybernetics applied to industrial management.) The project was designed to aid in the management of Chile's national economy, with one of its main goals to develop self-regulation of factories by way of empowering decision making by the workforce within industrial enterprises (in contrast to the command and control model of Soviet factories). An advanced prototype was completed and successfully tested in 1973 but was ordered dismantled and the operations room destroyed in the same year by the US-backed Pinochet regime, following the military coup on September 11, 1973.

In contrast to *Ecogame*, which was (at least in its various implemented versions) restricted to business and political leadership, Fuller envisioned *World Game* much in the same vein of Allende's and Beer's Cybersyn project: as a vehicle for popular participation in matters of communal stewardship. However, unlike *Ecogame* and Cybersyn, both of which presupposed strengthening existing democratic structures of government, Fuller's vision of collective global governance, which *World Game* embodied, implied their bypassing altogether. Fuller rejected direct political action as an effective approach to cultural, social, and ecological change. Instead, he envisioned the players of *World Game* as "artists" or "architects" to be guided not by political views but by science-based design. To this end, he sought to present the game in neutral terms, as a tool that could be used not for war or business but to help nongovernmental entities (rational individuals in the public) simulate and test with the aid of the computer. The processes of feedback and "automated" principles of self-regulation were to govern the total environment of "spaceship earth" (he was to call this approach synergetics, or the study of the patterns inherent in nature's systems, or "whole systems thinking," as he later wrote in the first issue of *Whole Earth Catalogue*). Fuller's framing of *World Game* as a tool of popular, sustainable self-reliance was one of its main countercultural draws, in particular within the context of the increasingly polarized and violent sociopolitical climate of the United States in the 1960s. Additionally, *World Game* was photogenic, with its centerpiece, the dymaxion map (fig. 3.1), vividly conveying the utopian vision of a planetary cybernetic ecology "all watched by the machines of loving grace," as The Diggers' poet Richard Brautigan put it in 1967.[19] Developed by Fuller, the dymaxion map depicted Earth as a continuous island surrounded by one ocean, thus literally as a utopian space evocative of More's island, *Utopia*.[20] The map could be rearranged in various ways to highlight various aspects of the world and, unlike conventional maps, did not have a right side. Land masses were represented according to proportion, and regions were indicated by colors, each of which would correspond to the prevalent colors of human skin in these regions. Fuller maintained that the Mercator map (developed in 1569), which is still the map most prevalently used today, was culturally biased, a product of linear thought (he never tired of denouncing the idea of infinity, in his view represented by this map, as the result of an antiquated perception of the earth as a flat surface). At the same time, the countercultural appeal of the dymaxion map, along with *World Game*, resided in its projection of a world beyond the hierarchies of arbitrary political borders and its promises of a decentralized, global stewardship of the earth by ordinary people schooled in synergetics. The utopian appeal of *World Game* was succinctly captured by Youngblood, an enthusiastic advocate, who devoted a series of articles to it in the *Los Angeles Free Press* and later in the *Whole Earth Catalogue*, two of the most significant countercultural publications on the West Coast at the time. According to Youngblood, "There are a lot of young people like me who were pretty uptight and didn't know what to do with their lives, who have now committed themselves to World Game. . . . It's really the only possible alternative for positive revolutionary action."[21] Echoing Fuller's rallying cry, "utopia or oblivion," which was itself a twist on Corbusier's dictum, "architecture or revolution," Youngblood concluded: "The young lives of mid-century America find themselves perched on the fulcrum of a cosmic balancing act with utopia on the one hand and oblivion the other."[22] In sum, from this point of view, the focus was on placing the products of industry and science, rather than as the handmaidens of consumerism and militarism, at the service of alternatives, bringing cybernetic thinking and digital technologies in line with ludic participation. As products of this long-standing project intersecting art and technology, *World Game* and *Ecogame* evoke utopian traditions in design, tracing through constructivist currents, the Bauhaus, and situationism. Their shared proposition, as the situationists had declared but never realized, was that the task of the counterculture was to harness cybernetics and cybernetic technologies (computers) to catalyze "the great game to come," as Dutch artist Constant Nieuwenhuys said in 1959.[23] At this juncture and a decade later, this project of détournement began to take shape in practice, as readaptations of game theory and computer simulations in service of cultural critique and the creation of sustainable alternatives to the control games of Cold War.

Figure 3.1. Fuller Projection Map™ Dymaxion Air © Ocean World with mean temperatures. © The Estate of Buckminster Fuller, represented by the Buckminster Fuller Institute. The Fuller Projection Map design is a trademark of the Buckminster Fuller Institute. ©1938, 1967 & 1992. All rights reserved, www.bfi.org.

Random War

Artists of the digital avant-garde, where collaborations between art and engineering were prominent, were not just conceptually inspirational to engineers but themselves initiated the first détournements of digital technologies, including computers and computer games. In the context of the increasing politicization of computers (i.e., their perception as tools of centralized control), these practices reflected a concomitant belief in their liberatory potential among collaborating artists and engineers. However, participators in collaborations were sometimes ambivalent, for instance by highlighting these technologies as instruments of dehumanization, as in the case of Charles Csuri's *Random War* (1967) (fig. 3.2), which to my knowledge is the first computer game designed by an artist (in collaboration with J. Shaffer, a programmer). Csuri (1922–), whose work in computer graphics was referenced in Youngblood as an exemplary aesthetic application of technology, is today recognized as a pioneer in the fields of computer art and animation. *Random War* was included in *Cybernetic Serendipity: The Computer in the Arts*, a landmark show about computer art and new technologies, curated by Jasia Reichardt, at the Institute of Contemporary Arts, London (August 2–October 20, 1968). The original game was programmed on an IBM 7094 and was exhibited as a silkscreen print.[24] *Random War* was not an interactive game because it lacked a user interface and could only be modified by changing the programming parameters. Focused on war rather than resources, like *World Game*, in concept, *Random War* invoked game theory, in this case not as a framework for rational and democratic ecology but to make an antiwar statement. A description of the game was included in *Cybernetic Serendipity*'s accompanying catalog:

Csuri made a drawing of one toy soldier, and this became the data deck. A computer programme which generates random numbers is called a pseudo-random number generator. Such a programme determined the distribution and the position of soldiers on the battlefield. One side is called the "Red" and the other one the "Black," and the names of real people were given to each soldier. Their military ranks were assigned by the random number generator. The random number generator also decided who is to die and who is to be wounded. The programme also has an automatic control for perspective. A picture 30 x 100 in. in colour of the battle was produced by the computer, and the "print out" gave the following instructions: 1. Total number of dead on each side[;] 2. Total number of wounded on each side[;] 3. The number of dead and wounded in each of forty sectors of the battlefield[;] 4. Identification of the dead and wounded in alphabetical order[;] 5. The survivors in alphabetical order.[25]

Figure 3.2. Detail of Charles Csuri, *Random War*, 1967. © Charles Csuri.

Literally conceived as a cold numbers game, in this case played with human lives, *Random War* mimics the zero-sum logic of game theory in order to critique its impersonal logic. To highlight this point, Csuri entered names of real people, including his own name and those of living fellow veterans. Additionally, he added Ohio State University administrators, faculty, and staff and contemporaneous politicians like Ronald Reagan (then Republican governor of California) and Gerald Ford (then a Republican member of the House of Representatives who opposed the Vietnam War).[26] In this way, *Random War* carries an eerie, even discomfiting resonance, as it points to the pervasive militarization of American society, spanning the social, military, academic, and political spheres during the Cold War period. It evokes General Dwight Eisenhower's misgivings about the potentially undemocratic impact of the swelling military-industrial complex expressed during his farewell presidential address in 1961.

It should be noted that, like Fuller, Csuri's interest in military simulation can be attributed to his background (Csuri fought in World War II and received a bronze medal for his service). Additionally, Csuri's work on computer graphics was made possible by defense-funded research. In his case, this research focused on the development of graphical interfaces, necessary to advance real-time computing within the context of Cold War defense systems such as the Semi-Automatic Ground Environment. In this sense, *Random War* was an inadvertent by-product of the well-endowed, public-funded military research laboratories of the Cold War, just as *Spacewar* was (developed as an MIT hack, or a fun side project by young computer engineers, *Spacewar* is today considered by many to be the first video game).[27] In contrast to the fun-filled fantasy space war scenario of *Spacewar*, *Random War* comments on war from a critical angle, as it correlates the militarization of simulation technologies with the dehumanization of human life under the aegis of Cold War's military-industrial complex. The game addresses the cultures of militarism and masculinity from the point of view of their shared appeal on play. The little green army men used by Csuri as a model to draw *Random War*'s soldiers were an integral part of most boys' toy sets until the late 1970s. As such, they were part of American male nostalgia. Csuri integrated this iconic figure in *Random War* to problematize militaristic child's play—in effect, to challenge commonplace assumptions that such play is inconsequential. Moreover, *Random War* is a game in which the boundaries between reality and fantasy dissolve to produce a distancing effect suggestive of alienation. As the description of the game in the *Cybernetic Serendipity* exhibition's catalog noted, *Random War* mimicked military (and political) simulacra, while itself representing a simulacrum of an imaginary war. The spectacle of automated simulations, that is, the passivity that they elicit, is what is at stake:

> *Random War* is an imaginary war, one with few variables, but it is a short step to a real situation with introduction of many more variables into the computer. One could introduce military intelligence reports into the programme with an estimate of the enemies' capabilities and the tactics they may use. The computer can handle information about the type of terrain, types and number of weapons, historical data which involved similar situations, weather conditions, physical condition of the troops and so forth. The battle can be simulated on the computer, and computer-generated movies would give a visual display of the contest. Then more decisions could be made before the event takes place in real time. Once the real battle starts, the computer can predict the outcome and its consequences many hours before the battle ends. It would show motion pictures as the battle progressed. The military computer could process one per cent of each of the variables and predict the outcome, much in the same way national television computers have recorded the final results of political elections.[28]

With *Random War*, Csuri pointed to the rise of hyperreality, as later theorized by Jean Baudrillard in his conception of simulations as spaces that work by imploding boundaries between the imaginary and the real, and their alienating effects and resulting detachment (from reality) that is produced.[29] In this sense, *Random War* departs from contemporaneous polarized cultural views of simulation technology, the computer: its embrace as a tool of ecological utopia, and conversely, its perception as an a priori instrument of dehumanization. As a counter to passivity, *Random War* looks toward détournement instead; it appropriates simulation technologies and resources meant for military research and employs them for opposite ends: to make an antimilitarist statement, or arguably, a stand against the encroachment of the military-industrial complex into every realm of civilian life, the more poignant a point as Csuri is a former soldier and decorated veteran familiar with the horrors of war.[30]

Random War was not initially conceived as a networked project, at least not in the sense that it implicated audience members as did Fuller's *World Game*. In 2011, however, the game was re-created on the initiative of curator Janet Glowski in collaboration with an Ohio-based independent video game company, Multivarious Games, as a *real-time interactive art object*, the term that Csuri coined in the 1960s to refer to his interactive works in computer graphics. This version of the game was developed as an application (app); it retained the historical, aesthetic, and conceptual framings of the original but was designed to be used on a social media network, Facebook. Players could upload selected Facebook friends into the application and let the game create itself over time. Just as in the original work, the program would randomly divide friends into two armies. Similarly, it would tabulate the various lists of those "survived," "dead," "wounded," and "missing in action," and assign each army medal winners such as "hero" and "medal for valor." This version of *Random War* was also displayed at Media Façade, as a projection of the game on the Museum of Contemporary Art in Zagreb as part of ISEA2011 Istanbul.[31] At this location, the project took on renewed significance, as it both pointed to the ongoing ties between simulation, play, and war, and functioned as a temporary war memorial, in this case, of the recent Balkan war (1991–1999). Intended as a recognition of Csuri's contributions to the field of media arts, the 2011 version of *Random War* also stands as a testimony to the long-standing politicized engagement of simulation technologies, including games, by artists (and collaborating engineers). Both as a statement about the personal and social implications of war and a game initially conceived as a collaboration between an artist and engineer, and later with game designers, to challenge the cultural inscription of violence through play, *Random War*'s historical significance spans interventions into masculinist and militaristic gaming culture from the inception of artists' access to computers to the spaces of contemporary social media networks.

Open Score

Similarly conceived as part of an art and engineering collaboration, *Open Score* (1966) (fig. 3.3), a game-based performance by artist Robert Rauschenberg (b. Milton Ernst Rauschenberg, 1925–2008) also made an antiwar statement in response to the escalation of the Vietnam War (1955–1975). In contrast to Csuri's *Random War*, however, *Open Score* combined technology with live performance to create an immersive space or an intermedial theater, blending performers, images, and sound. The work was part of a series of events titled *9 Evenings: Theater and Engineering*, staged on the grounds of the 69th Regiment Armory in New York City from October 13 to 23, 1966. Thirty engineers from Bell Telephone Laboratories in Murray Hill, New Jersey, under the direction of research scientist Billy Klüver (born in Monaco, Johan Wilhelm Klüver, 1927–2004) participated. The events of *9 Evenings* were conceived by Rauschenberg and Klüver and included a group of established multimedia artists, many of whom were associated with Fluxus networks, and members of the Judson School located at the Judson Memorial Church in New York, who were influenced by Merce Cunningham's notion of dance as chance-based processes. The artists included nine Americans—visual artists Rauschenberg, Alex Hay, and Robert Whitman; two composers, John Cage and David Tudor; dancers Yvonne Rainer, Deborah Hay, Steve Paxton, and Lucinda Childs—and Brazilian-Swedish multimedia artist Öyvind Fahlström. (*9 Evenings* would later lead to the founding of Experiments in Art and Technology [EAT], one of the first large-scale networks dedicated to fostering creative collaborations between artists, engineers, and scientists in the United States and abroad.)

Rauschenberg's contribution, *Open Score*, was performed twice, on October 14 and 23, 1966. The performance opened with a tennis match between artist Frank Stella and professional tennis player Mimi Kanarek, playing on a full-scale tennis court installed on the Armory grounds. The game was played with modified tennis rackets (similar to Fluxus's prepared

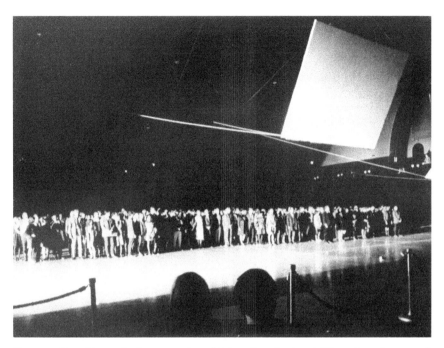

Figure 3.3. Peter Moore, Performance view of Robert Rauschenberg's "Open Score," presented as part of "9 Evenings: Theater and Engineering," NYC, 1966. © 2019 Barbara Moore / Artists Rights Society (ARS), New York. Courtesy Paula Cooper Gallery, New York.

rackets mentioned in chapter 2), which, in this case, were designed by engineer Bill Karninski to relay data by short wave (FM) to two receivers/transistors and from there to the Armory speakers. Each time Stella and Kanarek hit the ball, the audiences heard a loud, metallic-sounding bang reminiscent of a gunshot resonating throughout the cavernous space of the Armory. Each hit would turn off one of the thirty-nine lights surrounding the tennis court successively (due to technical problems, however, the lights were turned off manually during the first event). The game continued until the Armory was completely dark. In darkness, five hundred people entered the space and positioned themselves around a stage to perform choreographed movements. Lights with an infrared filter would suddenly illuminate the crowd as the infrared cameras manned by artist Les Levine picked up on their movements. The television images of the performers were projected onto three large screens in front of the audience. Though the audience could sense the presence of the crowd they could only see them as television images showing ghostly human faces and bodies moving according to a series of directives. Using flashlights installed on the balcony railings, Rauschenberg cued the movements' sequence inspired by Fluxus scores:

> 1. Touch somebody who is not touching you; 2. Touch two places on your body where you are ticklish (don't laugh); 3. Hug someone quickly then move on to someone else. Continue this until next cue. (Do this seriously, quickly and smoothly); 4. Draw a rectangle in the air as high as you can reach; 5. Take out a handkerchief and wipe your nose. (Do not blow); 6. Women brush hair; 7. Move closer together; 8. Move apart; 9. Men take off jackets; Replace them; Repeat; 10. Sing one of the 10 songs being sung (loudly) or sing one of your own choice.[32]

As the crowd moved according to instructions, Rauschenberg played a prerecorded soundtrack of the performers reciting their names one by one (this recording was omitted during the second staging of *Open Score*). The second act of the first event concluded when the lights slowly came on and then went off again, with Rauschenberg instructing the performers to leave silently in the dark. For the second staging of *Open Score*, Rauschenberg added a third act. With the lights out, a beam of light was projected on a cloth sack concealing Italian dancer and choreographer Simoni Forti, who began singing a Tuscan song from her childhood. As she sang, Rauschenberg approached, picking up her swaddled body and putting her down on different places on the Armory floor until she finished her song.

As extensions to the performers' actions, the technologies engaged in *Open Score*, including sensors, lights, speakers, and closed-circuit television, functioned to both amplify and disable readings of the event as spectacular theatricality. In this light, Rauschenberg wrote about *Open Score* that as "an event that is taking place in front of one except through reproduction," it highlighted the "sort of double exposure of action" that occurs in remote communication scenarios.[33] Like Csuri's *Random War*, *Open Score* recalled Jean Baudrillard's notion that simulation correlates with a world where the sign was not exchanged for meaning but merely for another sign "in an uninterrupted circuit."[34] In *Open Score*, Rauschenberg alluded to this circularity with surveillance technology. He achieved this effect by capturing images of the crowd of five hundred people in the second act of the performance via an infrared camera originally developed for surveillance purposes in situations of limited vision, such as the jungles of Vietnam.[35] Because infrared equipment was classified as top secret by the United States government at the time, a Japanese model was procured for *Open Score.* By evoking the panoptics of closed-circuit surveillance, also a new form of monitoring being installed during the 1960s in American cities, Rauschenberg's appropriation of surveillance technology also pointed to the passivity of our sheer fascination with the hyperreal and with manufactured images as tools of control. In this sense, *Open Score* illustrated literally Debord's thesis on the alienating (schizophrenic) effects of mass-media. "Imprisoned in a flat universe bounded on all sides by the spectacle's *screen*," Debord wrote, "the consciousness of the spectator has only figmentary interlocutors which subject it to a one-way discourse on their commodities and the politics of those commodities. The sole mirror of this consciousness is the spectacle in all its breadth, where what is staged is a false way out of a generalized autism."[36] On the background of a steady stream of media images depicting the mounting death toll of the Vietnam War, the ghostly human images and eerie soundscapes of *Open Score* held up a mirror to audiences, one that confronted them with their own detached spectatorship through an immersive environment that evokes Brechtian theater. Rauschenberg's *Open Score* thus complements Csuri's *Random War,* as both artists set contexts that together evidence the ties between play and leisure, simulation and war, with systems of control, and counters alienation by using simulation to frustrate cathartic spectatorship.

In addition to spectatorship, as scholar and curator Sylvie Lacerte has suggested, *Open Score* referenced space, as the Armory grounds' initial function was as a space to perform "military drills."[37] This "antagonist dimension" was similarly remarked on by art historian Michelle Kuo in reference to the "adversarial relationship between . . . Stella and Kanarek." Kuo linked this "agonistic conception of the subject" in *Open Score* with "the black box actors proposed by cybernetics and game theory."[38] *Open Score,* however, cannot in my view be solely reduced to an illustration of antagonism, as its open form, much like Brechtian theater and Fluxus games, suggests a mobilization of play for offering alternative ways of relating other than through control. As art historian Jack Burnham put it at the time, *9 Evenings* was conceived in the spirit of system aesthetics, in this case on behalf of a common interest of artists and engineers in investigating the possibilities of symbiotic relationships between humans and computers.[39]

Similar concerns were expressed by artist Öyvind Fahlström, who contrasted his own contribution to *9 Evenings,* titled *Kisses Sweeter Than Wine,* with Cold War game simulations. The latter, as he wrote, were "games seen either as realistic models (not descriptions) of a life-span, or the Cold War balance, of the double-code mechanism to push the bomb button . . . [involving] the thrill and resolution." Instead, he proposed games that have "both conflict and non-conflict," thus conceived as "'free form,' where in principle everything is equal."[40] The aim was to literally open the game, which in practice was achieved by withholding resolution. As such, Fahlström's performance, which he conceived as a game of "total theater," was, like *Random War* and *Open Score*, open-ended. As the artist explained, "There is no explanation. The spectator draws conclusions or not, as he chooses." However, like Csuri's and Rauschenberg's games, the piece took on political allusions and, in the case of *Kisses Sweeter Than Wine*, included overt political content. One of the nine acts included a film projection titled *Mao-Hope*, showing a street protest staged by Fahlström on New York's Fifth Avenue with seven people carrying placards displaying photographs of Bob Hope and Mao Tse Tung. The staged protest-happening also involved an accompanying performer masquerading as a local radio reporter who approached onlookers with the question "Are you happy?" in a parodic commentary on the spectacularization of direct action. Two characters, Space Girl, descending from the ceiling in a silver leotard, and Jell-O Girl, appearing to swim in a pool of gelatin, embodied the spectacle of happenings. In another act, Fahlström drew parallels between humans and computers through representations of autistic male characters. One played by Rauschenberg repeated sales and profit figures from stock exchange quotations as his face was filmed by a closed-circuit video camera. A Mylar "antimissile-missile" circling the Armory during the event, the gradual unveiling of a menacing portrait bust of Lyndon Johnson, and media footage from the Vietnam War were also overt allusions to contemporaneous socioeconomic and political conditions.[41] The piece concluded with a performer running onto the stage carrying smoke grenades and leaving plumes of smoke behind him. As the smoke rose, Fahlström pointed a laser beam at the genital area of a member of the audience, while in the background the New Christy Minstrels began singing *Kisses Sweeter Than Wine*.

Working with the concept of games as an open form, Fahlström would later create a series of détourned Monopoly games, or *variable paintings*, as he called them, that were painted on vinyl with magnets added on the surfaces. The magnets were movable and meant to be manipulated by audiences, such that new political and geographical mappings would emerge. Altogether, they were conceived to be mass-produced as quasi-didactic games that could be used to explore Cold War political, economic, and geographical dynamics in the 1970s (the latter goal was never realized).[42] In hindsight, it is interesting to note that by détourning the original game Monopoly, a symbol of American capitalism, Fahlström perhaps unknowingly restored Monopoly to its activist origins in The Landlord's Game, which was conceived by Elizabeth Magie, who first patented the game in 1904 to teach Americans about the ills of land rent and the need for antimonopoly legislation.[43] Fahlström's Monopoly games have similarly didactic underpinnings as they sought to impart information about the scope and dynamics of US military interventions into the Global South during the Cold War. From this perspective, they evoke the anticolonialist strand of utopian gaming culture, spanning from Xul Solar's *Panchess* to the intermedial chess sets of Yoko Ono and Takako Saito. In Brazil, Fahlström's anticolonialism was also contemporaneous with Augusto Boal's Brechtian-influenced participatory dramaturgy and games under the umbrella of the Theater of the Oppressed, which will be discussed in chapter 5 as a precursor of today's emergence of kindred video games in South America. In their time, the events of *9 Evenings*, including *Kisses Sweeter Than Wine* and *Open Score*, were provocative, playful games, politicized happenings sharing the Dionysian spirit of the participatory performances by the Dadaists fifty years prior.

These art historical resonances were appropriate to the events of *9 Evenings*, because as the artists were aware, the Armory was a significant site for the inception of avant-garde art in the United States. The first European and American avant-garde art exhibition in the United States took place on its grounds in 1913. Called the *International Exhibition of Modern Art*, this event was notorious for its controversial reception among the American public and critics at the time. In particular, Duchamp's *Nude Descending a Staircase* (1912), included in the show, was met with scorn. Like its avant-garde predecessor, *9 Evenings* was also a groundbreaking event. Not only was it the first large-scale collaboration between artists and engineers in the United States (they worked for ten months to prepare for the event), but their collaboration produced custom-designed systems for the theater and innovative uses of existing technologies. In addition, the event pioneered the use of closed-circuit television and television projection on stage, as well as fiber-optics and infrared television cameras, a Doppler sonar device, and portable FM transmitters and amplifiers that were readapted for artistic purposes. Ironically, *9 Evenings*, which like the *International Exhibition of Modern Art* fifty years earlier sought to expand the cultural vocabulary of the avant-garde, was also unfavorably received in its time by the public and critics alike (in total ten thousand people attended).[44] Art historian Sylvie Lacerte attributed the unfavorable tone of press reviews to the pervading influence of Clement Greenberg's "Kantian theories" based on the separation of the "aesthetic, social and scientific spheres."[45] As she noted, notwithstanding the happenings and performances realized in various venues on the East and West Coasts of the United States during the 1950s and 1960s, with which some were familiar, by and large critics were not prepared to analyze these events.[46] That the event was plagued by technical malfunctions, in large part because of unresolved technical problems due to time constraints, did not help matters since these mishaps frustrated attendees unfamiliar with the challenges of technology and art experiments. In response to criticism, a few months after the events, Klüver wrote that "critics and public had a field day at the engineers' expense. . . . Anything that was assumed to have gone wrong (whether it actually did or not) was attributed to technical malfunctions."[47] In effect, the artists involved in 9 *Evenings* were ambivalent about collaboration with engineers, though for reasons other than antiwar protesters denouncing the links between engineering and the US military.[48] Lack of a shared language and different world views were cited as challenges, as was, as choreographer Deborah Hay said, "the masculine" conception of technology and engineering culture.[49] Hay's remark was particularly revealing of one of the sources of tension, which was mismatched gender-normative conceptions of technology, since the artists involved, including Hay, Rauschenberg, Cage, Cunningham, Rayner, and others in the group shared queer and fluid notions of sexuality. Their identification as a queer and avant-garde community extended to the fluid, playful incorporations of technology in the 9 *Evenings* events, much in the same way that precursors in the early avant-garde, including Claude Cahun and Marcel Moore, used games as an extension of their engagement of the photographic camera for gender performativity. In addition, in the case of 9 *Evenings*, preconceived notions about technology as something magic were encouraged in publicity materials for the event and played into both the public's unrealistic expectations and the critics' views of the performances as "a circus."[50]

Cross-cultural mismatch, technological issues, and the public reception notwithstanding, 9 *Evenings* begat Experiments in Art and Technology (EAT), a nonprofit organization founded by Klüver, Rauschenberg, Robert Whitman, and Fred Waldhauer.[51] In this spirit, the organization was initially formed in order to facilitate one-to-one collaborations between artists and engineers by matching artists who had specific "technical problems or projects with engineers who could work with them."[52] As requests for assistance began arriving from various parts of the world (Europe, Japan, and South America), EAT began encouraging the creation of local EAT initiatives. In this manner a network of centers dedicated to serve as information sites was established (twenty-eight regional EAT chapters were founded throughout the United States in the late 1960s). Their joint task focused on promoting art and technology experiments by organizing events and exhibitions. Of these, the most iconic project by EAT was the *Pepsi Pavilion* for Expo '70 in Osaka, Japan. Sponsored by Pepsi-Cola, the project involved the collaborative effort of seventy-five artists, engineers, and scientists from the United States and Japan. Conceived as an immersive playground environment, the pavilion was in effect a large-scale version of existing projects, most notably *Game Room* (1967–1968) by artist Tony Martin, who also created the light system for *Pavilion*. Like *Game Room*, the inside of *Pavilion* was conceived as a participatory space in the form of a responsive environment, wired such that visitors could intuitively activate light and sound systems by way of their bodily movements.[53] Housed inside a large geodesic dome, the inside of *Pavilion* also contained a gigantic Mylar mirror, a kind of fun-house mirror reflecting visitors. Its outside, enveloped in a fog sculpture by Japanese artist and EAT collaborator Fujiko Nakaya, was likewise striking.[54] An impressive artistic and engineering feat even by today's standards, the project upped the stakes of *9 Evenings*, as it involved, in addition to engineering, negotiating corporate culture. From the onset, the project's sponsorship by Pepsi-Cola was fraught with tensions. Pepsi marketing representatives had little idea about what the project entailed, and, as a result, in face of disputes about funding, intellectual property, and equipment ownership, the artists withdrew and Pepsi took ownership of *Pavilion*, transforming it ultimately into a Disney-like environment.

In the aftermath of *Pavilion*, EAT refocused its initial mission as an organization primarily concerned with providing technological assistance to artists. The group's final statement, penned by Klüver, echoed situationist Constant, who suggested a decade prior that the shaping of ludic environments required a similar reorientation of all domains, including the economy. As Klüver stated, this shift was not a task of "the artist alone," but of everyone. He would thus rededicate EAT as a network working to empower the shaping of technology by ordinary people, a goal consonant with the countercultural outlook of the nascent digital counterculture, as Gere called them, consisting at this time of environmentalists, some academic engineers and entrepreneurial technologists, hobbyists, and emerging hacker communities on the West Coast of the United States. According to Klüver: "EAT is not organized for the benefit of the artist. Experiments in Art and Technology in a real sense is a revolutionary process to catalyze the individual's responsibility for the shaping of the new technology. We can no longer claim innocence for the human and social consequences resulting from technological change. . . . This responsibility implies the search for a technology directed towards pleasure and enjoyment. [I]t implies the elimination of the distinction between work and leisure."[55]

Klüver's statement was in effect a call for broadening the participatory potential of technologies in an effort to broaden their democratic impact. From this perspective, neither Csuri, nor the artists involved in *9 Evenings* events were entirely successful, as their focus was not primarily on pleasure or enjoyment. This focus was also a significant interest of some of artists of the digital avant-garde, however, and today one of their most lasting legacies, as it resonates in both the popular embrace of networked forms of digital media, including mainstream games, and in countercultural uses of such networks and media.

La Plissure du Texte: A Planetary Fairy Tale

On the West Coast, *La Plissure du Texte: A Planetary Fairy Tale* (LPDT, 1983) ("The Pleating of the Text") (fig. 3.4) by British artist Roy Ascott, represents a project exemplary of the collaborations between digital avant-gardes, counterculture, and the public in the early transnational context of digital networks. Deeply utopian in outlook, LPDT is one of the earliest examples of an online game by an artist and, most significantly, illustrates the contributions of artists to the reconceptualization of the computer and computer networks as spaces of pleasure and global, playful community. Created as a nonlinear narrative, the work was realized at the invitation of art historian Frank Popper, to be included in *Electra: Electricity and Electronics in the Art of the XXth Century*, an exhibition in Paris, at the Musée d'Art Moderne de la Ville de Paris. For LPDT, Ascott used Texas Instruments portable terminals donated by the company and shipped to each participant hub by Ascott and his team. Each terminal was connected to Planning Network (PLANET), one of the first conferencing systems, created by

```
FROM FRONT TO NEXUS SENT 01.10 14/12/1983
S
A
X
I
S
L
A
N
D
```

```
AMERICA                                             EUROPEEUROPEEUR
AMERIC                                              EUROPEEUROPEEUR
AME                                                 EUROPEEUROP
AM                        SAXISLANDSAXISLAND         EUROPEEUR
AMER                      SAXISLANDSAXISLAN          EUROPE
AMERICA                   SAXIALAND                  EUR
AMERICAAME                SAXISLAN                   AFRICAAFRICAAF
AMERICAAMER               SAXISLAND                  AFRICAAFRICAAFR
AMERICAAMERI              SAXISLAND                  AFRICAAFRICAAFRICA
AMERICAAMERIC             SAXISLAND                  AFRICAAFRICAAFRICAAF
AMERICAAMERICA            SAXISLAND                  AFRICAAFRICAAFRICAAFR
AMERICAAMERICAAM          AAXSSLAND                  AFRICAAFRICAAFRICAAFR
AMERICA AMERICAAME          SAXISLAND                AFRICAAFRICAAFRICAAFR
AMERICAAMERICAAMER          SAXISLANDS               AFRICAAFRICAAFRICAAF
AMERICAAMERICAAMER          SAXISLANDS               AFRICAAFRICAAFRICAAF
AMERICAAMERICAAMERI          SAXISLANDSA             AFRICA AFRICA AFRIC
AMERICAAMERICAMMERI          SAXISLANDSA             AFRICAAFRICAAFRIC
AMERICAAMERICAAMER    SAX     SAXISLANDSAX           AFRICAAFRICAAF
AMERICAAMERICAAM      SAXISLA    SAXISLANDSAX        AFRICAAFRI
AMERICAAMERIC         SAXISLANDD    SAXISLANDSAX
AMERICAAMER           SAXISLANDSAX     SAXISALANDSAX          AFRICAA
AMERICAAME            SAXISLANDSAXIS    SAXISLANDSAX          AFRIC
AMERICAA          SAXISLANDSAXISLAN  SAXISLANDSAXI            AFRIC
AMERICA             SAXISLANDSAXISALNDSAXISLAND              AFRI
AMERICA             SAXISLANDSAXISLANDSAXISL                 AFR
AMERIC              SAXISLANDSAXISLANDSAX                    AF
AMERI               SAXISLANDSAXISLAND                       A
AMER                SAXISLANDSAXI
AME                 SAXISLANDSAX
AM                    SAXISLA
A
```

```
S A X I S L A N D
PRINCESSE CHLOROPHYL
PADDLES HER CANOE MADE OF LETTRES WROTTEN ON BIRCH BARK.
UNDER THE EVIL EYE OF THE GGGGGGGGGG MAGICIEN
AS 4 BLACK RAVENS CIRCLE OVER HEARD.
SHE IS GOING TO THE BALL. " OH CHERE GRAND'MERE POUR EMPRUNTER
TA GRAMMAIRE, POUR IMPRIMER  L'INCANTATION SUR LA BETE".
!!!!!!!!!!!!!!WHEN SUDDENLY SWEEPS DOWN CALIGUALA  WHO STEALS HER
AWAY TO SAX ISLAND.
"YOU WILL BE MY DATE LINE SAYS HE. WE' LL TOGETHER TO THE BALL.
HAHAHAHAHAHAHAHAHAHA!!!!!!!!!!!!!!!!
SE
```

Figure 3.4. Screenshot of Roy Ascott, *La Plissure du Texte: A Planetary Fairytale*, 1983. © Roy Ascott.

Jacques Vallée, Roy Amara, and Robert Johansen, then at the Institute for the Future near San Francisco. PLANET ran on the ARPANET, many years before the internet was formed. The system had its inception partly at Doug Englebart's lab at the Stanford Research Institute, where Vallée, a recognized expert on UFOs, was engaged to build a database. (Englebart's lab is famous as one of the birthplaces of personal computing and, at the time, was a node between the counterculture, computer researchers, and incipient digital entrepreneurship on the West Coast.) Ascott, then dean and vice president of the San Francisco Art Institute, was in close contact with figures in these communities, including Vallée, who founded Infomedia, a company renting out the PLANET application to corporate clients. Ascott was attracted to the PLANET system because of its easy-to-use interface and because Vallée agreed to host LPDT for free for a period of twelve days, twenty-four hours a day, from December 11 to 23, 1983. Subsequently, Ascott posted a call for participants on the ARTEX system, an electronic-mail program for artists hosted by Vienna-based artist Robert Adrian X. Ascott collaborated with Adrian on the latter's project, titled *The World in 24 Hours*, which consisted of a networking event realized at Ars Electronica in 1982. Ascott's contribution to this event involved asking participants at computer terminals around the world to toss coins for the first planetary throw of the *I Ching*. In addition, previous to LPDT, the artist created *Terminal Consciousness* (1980), which was among one of the first art works to use computer conferencing, in this case between the United Kingdom and the United States.[56] The project made use of Infomedia's notepad system, which permitted storing and restructuring text. LPDT was a geographically expanded continuation of these prior events and similar to the text-based games that had been circulating in mainframe computers since 1961.

LPDT's subtitle, *A Planetary Fairy Tale*, referenced both the PLANET system it used and its conception as a project with global reach. According to Ascott, the work's main title, however, alluded to Roland Barthes's 1973 book *Le Plaisir du Texte*, a key poststructuralist view of textuality. Consonant with the turn to decentralization in both art and technology, Barthes proposed reconceptualizing the meaning of *text* (or "tissue"), conventionally understood as a "veil" or "closed mesh," toward its understanding as an open form, or a "generative idea" of "perpetual interweaving," in effect, a network.[57] Following this premise, LPDT was created by invited artists in different places in the world, who connected via PLANET and exchanged texts, each contributing a section of the story, although none had a total vision of where the narrative would lead. From an artistic perspective, as French media artist and theorist Edmond Couchot noted, LPDT reworked the surrealists' game of collaborative creation, the exquisite corpse, as a computer-aided, networked form.[58] Like the surrealists, Ascott's project explored expanded consciousness through collective authorship, and the use of networked technologies enabled him to do so on the transnational scale of *cyberspace* (a term referring to global computer networks popularized by cyberpunk author William Gibson, then writing *Neuromancer* contemporaneously; *Neuromancer* is as dystopic as LPDT is utopic, however).

In practice, the project included two languages, English and French, with participants located in eleven cities on three continents: Paris, Sydney, Pittsburgh, Vienna, Amsterdam, Alma (Quebec), San Francisco, Honolulu, Toronto, Bristol, and Vancouver. Each city or node in the network was assigned an archetypical fairytale character such as witch, prince, sorcerer's apprentice, villain, beast, and wise old man. In Paris, Ascott played the part of magician. According to Ascott, he conceived the roles of each participant after Russian semiotician Vladimir Popp's understanding of fairytale archetypes as "centers of action."[59] As such, each node was free to contribute as fitted its character's specific cultural interests, value systems, and artistic concerns. As a result, artists at different locations chose varied ways to engage LPDT. Some opted for collaborating with local artists and audiences, and other groups held regular meetings to develop collective texts, while others realized full-scale performances where texts were read and shared. Thus each hub in the network became itself a networking node acting locally. Online, participants could interact with the content of others by way of retrieving and adding to the existing narrative. Taken together, the resulting narrative resembled a complex textual interplay interweaving associative meanings that were witty, bawdy, clever, academic, philosophical, entertaining, inventive, shocking, or amusing; according to Ascott, each was a reflection of the "consciousness of the location."[60] LPDT's narrative, which, because it was produced within a networked, transnational environment where time and space were nonlinear, stood as a sign of utopian globality: an open, participatory, borderless, interconnected, and emergent environment in nature.

Long before numerous media scholars in the field of hypertext fiction, which includes text-based games, sought to connect this form to more democratic ways of conceiving textuality, LPDT testified to Ascott's utopian outlook on networked communication technology, especially the computer, which he viewed as a tool for global participation and interaction in line with his eclectic interests in nonlinear thinking and nonlinear forms. Exemplary of Ascott's overall work, which he characterized as concerning the realization of "telematics of utopia," the game was similarly, to paraphrase the artist, an articulation of his goal to create a field of consciousness greater than the sum of its parts.[61] Conceptually, Ascott's telematics of utopia drew on wide-ranging sources, spanning and combining historical and contemporary thought and practices in the arts and sciences. Artistically, this concept was indebted to the surrealists' interest in the collective or expanded unconscious, or as Ascott put it, "global consciousness," as a basis for cultural change (as opposed to one-way media). With regard to LPDT, Ascott cited kindred interests in telepathy, mystical thought (Kabalism and Sufism), and "hedonistic literature" (as exemplified by Marquis de Sade and Charles Fourier), along with the numinous-imbued landscape of his youth—the region around Stonehenge. In this vein, he wove in poststructuralist theory, which similarly drew on surrealism, as evidenced by Barthes's writings on literature, myth, and utopian thinkers, including Fourier. Ascott combined this legacy with developments in modern science and technology, in particular, second-order cybernetics as put forward by Francisco Varela, Humberto Maturana, and W. Ross Ashby. Of relevance to Ascott's practice were their notions about the relation between human consciousness and media ecology, and the idea that the world is brought forth through human processes, including language and the coordination of social interaction. In addition, he cited other "system thinkers," including Fuller and the popular media theorist Marshall McLuhan, as inspirations for his practice's global vision. Taken together, LPDT's conception and form referred to the potential of computer networks for overcoming doubts about the possibility of utopia. These notions were inscribed by analogy and by connecting myth, nonlinear (asynchronic) time, and boundless (global) space, games, and utopian thought, with computer networks and, by extension, collective or expanded consciousness.[62] Couchot referred to Ascott's work as being exemplary of how telematics networks "offer the artist the only medium really capable of breaking the barriers of time and space," which he predicted in utopian fashion, "will one day set one free of the limits of individual, national, and cultural intelligence."[63]

Similarly noting Ascott's use of telecommunication networks to allow "individual and cultural freedom," art historian Edward Shanken compared the game to the work of Fluxus member Nam June Paik, titled *Good*

Morning Mr. Orwell.[64] Intended as a rebuttal to Orwell's dystopian vision of television as a means of social control, the project was conceived as a satellite telecast to be broadcast, significantly, on the first day of 1984. Paik's goal was to disrupt the one-directional model of mass media, especially television, by way of enabling interactive, or two-way, communication. *Good Morning Mr. Orwell* was broadcast live from New York, Paris, and San Francisco to the United States, France, Canada, Germany, and Korea; it aired nationally in the United States on public television, and it reached a total audience of over twenty-five million viewers worldwide. Like LPDT, Paik's project was collaborative, including, among others, John Cage, Laurie Anderson, Peter Gabriel, Charlotte Moorman, Philip Glass, Merce Cunningham, Allen Ginsberg, and Salvador Dali. Paik wrote that the event stood as "a symbol of how satellite television can cross international borders and bridge enormous cultural gaps," thereby arguing that "the best way to safeguard against the world of Orwell is to make this medium interactive so it can represent the spirit of democracy, not dictatorship."[65] As Shanken suggests, Ascott's use of computers and computer networks and Paik's experiments with satellite television were kindred in utopian sensibility, born out of a "Brechtian desire to wrest the power of representation from the control of corporate media and make it available to the public."[66] Spanning these practices and those of contemporary artists and designers working with interactive media (among them the video game designers discussed in chapter 5), German dramaturg Bertolt Brecht's 1932 quasi-manifesto essay, "The Radio as an Apparatus of Communication," was written amid the rise of Nazi dictatorship. To counter the Nazis' centralized distribution mass-media model, Brecht envisioned decentralized networks, an example of which would be the radio as a "vehicle of communication [with] two-way send/receive capability."[67] Offered as a "utopian suggestion," as Brecht put it, this interactive model of communication would serve the dialectical function of the socialist society he hoped for, as all nodes in the system would be empowered to participate in the creation of such a world.

Likewise, artists using telecommunications in Europe, the United States, Australia, India, Japan, and Latin America during the 1970s and 1980s worked to mobilize media and media networks, this time in the face of corporate media control, typified by Youngblood as displaying "an irresponsible attitude toward the intermedia network," leading to "blind enculturation, confusion, and disharmony."[68] As their projects built on historical utopian notions of media, they also worked to expand these practices by way of mobilizing the interactive and multimedia capabilities of networked telecommunications technologies, including video, telex, fax, slow-scan television, satellite television, videophone, videotext, and computer networks.[69] Notable historical examples of artists working in this vein in the United States include EAT, who organized *Utopia Q&A* on July 30, 1971, as an international telecommunications project consisting of telex stations in New York, Tokyo, Ahmedabad in India, and Stockholm. Participants in the project posed questions and offered their views about changes that they anticipated for the next decade. Telematic arts pioneers Kit Galloway and Sherrie Rabinowitz cofounded Optic Nerve in Berkeley, California, and went on to realize experiments under a heading they called *Aesthetic Research in Telecommunications* (1975–1977), including the *Satellite's Art Project* in collaboration with NASA, and later, works including *Hole in Space* (1980) and *Electronic Café* (1984). Both of these latter events allowed remote and often playful two-way interactive exchanges (images and sound) between passersby on the streets of New York City and Los Angeles, and among residents of different neighborhoods in Los Angeles. The duo would go on to develop projects in the context of the democratic alternative media movement, leading to the founding of "Communication Access for Everyone" in 1989, with various locations on the West Coast of the United States.[70] In Europe, satellite television transmissions by artists trace to 1977, when Douglas Davis, Nam June Paik and Joseph Buys jointly produced a television program for *Documenta VI* in Kassel. The transmission reached thirty countries, ending with Davis inviting the spectators at home to step into the television screen and join. Other like projects in Europe include the previously mentioned work by Robert Adrian, *The World in 24 Hours/Die Welt in 24 Stunden* (1982), in which Ascott participated. This project consisted of exchange of visual materials and included wireless amateur operators connected via telephone, slow-scan television, and fax in various cities in the United States, Canada, Europe, Australia, and Japan. In Latin America, Brazilian and Argentine artists were among the most active in engaging telecommunications for similar purposes. Pioneering works include a fax exchange between artists Roberto Sandoval in São Paulo and Paulo Bruscky in Recife. Subsequently, *Arte pelo Telefone* (Art via Telephone) in 1982 involved a host of artists using videotext to exchange images. Participants and organizers of this event included Brazilian artists Julio Plaza, Carmela Gross, Lenora de Barros, Leon Ferrari, Mario Ramiro, Omar Khouri, Paulo Miranda, Paulo Leminski, Regis Bonvicino, and Roberto Sandoval.[71] In Argentina,

Marta Minujín (along with other artists associated with the Torcuato di Tella Institute in Buenos Aires) pioneered media spectacles and environments, starting with her *Cabalgada* (*Cavalcade*), a public happening involving horses for public television in 1964. Minujín relocated to New York in 1966 and participated in EAT, leading to *Minuphone* (1967), a project realized with Bell Labs engineer Per Biorn, which consisted of a phone booth that would turn into an immersive playground-like environment (colors would project on glass panels, sounds and drafts would be triggered, colored water would drip, and a television screen in the floor would activate, projecting the image of the caller back to her) in response to visitors dialing a number. These projects constitute just a few of the many works realized by artists working with telecommunications from the 1970s into the 1990s, when the internet became widely available, offering artists a broader reach.

These artists' shared utopian conception of telecommunication technologies also anticipated what has been termed *techno-utopian rhetoric* emerging as a popular discourse as computers and the internet became mainstream in the late 1980s and early 1990s. Liberatory notions about the computer and computer networks promoted in popular magazines, such as *Wired*, echoed the core ideas driving prominent artists to work with electronic communication in the 1970s. Their contention was that the exchange of text, sound, and images among geographically dispersed and culturally diverse strangers would increase human understanding and empathy and even facilitate global peace. This argument would reappear in the writings of early 1980s and 1990s electronic media theorists like Howard Rheingold, who coined the term *virtual community*, and become the crusade of digital rights groups, including the Electronic Frontier Foundation. Before them, the practices of artists like Ascott (and his counterparts in Australia, Latin America, India, Europe, the United States, and Canada), as Shanken observed, offered a model of "life-as-it-could-be," to inspire "the collective imagination to create it in the present."[72]

The Beginning and End of the Digital Avant-Garde's Games

As part of practices of artists engaging cybernetics and new technologies, the games of the digital avant-garde were briefly embraced by the mainstream art world, but subsequently marginalized. With the exception of artists such as Ascott, who would exhibit *Planetary Network* at the Venice Biennale in 1986, the mainstream art world's support of artists working in this vein was brief, peaking and then disappearing by the 1970s. An expanded follow-up on LPDT, *Planetary Network* was conceived as an extension of the Biennale, a live telematic performance themed on the daily news and involving one hundred artists on three continents. Its inclusion in the 1986 Venice Biennale was unusual, however. The period from the 1970 Biennale until Ascott's exhibition in 1986 saw scant attention paid to digital art, save for video art, which gained wide acceptance in the art world at the end of the 1960s and was regularly shown from then on. The introduction of cybernetic concepts and computers in art was acknowledged at the 1968 Venice Biennale, signaling a break with its curatorial model, which had been based on the nineteenth-century world's fairs. This shift was a response to pressure from protesters emboldened by the student-led revolts of 1968 in universities in Europe and elsewhere. The 1968 Biennale included cross-disciplinary projects by artists such as Argentinean David Lamelas and French cybernetic-art pioneer Nicolas Schöffer. Computer art took center stage as the 1970 Biennale's major show, exhibited at the Giardini. Titled *Ricerca e Progettazione: Proposte per una Esposizione Sperimentale* (Research and Planning: Proposals for an Experimental Exhibition), the show was entirely devoted to "experimental art" and included a large selection of early computer art arranged historically and thematically. Artworks using computer-generated programs included *Return to a Square* by the Computer Technique Group; *Electronic Graphics* by Herbert W. Franke, using a Siemens System 4004; works by Auro Lecci, using an IBM 7090 machine and a plotter Calcomp 563; *Matrix Multiplication* by Frieder Nake; *Computer Graphics* by Georg Nees; and a computer-generated sculpture by Richard C. Raymond. In hindsight, this show proved to be an anomaly. Since the 1970 Biennale, computer-aided art, with the exception of video installations, has been peripheral to Biennale's spaces. Similarly, the heyday of cybernetic-inspired and computer-aided art was marked by large exhibitions such as *Cybernetic Serendipity* in Britain in 1968, which included Csuri's *Random War*. In the United States, *The Machine as Seen at the End of the Mechanical Age* was exhibited at the Museum of Modern Art (MoMA) in New York in 1969, which included a project by EAT consisting of commissions of winning works in this category. Despite this attention, exhibitions exclusively focused on practices in computer arts would not return until the 1990s, when the internet and the World Wide Web offered new possibilities for artists working with digital media, including computer games.

Contemporary game-themed exhibitions at mainstream art venues can be traced to a different exhibition. *Play Orbit* was curated by Jasia Reichardt in 1969, a year after she curated *Cybernetic Serendipity*. Conceived as "an attempt to narrow the gap between art" and design, *Play Orbit* was shown at the Royal Eisteddfod of Wales and at the Institute of Contemporary Arts in London.[73] The works shown included toys, games, and playables contributed by one hundred invited artists. With a participatory audience in mind, Reichardt asked artists to produce a toy no larger than six feet in any direction and avoid the use of fragile materials. With the exception of Phillip Hodgetts's *55 Point Light Structure*, a hanging structure with blue spheres responsive to audiences' movements by way of light and sound, the games in the exhibition did not incorporate technology. Interest in electronic games by artists and designers would emerge as a programming trend at mainstream art institutions beginning at the dawn of the 2000s and continuing today with no signs of abating. The first wave of exhibitions dedicated to artists using video games include *Beyond Interface* (1998) at the Walker Art Center in Minneapolis, Minnesota; the online *Cracking the Maze: Game Plug-Ins as Hacker Art* (1999) for Kiasma Museum in Helsinki, Finland; and the University of California at Irvine's Beall Centre's *Shift-Ctrl* (2000). In the 2000s, large art institutions such as Massachusetts Museum of Contemporary Art, MoMA, Whitney Museum, New York Museum of the Moving Image, Smithsonian American Art Museum, and Tate Museum in London featured exhibitions showcasing video games by artists and designers. Additionally, in 2012, MoMA began acquiring video games for its permanent collection, an ongoing project, although one without unanimous approval by some who question whether video games can be seen as art.[74] In an unforeseen twist, however, this trend may be the forerunner of a new wave of interest on the part of art institutions in historical practices of computer art, as MoMA hosted its first exhibition (November 2017–April 2018) entirely devoted to computer art whose title, *Thinking Machines: Art and Design in the Computer Age, 1959–1989*, obliquely recalls its 1968 show, *The Machine as Seen at the End of the Mechanical Age*.

In hindsight, the mainstream art world's withdrawal of support for computer art in the late 1960s can be attributed to several factors, including the decline of cybernetics' influence. Indeed, on the backdrop of military and corporate use of cybernetics and computers, the artists' belief in their liberatory potential may have resonated as tenuous or even naive to some.[75] Yet in light of controversy about the relationship between art and video games, such as critiques accompanying MoMA's acquisition of video-games for its collections starting in 2012, the rejection of computer art and cybernetically inspired work may also be understood as similarly linked to lingering anxieties about the transgression of the autonomy of the art sphere leading to its conflation with and subsuming by mass media.[76] That such practices successfully straddled the spheres of art, science, and counterculture was both their success and their downfall. Though some artists continued to develop work in this vein throughout the 1970s and 1980s, the withdrawal of support by the mainstream art world signaled their absorption in and eventual reformulation as the mainstream, as consumer culture. As the utopian impulses underlying digital avant-garde practices, including games, were taken up outside of the bounded spaces of the art world into the public spaces of popular culture, parks, plazas, schools, and mass media, they would become the building blocks of the postindustrial reconstitution of capitalism. At the crux of this transformation was the digital countercul-ture, then a small subset of the broader countercultural movements of the 1960s. Located in close proximity to Silicon Valley, the digital countercul-ture would work to promote the ideas and practices developed in the digi-tal avant-garde through networking previously separate communities and their value systems, in the process creating the circumstances for much of today's digital cultural forms and industries, including video games.

Game Hackers

As Gere and other cyberculture historians, including Fred Turner and Andrew G. Kirk, have documented, between the late 1960s and 1970s, the notion of the computer as a tool of global consciousness expansion (via the exchange of information) functioned to interweave two seemingly anti-thetical Bay Area communities: "establishment" engineers and the "New Communalists."[77] This convergence evolved into a network of intentional communes, art and music communities, alternative living and media centers, and academic, engineering, and entrepreneurial individuals and groups, which together formed the digital counterculture. More recently, an extensive exhibition titled *Hippie Modernism: The Struggle for Utopia* associated this network within the context of *hippie modernism*, a term denoting both hybrid and bricolage forms and alternative applications of technologies for social and ecological change by the counterculture in anal-ogy to the practices of the digital avant-garde.[78]

Exemplary of the heterogeneous ethos of hippie modernism was the *Whole Earth Catalogue*, a catalog published regularly from 1968 to 1971 and intermittently until 1998. Originally conceived as a West Coast countercultural magazine, the publication was founded by Stewart Brand, a central figure in California's digital avant-garde. The catalog's funder, the Portola Institute, was a nonprofit alternative education organization started by engineer Bob Albrecht, whom Steven Levy named as a key figure (a "true hacker") in the history of microcomputing in his historical 1984 account of hacker culture, *Hackers: Heroes of the Computer Revolution*. In contrast to Albrecht's background in engineering, Brand's background was eclectic and typical of privileged white male hippiedom. In addition to studying biology at Stanford University, Brand studied design at San Francisco Art Institute and photography at San Francisco State College. He was also a member of the Merry Pranksters, a California cult group led by LSD guru and Beat/hippie poet Ken Kesey, and held close relations with USCO ("The Company of Us"), a group of artists and engineers noted by Youngblood as pioneers of "multimedia performances" and "Kinasthetic events" (effectively light and sound shows laced with psychedelic drugs).[79]

Created out of a collaboration between an enterprising hippie and a hacker, the *Whole Earth Catalogue* would cater to both communities, as it offered advice and reviews of tools and literature to back-to-the-land hippies and survivalists, as well as to those in the nascent hacker movement. As such, the catalog was a great success and, in hindsight, a significant node for synthesizing concerns with sustainability and technology from within a shared decentralist ethos. Evocative of Fluxus catalogs, *Whole Earth Catalogue*'s typographic style and collage layout, including its oversized mailing format, embodied the integrative lexicon of hippie modernist design. Likewise, its content, which consisted of reviews of products, ranged from farming and survivalist tools to educational materials, including books on cybernetics and systems theory. Brand presented the catalog's form and content in light of Fuller's "understanding of whole systems," which he introduced in the original catalog as a framework to think about issues of ecology (whole systems became the title of a recurring rubric in subsequent catalogs).[80] Fuller was upheld as one of the vocal advocates of *appropriate* or *soft technologies*, essentially decentralized, personal, and cheap tools reviewed in the catalog and thought to be vital for enabling people to create an environmentally and socially sustainable world, a focus consonant with Klüver's call to adapt technology toward pleasure and enjoyment.[81]

Per this ludic orientation, an entire issue of the March 1970 catalog was devoted to introducing readers to Fuller's *World Game*, including an article by Youngblood.

Prior to the publication of the *Whole Earth Catalogue*, Brand's interest in games as tools for cultural and social change formed out of his collaboration with the War Resisters League at San Francisco State College, which asked him to stage a public event in response to the Vietnam War in 1966. Drawing on his military training and consonant with the idea of soft technologies, essentially tools of systems ecology, Brand conceived *softwar* games designed to explore and learn about conflict.[82] As such, like other mobilizations of game theory, these games employed play to build on participatory and sustainable forms of community. For example, Slaughter, a Fluxus-inspired game involving forty players, four moving balls, and two moving baskets on a large wrestling mat, pivoted on intense physicality. The rules were simple: anyone pushed off the mat was eliminated. The goal was to provide a context in which aggression could be safely expressed. As a counterpart, Brand designed Earth Ball as an ecologically themed game, involving hundreds of players and a six-feet-diameter canvas "earth ball," which was painstakingly inflated by the players' breath. In the role of referee, Brand would announce the rules: "There are two kinds of people in the world: those who want to push the Earth over the row of flags at that end of the field, and those who want to push it over the fence at the other end. Go to it." Choosing neither role, players began switching sides to prevent both sides from scoring a goal as the ball neared one end or the other of the field, opting for continuing the play instead. Subsequently, Earth Ball became a symbol of the New Games Foundation, a San Francisco–based organization hosting free community play events in public spaces, including city and national parks and schools. This foundation emerged as an offshoot of an earlier commune named Games Preserve, located in rural Pennsylvania. Founded by Bernie de Koven, the commune sustained itself through workshops designed to train youth groups, couples, scholars, and local prison guards to work through conflict through games. As an extension of these experiments, the New Games Foundation advocated for the integration of play in everyday life with slogans such as, "In New Games there are no spectators," and by rejecting fixed rules, instead encouraging games that could be readily adapted or changed by players. As news about the tournaments spread through mainstream media and requests began pouring in from other parts of the United States, Australia, and Britain, New Games began producing materials, including books and instruction videos, eventually folding in 1981. The utopian legacy of the New Games movement, however, was revived by contemporary game designers looking for models to address what game designer Celia Pearce called "the creative crisis in mainstream videogame production."[83] Pearce cited the similarities between the context against which the New Games movement developed and the present moment, which, as she contended, is similarly afflicted by "climate change, a controversial war, political upheaval and complex gender issues."[84] For his part, Brand opined in echo of Fuller's dictum and the decentralist ethos that such games stood for the notion that "you can't change a game by winning it . . . or losing it or refereeing it or spectating it." Rather, "you change a game by leaving it, going somewhere else and starting a new game. If it works, it will in time alter, or replace the old game."[85]

As the heyday of commune experiments drew to a close, Brand followed through, folding the *Whole Earth Catalogue* and turning to hacker networks in close proximity. (The catalog would be resurrected in different forms, first as the WELL, a virtual community founded by Brand in 1985, and as *Wired*, a magazine founded by Kevin Kelly, a former editor of the catalog, in 1993.) Likewise, Brand's interests in games shifted from performative, embodied theater to virtual, networked forms of play. Among other sites, Brand traced hacker games to Douglas Engelbart's Augmentation Research Center, located at Brand's alma mater, Stanford, which he highlighted in "*Spacewar*, Fanatic Life and Symbolic Death among the Computer Bums," an article that appeared in *Rolling Stone* in 1972. Written as part reportage, part manifesto, Brand began by pointing to the significance of the computer as a tool of personal and social change post-LSD culture, highlighting the ludic ethos of Engelbart's young research assistants meeting to play *Spacewar*.[86] Adorned by photographs of the long-haired "freaks" at the lab and adjacent like-minded hacker communities taken by New York photographer Annie Liebowitz, Brand couched hacker culture seductively, in countercultural terms, dubbing the gathering of players the "Intergalactic *Spacewar* Olympics." The article's crux, however, was praise for the development of the microcomputer, the holy grail of Engelbart's group's research. Brand's support for this project dated to his role in advising Engelbart on the choreography of the "mother of all demos" in 1968, for which he drew on his experiences with USCO, taking on the role of camera operator. The "mother of all demos," titled retroactively by Brand, was a live presentation by Engelbart to the Computer Society's Conference in San Francisco, which is today considered a landmark event in the history of the personal computer. During the event, Engelbart demonstrated almost all the fundamental elements of modern personal computing: windows, hypertext, graphics, navigation and command input, video conferencing, the computer mouse, word processing, dynamic file linking, revision control, and a collaborative real-time editor. Brand's article was an extension of this role and a testimony to his unwavering belief in the liberatory potential of the computer consonant with the decentralist focus of the digital avant-garde. Brand concluded the article in echo of the New Games movement's replicable model, urging the reader to join in and become a hacker. In this spirit, he provided *Spacewar*'s source code as an incentive.[87]

Computer games were already available as learning resources at low cost through the network of community sites funded by hacker groups to provide information and public access to computers in the Bay Area. Such groups were described by journalists Paul Freiberger and Michael Swaine as "technological revolutionaries . . . actively working to overthrow the computer hegemony of IBM and the other computer companies, and to breach the 'computer priesthood' of programmers, engineers, and computer operators who controlled access to the machines."[88] The political gist of this quest was succinctly captured by Theodor Nelson's *Computer Lib* (1974) slogan: "COMPUTER POWER TO THE PEOPLE! DOWN WITH CYBERCRUD!" (Nelson's own term, *cybercrud*, referred to the centralized model of the computer, such as practiced by IBM at the time).[89] In turn, Levy referred to Nelson's book as "the epic of the computer revolution, the bible of the hacker dream."[90] One of the epicenters of hacker activity, the People's Computer Company, was founded by Bob Albrecht, the initial funder of Brand's *Whole Earth Catalogue*. In addition, the company included the Whole Earth Truck Store, the Portola Institute, the Free University store and print shop, and the Briarpatch food co-op, among other locations concentrated in Menlo Park.[91] Incidentally, the Homebrew Computer Club, which included future Apple founders Steve Jobs and Steve Wozniak as members, grew out of this network, as a like-minded group of hobbyists freely sharing information and materials on computing (the free sharing of software among members was famously denounced as theft and parasitism by Microsoft founder Bill Gates in a public statement at the time).[92] Another militant multidisciplinary group, Project One, in San Francisco ran a community center housed in a space among "200 artists, craftsmen, technicians and ex-professionals, and their families."[93] Among the artists at

Project One was Sherrie Rabinowitz, then working on her telematics projects in collaboration with fellow artists in her group, as noted previously in the chapter. Rabinowitz's friend and co-resident at Project One (as well as cofounder of the hacker group Resource One), was computer programmer Pam Hart. Brand had interviewed Hart for his *Rolling Stone* article. In it, Hart described how Project One was working to adapt a computer, the XDS-940, to the needs of researchers investigating "corporations, foundations" and state's statistical data on the city. Additionally, the machine was also to serve as accounting support for the city's system of free clinics and as a gaming platform meant to teach programming to anyone interested.[94] This is the computer that Lee Felsenstein would use to create in 1973, with other like-minded hackers, the first version of the publicly accessible Community Memory, a computer network housed in a record store across the bay near the University of California, Berkeley, campus. It was the People's Computer Company who published one of the first computer game books designed to teach children how to program in 1975, however.[95] The book was part of a fundraising effort to create more community computer centers and consisted of a list of text-based games designed to teach children BASIC (Beginner's All-purpose Symbolic Instruction Code) programming. These games were "fun" teaching tools meant to attract and shape the next generation as participants of the hacker dream of a different world: a collaborative and digital utopia, modeled, even if not recognized by later generations as such, on the participatory media and utopian ideals of the art avant-garde.

Born out of this utopian spirit, video games, as typified by *Spacewar*, were literally conceived as open, playful environments, as source code was freely shared, adapted, and changed by players. To outdo others' adaptations and share new ones was itself the fun and point of the game. In contrast, the video games that Levy associates with the "third generation of hackers" of the early 1980s, were conceived as closed spaces, as copy protection mechanisms to prevent software from being used without permission, as called for by Gates, became the rule.[96] Levy typified this shift against a background in which personal computers, and by extension video games, were becoming repackaged as consumer products and in relation to the emergence of a new generation that, in contrast to the antiestablishment attitude of earlier hackers, was business-oriented and competitive.

Ironically, however, the cultural and economic success of the video game industry would, in time, increase the significance of video games as platforms to mobilize the counterculture slogan "power to the people." The hackers' notion of using video games to undermine the goals of the Cold War game theorists, to engage and mobilize people in processes of social change, resonates today in the work of artists and designers emerging in response to the regressive control culture of entertainment video games, leveraging mainstream video games and/or networks for this purpose. In the 1990s, the virtual spaces of video games became one of the foci of art-activist interventions by tactical media practitioners. These interventions built on the legacy of the digital avant-garde and the digital counter-culture; that is, their joint conception of the computer as a symbiotic tool of utopia, against the background of postmodernism, and alongside the development of the World Wide Web in the Global North providing attractive spaces for artists, activists, and corporations.

Notes

1. The notion of *systems ecology* was developed by scholars across various disciplines, including Gregory Bateson (anthropology) in *Steps to an Ecology of Mind*, 1972, Jack Burnham (art history) in *Beyond Modern Sculpture*, 1968, Gene Youngblood (cinema and media studies) in *Expanded Cinema*, 1970, and György Kepes (art) in *Arts of the Environment*, 1972), among others.

2. Youngblood, *Expanded Cinema*, 341.

3. Burnham, "Systems Esthetics," 15.

4. The geodesic dome was invented by German engineer Walther Bauersfeld in the 1920s, though Fuller was granted its patent in the United States.

5. Blauvelt, *Hippie Modernism*, 11.

6. Such communities sprang up in rural areas in the United States during the 1960s, as young people sought to create alternatives to consumer culture. One of the most famous was Drop City in southern Colorado, created in 1965. The novel *Ecotopia* (1975) by Ernest Callenbach articulates the perspectives animating such communities from the point of view of northern California counterculture, describing the state transformed in an ecological utopia integrating "green" technologies and communal living.

7. R. Buckminster Fuller, *World Game*, 17.

8. Ibid., 8; Schank, *Avant-Garde Video games*, 12–121.

9. R. Buckminster Fuller, *World Game*, 10.

10. Ibid., 2.

11. Ibid.

12. Von Neumann and Morgenstern, *Theory of Games and Economic Behavior*.

13. R. Buckminster Fuller, *World Game*, 2.

14. Ibid., 160.

15. Ibid., 177. The political support for research into interactive computing took place against the dystopian backdrop of the Cold War arms race, which accelerated with the launch

of Sputnik 1 by the Soviet Union in 1957. In response, the US government began massive funding of academic and industry research into long-term projects aimed at the development of complex network systems such as ballistic missile defense, satellite-surveillance radar, and nuclear test simulations (e.g., the Semi-Automatic Ground Environment). The transformation of computing from the batch-processing model employed in computing at the time, which used punch cards, into "real-time" computing was required for an efficient and rapid response in the case of nuclear defense. This shift also necessitated rethinking the relationship between human and computer. "Man-Computer Symbiosis," the title of a 1960 essay by American engineer and psychologist Joseph Carl Robnett Licklider, captures the pivot of this change as a break with the traditional separation between human and machine. The essay, addressed to engineers, argued against the mechanist perspectives underpinning the notion of "mechanically extended man" in favor of bringing human and computer into a mutually beneficial relation premised on collaboration: Licklider calls these machines statistical-inference, decision-theory, or game-theory machines. In this vein, "human-computer symbiosis" also framed the management of scientific knowledge in terms of collaborative, interdisciplinary interchanges between engineers and researchers regardless of geographical location. This new type of work-group community was envisioned by Licklider as an "intergalactic computer network." The precursor of today's internet, the ARPAnet was established in 1969 to facilitate such exchanges. As the director of the Information Processing Techniques Office, Licklider oversaw funding toward the development of real-time computing, including the work of John McCarthy, who developed the concept of time-sharing, allowing the use of the computer on a one-to-one engagement, eventually leading to the personal computer. He also funded the work of Ivan Sutherland, who developed Sketchpad, an interactive graphics program that showed that the computer could be used as a visual medium. Licklider, "Man-Computer Symbiosis," 74–82; Waldrop, *Dream Machine*. For a succinct overview of the cybernetic era, see Gere, *Digital Culture*, 47–74.

16. Mallen, "Bridging Computing in the Arts," 190–202.

17. Mallen had also been involved in the construction of Pask's iconic work, *Colloquy of Mobiles*, an interactive sculptural work built for the cybernetic Serendipity exhibition in 1968, curated by Jasia Reichardt at the Institute of Contemporary Arts, London. Fernandez, "'Aesthetically Potent Environments,'" 53–70.

18. Stafford Beer devoted parts of his books, *Brain of the Firm* (1972) and *Platform for Change* (1975), to the Cybersyn project. After Chile, Beer continued working in Latin America, consulting for the governments of Mexico, Uruguay, and Venezuela. Medina, *Cybernetic Revolutionaries*.

19. Richard Brautigan's poem titled "All Watched Over by Machines of Loving Grace," is quoted in Turner, *From Counterculture to Cyberculture*, 38–39.

20. For Fuller's description of the dymaxion map, see R. Buckminster Fuller, *World Game*, 75–81. The word *dymaxion* was a Fulleresque neologism combining syllables relating to the words *dynamism*, *maximum*, and *ions*. For a short examination of Fuller's iconic status in counterculture, see Turner, "R. Buckminster Fuller: A Technocrat for the Counterculture," 146–159. In his discussion of "spaceship earth," Fuller argued that cybernetics and systems theory held the key to the solution of world problems. See Fuller, *Operating Manual for Spaceship Earth*, 87. Fuller's view of the world as one island as well as his perspective on computers were closely related to McLuhan's concept of the "global village" and ideas about technologies as extensions of humans: in *Operating Manual for Spaceship Earth*, Fuller stated that computers were extensions of the human brain, a view that he repeated in his *World Game*.

21. Youngblood, "World Game: Escape Velocity," 24.

22. Youngblood, "World Game: Part Two: Ecological Revolution," 55.

23. Nieuwenhuis, "The Great Game to Come."

24. Glowski, *Charles A. Csuri*, 18–19.

25. Efland, "An Interview with Charles Csuri," 81.

26. Glowski, *Charles A. Csuri*, 76.

27. *Spacewar* was designed by three engineering students at the Artificial Intelligence Laboratory housed at the Massachusetts Institute of Technology (MIT): Steve Russel, Martin Graetz, and Wayne Witaenem. The laboratory was an epicenter of Cold War military-funded research into real-time computing. At the time, *Spacewar* was not particularly exceptional but one of many "curious" by-products of a "utopian situation," as one of the MIT hackers characterized this particular moment in the development of networked computing (others included the creation of new forms of debugging, text-editing, music, and various other game programs). Levy, *Hackers*, 150–151.

28. Efland, "An Interview with Charles Csuri," 81.

29. As a meditation on hyperreality, *Random War* underscored Baudrillard's challenge to McLuhan's famous statement that the "media is the message." In contrast, Baudillard held that hyperreality, or the simulation and imitation of reality, had come to stand for reality itself. In other words, the message, the medium, and the real were undistinguishable. In this sense Baudrillard disagreed with McLuhan's argument that simulation would produce empathy. On the contrary, for Baudrillard, simulation spelled the impossibility of mediation, as fascination took over, resulting in "the neutralization and implosion of the social." Baudrillard, *Simulacra and Simulation*, 83, 89.

30. Among the majority of the counterculture in the United States, the computer was widely perceived as a tool of the industrial-academic-military research system, as, for instance exemplified by the 1964–1965 free speech demonstrations at Berkeley, with students marching with computer cards around their necks on which punched patterns of holes read "FSM" (an acronym standing for Free Speech Movement), "Do not fold, spindle or mutilate," and "Strike." The warning "Do not fold, spindle or mutilate" was printed on IBM punch cards used for public purposes, such as student registration, since the 1930s (statistician Herman Hollerith used punch card to tabulate the 1890 census in the United States and was the founder of one of the companies that later merged to form IBM). By the 1960s, the cards became symbolic of the alienation and hostility felt against centralized systems: the state, the corporate world, and the university. Lubar, "Do not Fold, Spindle or Mutilate."

31. Aceti, *Dislocations*.

32. Rauschenberg, "Instructions for Participants in 'Open Score,'" 36–37.

33. Rauschenberg's note for the then-unnamed concept of *Open Score*.

34. Baudrillard, *Simulations*, 10.

35. In reference to such sensor-based surveillance systems, Paul N. Edwards theorized the notion of the *closed world* logic of Cold War politics of simulation: "pure information" promising "certainty in command, combat without (American) casualties, total oversight, global remote control." For instance, Edwards described how the American military in Vietnam used sensors shaped like twigs, jungle plants, and animal droppings designed to detect any human activity: the noises of truck engines, body heat, even the scent of human urine. Ironically, as he indicated, the panoptic battlefields of the Vietnam War proved, in the end, vulnerable to simulation, as American soldiers would fake the data and override sensors,

and Vietnamese resistance fighters would develop low-tech ways to confuse the sensors. Edwards, *Closed World*, 120.

36. Debord, *Society of the Spectacle*, 153.
37. Lacerte, "9 Evenings and Experiments in Art and Technology."
38. Kuo, "9 Evenings in Reverse," 33.
39. Burnham, *Beyond Modern Sculpture*, 359–362.
40. Quoted in Kuo, "9 Evenings in Reverse," 33.
41. Ibid., 11.
42. Mesquita, *Mapas dissidentes*.
43. Pilon, *The Monopolists*.
44. Lacerte, "9 Evenings and Experiments in Art and Technology."
45. Ibid.
46. Ibid.
47. Klüver quoted in Wardrip-Fruin, "The Pavilion," *The New Media Reader*, 212.
48. Ibid.
49. Hay quoted in Dyson, "Art and Technology."
50. Ibid.
51. Klüver, "Four Difficult Pieces," 86.
52. Ibid.
53. Glass, "Stirring the Intermix: An Interview with Tony Martin," *Hippie Modernism*, 406–408.
54. Experiments in Art and Technology, *Pavilion*.
55. Klüver quoted in Dyson, "Art and Technology."
56. The first work of art to use computer conferencing was the *Sat-Tel-Comp Collaboratory* in 1978, which was organized by the Direct Media Association, an artists' group formed by Canadian artist Bill Bartlett.
57. Quoted in Ascott, "Distance Makes the Art Grow Further," 282.
58. Couchot, *Images*, 187.
59. Ascott, "Distance Makes the Art Grow Further," 288.
60. Ibid., 290.
61. Ibid., 288.
62. Ibid.
63. Quoted in Shanken, "From Cybernetics to Telematics," 66–67.
64. Ibid, 68.
65. Ibid.
66. Ibid., 57.
67. Brecht, "The Radio as an Apparatus of Communication."
68. Youngblood, *Expanded Cinema*, 42.
69. The use of video in these practices, subsequently emphasized in the art historical record as *video art*, gained broad acceptance in the art world from the end of the 1960s going forward. Hence, this history is better known under this category, with Nam June Paik often cited as a pioneer of the genre, using the Sony Portapak in 1965 for artistic ends. In practice, the use of video was part of a broader interest in various forms of communication technologies on the part of artists but also alternative media activists. In the United States, *Radical Software* (1970–1974), a journal dedicated to "media ecology," exemplified the decentralist ethos of artists and hackers of this new technology, with video being one of

the new low-cost, portable consumer products at the time. Despite its title, Youngblood's account acknowledges the importance of video (and television) over cinema, calling its global networks the "videosphere." The Apollo missions, which culminated in 1969 with the *Apollo 11* moon landing's live televised feed, demonstrated how the medium had transcended planetary boundaries. Meigh-Andrews, *History of Video Art*. The Apollo missions unwittingly contributed to cybernetic environmentalism. Most significantly, the famous photograph showing the globe in its entirety, *Blue Marble*, which was taken aboard *Apollo 17* in 1972 by the crew as they left Earth's orbit on their way to the moon, would become significant among environmentalists, including the digital counterculture.

70. Youngblood documents a large sample of artists working with telecommunications in his book *Expanded Cinema*, including television, video, film, holographic cinema, telex, and computers, among other media. Youngblood, *Expanded Cinema*.

71. Prado, *Arte Telemática*, 45.

72. Shanken, "From cybernetics to Telematics," 88.

73. Reichardt, *Play Orbit*.

74. Jones, "Sorry MoMA, Videogames Are Not Art."

75. The situation in Latin America was somewhat different, as the ushering of US-backed military regimes in the 1960s—due to Cold War deterrence strategies—effectively put an end to freedom of expression, leading to censorship of artists and exodus abroad, including to the United States and Europe.

76. Jones, "Sorry MoMA, Videogames Are Not Art." Jones is the *Guardian*'s art critic. His adversarial stance on MoMA's acquisitions of videogames for its permanent collections was propagated widely on social media platforms in 2012.

77. Turner, *From Counterculture to Cyberculture*, 4.

78. Blauvelt, *Hippie Modernism*. In her study of adolescents playing video games, Sherry Turkle suggested the notion of bricolage as a way to name bottom-up approaches that hinge on "playful exploration" in relation to programming. Turkle, *Life on the Screen*.

79. Youngblood, *Expanded Cinema*, 347.

80. In later catalogs, Fuller was replaced by Gregory Bateson, an anthropologist associated with second-order cybernetics. Bateson developed concepts, such as whole systems, mind-body interaction, and co-evolution, in relation to questions regarding the observer and reflexivity in ecological systems. In the second decade of the 2000s, the work of Bateson and others involved in systems ecology has been revived in art history due to the contemporary emergence of ecological arts, for instance by art historians T. J. Demos (*Decolonizing Nature, Contemporary Art and the Politics of Ecology*, 2013) and James Nisbet (*Ecologies, Environments, and Energy Systems in the Art of the 1960s and 1970s*, 2014).

81. The idea of *appropriate* or *soft technologies*—low-cost, small-scale DIY, and environmentally friendly technologies managed and controlled by ordinary people—traces to Mahatma Gandhi's advocacy for such technologies in the context of anticolonial struggles in India. Inspired by these ideas, British economist E. F. Schumacher first articulated them in the Global North through the concept of *intermediate technology* in his work *Small is Beautiful, Economics as if People Mattered* (1973). Catholic priest and philosopher Ivan Illich termed them *tools for conviviality* in his 1973 book of the same name. Contemporary terms, including *alternative technology* and *open source appropriate technologies*, reference these and related ideas.

82. Fluegelman, *The New Games Book*, 7–20.

83. Pearce, Fullerton, and Morie. "Sustainable Play," 261–278.

84. Ibid.

85. Fluegelman, *More New Games!*, 137.

86. Brand, "*Spacewar*"; Turner, *From Counterculture to Cyberculture*, 41–68; Freiberger and Swaine, *Fire in the Valley*, 100–101.

87. *Source code* is the written instruction specifying the actions to be performed by the computer.

88. Freiberger and Swaine, *Fire in the Valley*, 99–100.

89. Nelson, *Computer Lib*, 8. *Computer Lib* was inspired by Brand's *Whole Earth Catalogue*.

90. Levy, *Hackers*, 174.

91. Markoff, *What the Dormouse Said*, 262.

92. Freiberger and Swaine, *Fire in the Valley*, 132–135; Gates, "An Open Letter to Hobbyists."

93. Project One was organized at Berkeley Computer Corporation during the protests against the Cambodian invasion, designed around "a retrieval program for coordinating all the actions on campus," and went on to form Community Memory, a computerized community network lasting until the 1980s. Brand, "*Spacewar*."

94. Chun, *Programmed Visions*, 81; Markoff, *What the Dormouse Said*, 206. The time-share computer was a massive behemoth the size of seven refrigerators and worth $300, 000. It was donated by the Transamerica Corporation. Incidentally, Project One received a loan from the *Whole Earth Catalogue*'s leftover funds, handed out at the publication's "demise party" in San Francisco.

95. Albrecht, *What to Do After You Hit Return*.

96. Levy, *Hackers*, 313–331.

4

GAMING ELECTRONIC
CIVIL DISOBEDIENCE

EMERGING ON THE BACKDROP OF THE UTOPIAN PROMISES of decentralization that accompanied the mainstreaming of digital networks in the 1990s, interventions in digital games associated with tactical media (TM) took the form of playful electronic activism. Like their predecessors, the digital avant-gardes and counterculture, tactical media practitioners promote digital spaces and technologies as the most suitable environments for social mobilization. However, they depart from the contention of some digital artists and hackers that participation in online communication is inherently an emancipatory or democratic act. In contrast, artists and activists associated with TM believe that the replacement of the centralized media model with a more rhizomatic paradigm is tied to the restructuring of power, as theorized by Gilles Deleuze, heralding the emergence of control societies. Writing in the early nineties, Deleuze argued that control societies represented a shift from what Michel Foucault described as disciplinary societies. Whereas the latter correspond to centralization and are associated with the architectures of the industrial society, including the factory, the school, and so forth, the former employ decentralization and are typified by the architectures of information technologies and computer networks. Control societies project the appearance of an unparalleled freedom, but this is an illusion; in Deleuze's words: "The diffusion of power places us all the more under the forces of capitalism," adding that "everywhere surfing has already replaced the older sports."[1]

Control societies thrive on modulation, or the decentralized control of information and knowledge. For example, mainstream video games are commodities conceived with the expectation of a new kind of consumer in

mind: one that wants products (video games) that actively support the creation of the consumer's own means of responding to needs and desires. On
one hand, as Sherry Turkle passingly argued, video games are consonant
with this consumer's postmodern sensibility, spaces to play with and try out
multiple and flexible identities.[2] On the other hand, in game studies, much
has been written lately, often in denunciatory terms, about video games as
representing capitalist exploitations of play and players and the internaliza-
tion of control culture. This literature echoes Deleuze's comparisons of old
and emerging forms of capitalism: "Capitalism in its present form is no
longer directed toward production. . . . It's directed toward metaproduc-
tion. . . . What it seeks to sell is services, and what it seeks to buy, activities.
It's capitalism no longer directed toward production but toward products,
that is, toward sales or markets."[3] Deleuze's concern, however, as he empha-
sizes in his essay, is with the need to develop new forms of resistance, all the
more urgent a project because older forms developed during industrializa-
tion, such as workers' unions, are of limited use in the face of the decentralized power of control societies. As he states: "It's not a question of worrying
or of hoping for the best, but finding new weapons."[4] TM activism, including digital games, is a response to this call.

In practice, TM interventions in gaming culture were developed as a
way to hijack both virtual and physical play spaces, in line with techniques
developed in avant-gardism and counterculture, from détournement to
hacking, and in consonance with contemporaneous alterglobalization
activism. TM involves play to both slow down and make visible the workings of ideology and to catalyze immanent social desire for individual and
collective transformation. At the same time, TM games testify to a postmodern project premised on rethinking and reinvigorating the ludic impetus of historical avant-garde and countercultural currents as both antidotes
to the dominant culture and as grounds to envision alternatives to it. In
their own historical time, TM games are aimed at creating disturbances
designed to raise questions about the unique way that the categorization
and exploitation of individuals intertwines with the digital game environment. Additionally, they are also understood as spaces that can be leveraged
to spread dissent virally and cross-culturally, most significantly through
alliances among artistic, technologist, professional, and activist and social
networks. As part of its broader set of practices, and as a subset of postmodern forms of activism, mobilizations of electronic games and environments enabling collective and transnational forms of collaboration and

participation speaks to the overall aims of TM: to exploit the potentials of digital technologies and cultural forms for resistance in control societies.

The New Avant-Garde Leaves the Streets

Tactical media emerged within state-funded institutions and initiatives supporting and promoting open forms of media distribution and electronic media arts in Western Europe at a time of increased cultural mobility and access to digital technologies and networks, post-1989. The term *tactical media* originated at the Next Five Minutes (N5M) festivals in Amsterdam and Rotterdam, events convening politicized media artists, theorists, and alternative media communities interested in "exploring connections between art, electronic media and politics."[5] N5M festivals took place in 1993, 1996, 1999, and 2003, and revolved around notions of tactical media and the merging of art, politics, and media. Organizer Felix Stalder would characterize these events "as tactical because they were not geared towards setting up long-term structures, but towards quick interventions that could be realized with high ingenuity and low budgets . . . partly as an attempt to sidestep the exhausting debates about identity and representation that had been raging for more than a decade."[6] Other important venues for tactical media were located in Germany and Austria. These included the influential Ars Electronica Festival held in Linz, Austria, since 1979. Ars Electronica had a long-standing engagement with digital avant-garde artists, including Nam June Paik and collaborator Charlotte Moorman; Dadaist currents including the Cabaret Voltaire; feminist performance artists such as Valie Export and Diamanda Galas; conceptual artists including Dan Graham; and other intermedial artists working on the intersections of experimental cinema, video art, and computer arts, such as Woody and Steina Vasulka, and Peter Weibel. A pioneer of expanded cinema, Weibel was then the director of the Center for Art and Media Karlsruhe, a public-funded institution dedicated to new media arts. Alternatively, art venues and media initiatives in Europe like Documenta (Kassel, Germany), and Public Netbase (Austria) offered international artists and activists ample opportunities to develop transdisciplinary work in digital media.

The generous funding of media-arts institutions by governments in Western Europe in the 1990s contrasted sharply to the situation in the United States, where federal funding of the arts was increasingly diminished under pressure by conservative policy makers. The Reagan administration presiding over the 1980s is synonymous with the so-called culture wars led by Republican politicians and religious fundamentalists against the activism of feminists, artists of color, and queer artists responding to the AIDS epidemic.[7] This heightened activism in art at this time was formative for many of the initial TM practitioners from the United States, who were invited by their European counterparts to festivals and events in the early 1990s. The most prominent group of TM artists was the Critical Art Ensemble (CAE). The group formed in 1987 in Tallahassee, Florida, and included members versed in performance, computer graphics and web design, film and video, photography, text art, and book art. Self-described as situationist-inspired street guerrillas, early multimedia performances and exhibitions by the group consisted of public screenings of situationist-style film collages and collaborative interventions with various activist groups on issues concerning homophobic evangelizing in face of the HIV epidemic in the United States. These performances took place in the context of nonprofit public art events like *Highway Culture* (1992), in which the CAE addressed issues relating to agricultural labor and Latin American immigration in Florida.

The CAE's focus shifted to the internet in 1991 with the publication of *The Electronic Disturbance*. In it, the CAE calls on artists and activists to forget about the streets as the terrain of their political work and instead focus on digital spaces. The goal: to develop *electronic resistance*. After all, the streets, as they judged it, were no longer the primary site of public life, as the public retreated to private spaces, living behind their screens. This withdrawal, already set in motion with television and its constant portrayal of the streets as unpredictable and unsafe places, was to become even more pronounced with the advent of the internet. The street, once useful as the central arena for negotiating the conditions of collective life, was now deserted and had ceased to be of use for artists-activists. Mainstream media now not only dominated the public sphere but also offered the illusion of security with remote instant communication. Under these conditions, the task of artists and activists was to devise ways to disturb and tap into this corporate monopoly on public life. In addition to noting the decreased impact of street protest, the CAE cited the inadequacy of online disruptions by depoliticized hackers. As the group saw it, even if hackers were the best equipped for this project, their adherence to the utopian notion of decentralization as a democratic force in itself suggested that they would likely be unwilling (or unable) to develop the principles of electronic disturbance. This made the development of interventions into electronic spaces by artists and activists all the more urgent; as they put it: "developing systems of communication may provide another utopian opportunity. . . . If cynical power has withdrawn from the spectacle into the electronic net, then that is also where pockets of resistance must emerge."[8]

In effect, the CAE's proposal mimicked the modus operandi of postmodernist informational capitalism, as typified by Deleuze's concept of the control society, as a decentered formation and referred to by the group as "nomadic capital."[9] Its corresponding "transcendent cyberelite," they characterized as an opaque entity that was anonymous, fast, and operated beyond national and urban bases. As the CAE suggested, their counterparts, the electronic resistance, would likewise take this dispersed form of small groups or "cells" thriving on the mobility, global reach, and opacity afforded by networked technologies. Cells would be formed by those already working with new technologies, including activists, artists, theorists, hackers, and lawyers, who were well positioned to intervene. Electronic resistance would, in practice, be a translation of the techniques developed for interventions on the streets, which in various forms, including pamphleteering, postering, barricades, demonstrations, street theater, and public art, effectively slowed down and disrupted the spaces of industrial capital. Electronic disturbances would be likewise conceived as disruptions of the informational flows vital to postindustrial capital and, by extension, adapted for electronic spaces and networks.

As the CAE stated, drawing on the "historical tendency" of recombination found in various forms in countercultural and avant-garde currents, TM cells would work to adapt, refine, theorize, and intensify electronic civil disobedience.[10] These cells would join to form the new avant-garde of electronic resistance, which they understood in contrast to the transcendent identity and grand narratives (the march toward future utopia) of these previous currents. As the CAE described it, "The avant-garde today cannot be the mythic entity it once was. No longer can we believe that artists, revolutionaries, and visionaries are able to step outside of culture to catch a glimpse of the necessities of history as well as the future. Nor would it be realistic to think that a party of individuals of enlightened social consciousness (beyond ideology) has arrived to lead the people into a glorious tomorrow. However, a less appealing (in the utopian sense) form of the avant-garde does exist."[11]

In this way, the CAE envisioned the new avant-garde as an open-ended and emergent formation akin to a network, rather than a stable or centrally structured form or organization. In practice, this model replicated the decentralized model of some of the earlier digital avant-garde, including Fluxus, organizations like Experiments in Art and Technology, and hacker groups associated with the digital counterculture. In its own time, electronic civil disobedience mirrored the performative identity and decentralist focus of postmodern activism, of which the Zapatistas are exemplary. The Zapatistas rose to prominence in 1994 as the first postmodern guerrilla movement due to their effective use of electronic networks from deep within the Lacandon jungle to report on corporate and governmental abuses in Chiapas, Mexico, and their energizing of alterglobalization movements across the world, not least by way of highly ironic and theatrical identity performances of the *guerrillero* by Subcomandante Marcos in the media. Deleuze's call for new forms of resistance to the society of control in 1990 was echoed four years later in the Zapatistas' proposal to the global civic community to develop "intercontinental networks of resistance."[12] As a subset of these networks, TM would focus on developing cross-cultural collaborations from within digital spaces and networks. Such projects would, in practice, take forms akin to détournements and, in hacker terms, exploits and viral campaigns. Ultimately, the goal was to disrupt and render vulnerable to semiological deconstruction the smooth workings of neoliberal informational capitalism.

As a network chiefly operating in digital spaces, TM was conceived as a refinement of historical avant-gardist and countercultural models of organization and techniques, as a subversive replication of informational capitalism, and as a small network within larger alterglobalization networks. TM's flexible, decentralized, and cellular configuration was summed up at the time by anarchist poet Hakim Bey as a form of organization that, because it was "devoted to the (immediate) overcoming of separation," pertained to *ontological anarchy*, his term for autonomous politics whose unfolding is immanent on being/doing/becoming. Bey suggested that the task of such an organization was to create a temporary autonomous zone (TAZ), a notion often invoked by TM practitioners at the time as a fitting characterization of TM practices.[13] For instance, a group working alongside the CAE, the cyberfeminist collective Subrosa, would argue that activist disruptions of digital culture (its forms and spaces) embody a political space, which evocative of the Zapatistas' liberated zones, they deemed a becoming autonomous zone or BAZ, their feminist adaption of Bey's TAZ.[14] To paraphrase the group, such a space stands in contrast to the spaces controlled by informational capitalism in which separation and exclusion based on gendered, racial, and social and economic hierarchies is upheld by proprietary knowledge, and accumulation of resources and competition is the rule. Instead, the space of the TAZ/BAZ/Zapatista autonomous zones is dedicated to a politics of autonomy thriving on openness, on welcoming difference, on the exchange of skills, and on collaboration as the basis to develop a "common wealth of knowledge and power."[15]

In sum, TM's interventionist project, including disturbances of mainstream gaming culture, does not represent an attempt at uncritically reinstating the historical avant-garde identity and revolutionary grand narratives as the grounds of a progressive political project, rather its development and redefinition within the context of consumer-market-driven digital culture. In practice, this project required thinking through collaborative and participatory formations capable of enabling cultural and political change in the aftermath of the mobilization and refashioning of the historical digital avant-gardes and countercultural legacies and harnessing of Cold War's digital technologies, as art historian Charlie Gere notes, for "the reconstruction of capitalism into a more flexible and responsive mode."[16] With this in mind, the task set out by TM artists and activists was to test the potentials of decentralized spaces and media forms, the new loci of control, for derailing and disabling consumer digital culture. This line of research, as one of the former members of Subrosa once pointed out to me, is akin to Deleuze's and Guattari's concept of philosophy's aim, which is not to rediscover the eternal or the universal but to find the singular conditions under which something new could be created.[17] In their words: "Philosophy takes the relative deterritorialization of capital to the absolute; it makes it pass over the plane of immanence as movement of the infinite and suppresses it as internal limit, turns it back against itself so as to summon forth a new earth, a new people."[18] In this spirit, TM is best playfully articulated in Bey's words, as "a game for free spirits."[19]

Identity Corrections

TM interventions in digital games were largely realized in the 1990s during a period in which internet environments were rapidly emerging but still mostly unstable. Net-artist Olia Lialina speaks of a "vernacular web," describing the growth of the World Wide Web during this time as the work of amateurs "soon to be washed away by dot.com ambitions, professional authoring tools, and guidelines designed by usability experts."[20] This window in time provided an ideal environment for artists and activists already organized around the spaces and environments of new forms of entertainment culture germane to the medium, including digital games, who were intent on reaching broad and transnational audiences. Conceived as electronic civil disobedience, early TM interventions in games take various forms, ranging from media stunts, provocations, and covert infiltration, to the overt implications of the player as a participant in interventions.[21] More recently, artists and activists working in TM have extended these forms to synchronize dissent in virtual and physical spaces. Then and now, TM interventions in gaming culture seek to disrupt the relationship between mainstream play and power and to empower the player to change the game.

One of the earliest TM interventions into gaming culture was a hack targeting *SimCopter* (1996), a video game developed by Maxis (the company was also developing *The Sims* at this time). Initially, Jacques Servin, a gay programmer, made the news in 1997 when he was fired by the company after he modified fifty thousand *SimCopter* units that were shipped across the country during the 1996 Christmas season, by inserting scantily clad male characters kissing each other.[22] The characters, as the programmer explained, were coded to be triggered at certain times: on Servin's birthday, on his partner's birthday, and on Friday the 13th, but according to players' later reports, a glitch made it such that characters appeared frequently and randomly.[23] In game culture, this is referred to as an "Easter egg," and it is likely that the timing, before Christmas, was both a pun on this and a date calculated to have maximal effect since there is such a high demand for video games at Christmas.

The action was later claimed by RTMark (derived from "registered trademark"), an anonymous group registered as a corporation and represented by a website. RTMark was essentially a spoof of the proliferation of dot.com companies online and designed to exploit the protections conferred to a corporation to match activists who plan projects with donors who fund them. Historically, this modus operandi traces back to Berlin Dada's spoofs of commercial entities and religious organizations as forms of cultural sabotage. (In their own time, it recalls the Zapatistas' ironic imitations of the modernist guerrilla, à la Che Guevarra).[24] In the movie *The Yes Men*, Servin (who is one of the Yes Men, RTMark's performative counterparts) claimed the *SimCopter* hack and recounted how he heard about RTMark from a friend. According to Servin, he dialed RTMark's BBS

(Bulletin Board System), signed up for a project that proposed video game designers to hack video games, and was eventually paid $5,000 in the form of a money order as a reward for the risk (the funds were provided by an anonymous donor that RTMark claimed was actually an organization of war veterans).[25] But the real reward came as Maxis was publicly embarrassed by the prominent media coverage about the hack on national and international channels. Servin soon got another job that paid twice what his old job had and, in retrospect, gained something far more rewarding than monetary compensation—a sense of empowerment. As he described it, "I felt more powerful. I brought down a system a little bit. I embarrassed a whole company. I affected a stock."[26] In the movie, Servin states that the *SimCopter* hack was motivated by his frustration with working conditions at Maxis, where he was employed as a game designer working sixty-hour weeks with no vacation and with his dissatisfaction of the company's masculinist stereotyping in mainstream macho-action games.[27] According to Servin, the scantily clad "boys" were meant to offset the prominence of their female counterparts, the "female bimbos" in mainstream video games. RTMark and the Yes Men call these Dadaesque targetings of corporate branding "identity correction," performed with the aim of giving "a more accurate portrayal of powerful public figures and institutions than they themselves do."[28] In this case, Maxis was exposed for its exploitation of labor (a gay coder) and its militarism and sexism (gender normative stereotypes of male characters).

About the time of *SimCopter*, Mongrel, a UK- and Jamaica-based art collective, released *BlackLash* (1996) (fig. 4.1) as part of the Natural Selection search engine designed to intercept and redirect query terms for sex, race, and eugenics to content commenting on racism on the internet.[29] Mongrel used the explosion of search engines in the 1990s to disguise their intervention (*BlackLash*) through camouflage. Natural Selection linked racialized terms (e.g., white, paki, nigga, etc.) to the group's server that held a database of websites contributed by artists and collectives, such as CAE, Stewart Home, Daniel Waugh, Hakim Bey, and poet Dimela Yekwai. The database included parodies of white supremacist music, sites offering advice to prospective undocumented immigrants to Britain, poetic histories of eugenics, specifically targeted heritage software meant to locate one's nonwhite relatives, fake biotech companies offering their services to those wishing to racially engineer their offspring, and *BlackLash*, a game designed as an inversion of the shoot-the-alien action of *Spacewar* spinoffs such as *Space*

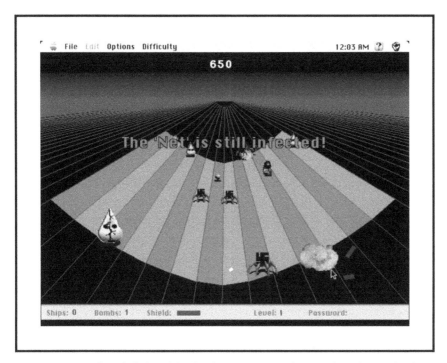

Figure 4.1. Screenshot of *BlackLash* (Richard Pierre-Davis and Mongrel, 1996). © Richard Pierre-Davis and Mongrel.

Invaders (Taito, 1978) and *Tempest* (Atari, 1981). In *BlackLash*, the player in clichéd black-male roles, like crime lord or lover, is pitted against aliens who are represented as swastika-adorned spiders, policemen, and Ku Klux Klan members on a sonic background provided by Wu-Tang-Clan.[30] According to author and Mongrel member Richard Pierre Davis, *BlackLash* was conceived "to encourage the black community through game culture that it is possible to break into different areas apart from music, and create games that have something to say."[31] Mongrel member Mervin Jarman spoke about the game as "a serious wake 'em up call. It is all about 'REPRESENT' and who is representing whom."[32]

Along with challenging stereotyped portrayals of black men in media, particularly video games, Natural Selection questioned the neutrality of the algorithmic structure of information technologies that frame the relationship between the organization of data/information and the user's experience. In her discussion of the project, Wendy Hui Kyong Chun writes:

"Mongrel's interfaces and software reverse the usual system of software design: it produces interfaces and content that are provocative—even offensive—in order to reveal the limits of choice, to reveal the fallacy of the all-powerful, race free user. . . . Mongrel's projects also play with the relationship between software and ideology in order to make us question the reduction of race to a database category."[33]

Mongrel collaborator Matthew Fuller relates the project to "second-order memetics," a playful reference to memetics, a theory of cultural transmission peaking in the 1990s, that sought to explain human behavior on the basis of information theory as a result of preprogrammed memetic (i.e., informational) replication.[34] As a deliberately biased software, Natural Selection was conceived to meet the resurgence of positivist ideologies in techno-environments with a strategy of ridicule akin to the identity correction of Servin and RTMark. *BlackLash* brought to the fore the racial undercurrents of mainstream media culture, in this case provocatively asking the player to play the game as a stereotyped black male, employing cross-cultural collaboration that surpassed the one-off, solitary actions of a disgruntled programmer.

Similarly, the notion of identity correction was central to one of the calls coming out of the Cyberfeminist International meetings at Documenta X in 1997 that proposed "creating new avatars, databodies, new self-representations which disrupt and recode the gender biases usual in current commercially available ones."[35] This suggestion was put into practice in *The Intruder* (1999), a viral game by Natalie Bookchin, former member of RTMark and currently a Los Angeles-based net artist. The title of the game is a double entendre that signals the maker's disruptive intent and the work's basis on a short story by Jorge Luis Borges, titled "The Interloper" (1998). The story is a parable of misogyny that transposes a biblical passage (Matthew 1:26) onto gaucho (cowboy) culture in Argentina. The plot revolves around two gaucho brothers, Christian and Eduardo Nilsen, with Juliana, a young peasant woman referred to by the anonymous narrator as a "beast" and a "thing" subject to the brothers' jealous competition, bigamy, sexual slavery, and, ultimately, murder, leading to the narrative's resolution in fraternal reconciliation. It is a tale about the erasure of the voices of women in male-dominated culture through objectification and exclusion, extended by Bookchin in *The Intruder* to show how this dynamic is an historical constant, spanning analogue and digital media. Like Natural

Selection, *The Intruder* was set for random discovery by internet users. Bookchin explains:

> People who come to the computer for entertainment are mostly coming through games, and I wanted to lure people in who wouldn't otherwise be interested. For this reason I thought it could work on the net . . . I inserted keywords, at a time when that still worked, so that people looking for "sex" or something else would end up at "The Intruder." I don't know how long people would stay, but it did end up being something that did insert itself into all these different contexts: art, literature, hypertext, people who were just interested in playing . . . that was my interest, in having something that was not automatically framed as "art," so that people would end up being surprised . . . because I think when you walk into an institution that frames itself as art . . . you already have the expectation that you are going to be shocked, or surprised, or in some way moved.[36]

Additionally, by drawing parallels between cowboy and gaming cultures, Bookchin not only situates them in relation to their shared appeal to the normalization of hypermasculinity but also points to the cultural form typifying this identity: that is, its drive toward closure. To make this point, the artist positions the player to act unwittingly as an accomplice in the unfolding of Borges's story. The game's ten levels combine a soundscape composed of narration by a female voice, atmospheric sounds, and soundtracks of early video games, with typical closed or goal-driven actions such as competing, shooting, chasing, and conquering. In this way, the game suggests that the coding of stereotypic masculinist identity in video games—reducing the complexity of gender and intra and intersexual interactions to impersonal units, separating Self from Other, and exerting power over—is tied to the use of closure.[37] To finish *The Intruder* the player is positioned to enact the story's ending, shooting at Juliana from behind the sight of a gun aimed at her diminutive figure running in the woods. Conversely, the game also denies closure, as it ends by leaving the player to consider open-ended questions about both the othering inscriptions of the female body and female difference in cultural forms (such as text and games), and the potential of these forms for developing and creating alternative understandings, images, and representations of women by women. In the latter sense, *The Intruder* pays homage to and adapts the notion of *écriture féminine*, or women's writing, adapting what Lucy Sargisson calls feminist utopianism to the medium of the video game, reshaping it likewise as an open-ended form that reaffirms its potentialities for transformation.[38]

In a similar vein, Bookchin used *The Intruder* in workshops designed to teach children game modding (the alteration of aspects of the game by players, including visuals and behaviors). As a teaching tool, the work functioned similarly, as a means of empowerment, since the artist invited young attendees, including children of Muslim immigrants to France in Marseille, to use *The Intruder* as a placeholder for their own purposes, as a conduit for self-understanding and self-representation based on the exchange of skills and knowledge in the spirit of cyberfeminist projects aimed at becoming autonomous.[39] In this case, the goal was to ultimately recode video games counter to their marketing as white, cisgender male domains as spaces welcoming of difference.

While the Yes Men, Mongrel, and Bookchin's interventions effectively bring the gender and racial stereotypes in the form and content of video games to the fore, these projects are limited to singular actions by artists and designers. To increase the number of individuals able to undertake or replicate similar projects, other TM artists concentrated on strategies designed to impart knowledge to empower individuals routinely excluded and/or misrepresented in video games and the video games industry, much as Bookchin began doing in her later workshops with *The Intruder.*

The use of video games as pedagogical tools is central to *Super Kid Fighter* (1998), a project developed by the CAE and Carbon Defense League as a hack of a Nintendo's GameBoy ROM aimed at boys between the ages of ten and fifteen, the target market of Nintendo products at the time.[40] Instructions on how to replicate the hack were included in *Child as Audience*, a media kit containing a CD-ROM, a pamphlet on youth oppression, and a hardcore music CD by the band Creation is Crucifixion, the Carbon Defense League's musical persona (kits were initially distributed at concert venues). *Super Kid Fighter* is a role-playing game in which the player plays as a student siding with "deviants" to escape authority (school, church, family, etc.) and earn money and information leading to the final reward, the entrance to a brothel where two images of a male and a female could be bared (the score determines the degree of exposure). The project, which is exceptional in that it was conceived prior to children gaining widespread access to the internet, additionally aimed to counteract the "ideological influence of games in childhood" by way of raising the possibility of provoking a company (Nintendo) to speak publicly against the (modified) cartridges sent in by alarmed parents.[41] A potential public acknowledgment of the hack would have a tremendous reverberation in the gaming community because GameBoy (1989) was the top-selling video game device at the time, because it encouraged children and politicized programmers to create games for their own subversive purposes, and finally, as a retort to Nintendo's obsession with control over its products, *Super Kid Fighter* demonstrated that piracy and reverse-engineering of products is always possible.[42] The pedagogical frame of the project evokes the work of Brazilian activist-pedagogue Paulo Freire, whom the CAE cites in another context as an inspiration for devising their performative practices of "recombinant theater" aimed at educating and imparting basic information on biotechnologies to the public.[43] Freire's framing of pedagogy as a means to critical consciousness are echoed in the hack's attempt to create awareness of the exploitative strategies of video game entertainment corporations and the audience's agency to respond to them. In addition, the narrative of *Super Kid Fighter* pays homage to the Austrian American psychoanalyst Wilhelm Reich, whose research on the rise of fascism in Germany led to his idea that sexual or libidinal repression in childhood and adolescence leads to frustration and anxiety, and ultimately produces the type of individual amenable to authoritarian systems.[44] (Deleuze and Guattari later reprised Reich's arguments in their discussion about the formation of fascism as a response to capitalism, that is, a reactionary attempt at imposing order on the chaos of utopian desire.) These influences converge in a game designed to thwart the asexual and heterosexist roles inscribed in the rules of Nintendo's video games for children by encouraging their sexual curiosity and their propensity for discovery—and capabilities, in this case—to play (fool) a powerful video game company.

The rapid development of the World Wide Web in the late nineties transformed the internet, ushering in a phase of enclosure (privatization) expressed in the rise of new forms of commerce, so-called e-commerce, and the professionalization of digital spaces. These developments and the increased global reach of internet networks gave rise to the growth of mainstream online games and, at the same time, brought new opportunities and impulses to the development of games of electronic civil disobedience. The high-profile tactical event Toywar exemplifies how increasingly robust digital networks provide a context in which transnational artists, allies, and audiences combine in collaborative protest. The event was launched as a large-scale multiplayer game campaign in 1999 in response to a legal dispute between Etoy.org, an art website by the Swiss art group Etoy, online since 1994, and eToys.com, a relatively new dot.com selling children's toys online.[45] The toy retailer filed the lawsuit in California following Etoy.org's operators' refusal of a monetary offer for the Etoy.org domain name. The toy company accused the artists of "unfair competition, trademark dilution, security fraud, illegal stock market operation, pornographic content, offensive behavior, and terrorist activity."[46] The strategy was successful, leading to a court injunction shutting down the Etoy.org website. Etoy.org's solicitation for support on various lists like the Thing, Rhizome.org, nettime, hell.com, and others, resulted in *The Twelve Days of Christmas*, a game campaign designed by RTMark in collaboration with the Electronic Disturbance Theater, a digital performance group founded and led by Ricardo Dominguez, a former member of the Critical Art Ensemble.[47]

Using FloodNet, a software application first launched by Electronic Disturbance Theater in support of the Zapatista uprisings in the south of Mexico, large groups of gamers repeatedly reloaded the eToys.com website manually at selected times, causing access to slow down for long periods. The campaign developed over time with added features such as the automation of the check-out process on the eToys.com website by "Etoy soldiers" and the loading of pages, including financial documents, on the eToys.com server in order to overload its capacity for response.[48] Alexander R. Galloway, a Rhizome.org affiliate at the time, described Toywar as a "complex, self-contained [system], with [its] own internal email . . . [its] hazards, heroes and martyrs." He added that, "similar to a simulation or training game, Toywar constructs a one-to-one relationship between the affective desires of gamers and the real social contexts in which they live."[49] According to the Etoy group, in its entirety the campaign involved regular internet users as well as "1798 activists, artists, lawyers, celebrities and journalists . . . filing counter court cases, infiltrating customer service, pr [*sic*] departments, the press, investor news groups and also on the level of Federal Trade Commission."[50] Play was extended for several months, into the Christmas season, which resulted in a drop of eToys.com's already inflated stock from $67 at the beginning of the launch of Toywar to $15 when the company (eToys .com) stopped the virtual eviction and was ordered to pay court restitutions.[51] The Etoy group commented ironically post-event, declaring Toywar to be "the most expensive performance in art history: $4.5 billion dollars."[52] Most significantly, in surpassing the effects of the one-time interventions and analogue projects, Toywar demonstrated that electronic technologies can be important tools in the organization of collective, global forms of resistance, as proposed by the Zapatistas. As forms of electronic civil disobedience, electronic games can facilitate the participation of wide audiences and as a result, as the project made evident, empower the negotiation of issues of self-representation and public access to digital media and networks. This insight is one of the legacies of early TM interventions, at their apogee during the last decade of the twentieth century but still reverberating in gaming culture today.

After Tactical Media

Kindred projects would extend electronic civil disobedience into new game environments that emerged in the late 1990s, like the popular massively multiplayer online games, which inadvertently brought new and significant opportunities for dissent. Artists familiar with TM recognized that these spaces provided ready-made platforms, the more attractive for their verisimilitude, with technical capabilities involving hundreds or thousands of players and including relatively user-friendly options for modifications. Additionally, these new game environments' capabilities for real-time communication lent new and innovative opportunities to artists interested in speaking to the connections between virtual play spaces and real spaces, in particular vis-à-vis the militarization of both these environments under the aegis of the empire-driven, bold, global mandate of the war on terror. After the 9/11 attacks in New York City, these interventions focused on the militarization of gaming culture as exemplified by both the proliferation of anti-Muslim and prowar-themed games on the internet, often authored by gamers, and the adoption of video games by the US military for the purpose of recruiting and training gamers as future soldiers for drone war, the preferred method of warfare in the war on terror. This trend entrenched realism as the aesthetic ideal of mainstream video games, with immersion in the game as the goal.

Conceived inside this background, the games of artist Anne-Marie Schleiner are significant examples of interventions situated on the intersections of video games, militarism, gender and racial categories, and their relation to realist constructions of online and off-line spaces during this historical period. Working after the heyday of TM, Schleiner's practice differs from the broader scope of TM projects in that it focuses exclusively on video games and video game culture, though it shares similar conceptual and transnational collaborative underpinnings. Schleiner herself characterizes her work as "situationist gaming," in reference to the situationists' employment of play as a "freeing and transformational" force acting to suspend the dominant order.[53] *Velvet-Strike* (2002) was her first collaborative intervention with Joan Leandre (Spain) and Brody Condon (Mexico-US). The project took advantage of the popularity and the modding capabilities of *Counter Strike* (Vivendi Universal, Microsoft Game Studios, 2000) to solicit the participation of players in making alterations to the appearance of the game's environments. The choice of *Counter Strike* is also significant, as it is an example of the strong militarist sentiment taking hold in gaming culture post-9/11. *Counter Strike* originated as a gamers' mod of *Half-life* (1998) and was subsequently commercialized due to its popularity; play revolves around pitting a team of counterterrorists against a team of terrorists in a narrative reminiscent of the framing of the global war on terror after the 9/11 attacks, the height of the game's popularity.[54] The *Velvet-Strike* mod provides gamers with the ability to post and download spray-paint skins modeled on graffiti, with antiwar messages that can be placed on the walls, ceilings, and floors of the game environment.[55] In his discussion of the project, Mateo Bittanti notes: "By destabilizing the intended, expected uses of the game by means of virtual protest, Schleiner's approach can be linked to the long tradition of player empowerment."[56] To this point, Condon's sprays (*Love 1, 2, 3*), which are part of *Velvet-Strike* and altogether show two male combatants engaged in various homoerotic poses, evokes a playful homage to *SimCopter*'s kissing soldiers, and as Schleiner remarked in an interview, these images were especially provocative with the heightened masculinist context of *Counter Strike*.

Velvet-Strike also speaks to Schleiner's personal background, as the granddaughter of a German immigrant who told her stories of the devastating consequences of war and the mobilization of youth through the use of games by the Nazis. In terms of art, the game speaks to Schleiner's pioneering role as a curator of various online shows on digital games and internet folklore. These exhibits began with *Cracking the Maze* in 1998, which consisted of game mods by artists and art collectives on gender, race, and politics in and out of gaming, and included *Mutation.fem*, a collection of female character game hacks and skins first exhibited in Helsinki, Finland, at the Kiasma Museum show *Alien Intelligence*, curated by Erkki Huhtamo in 2000; *Lucky Kiss*, an online exhibit of interactive erotica designed and freely distributed by networks of fans dedicated to develop and share these works; and *Snow Blossom House*, which is a collection of hentai games based on adult manga developed by artists and fan communities.[57] In this same vein, *Velvet-Strike* uses the *Counter Strike* environments as the exhibition backdrop of sprays (or graphics) freely contributed by artists and the public, thus repurposing *Counter Strike* as a gallery. Keeping in mind the modding or fan culture from which *Counter* Strike itself originates, *Velvet-Strike* pays similar homage to net art as an extension of free culture on the internet. In this spirit, among others, it includes sprays contributed by Australian producer Rebecca Cannon, a fellow artist and cocurator with Julian Oliver of the now off-line online game archive Selectparks.net, one of the first initiatives to preserve and make available electronic games with progressive messages.[58]

In addition to sprays, the *Velvet-Strike* website contains instructions for specific tactics that gamers can deploy to undermine the trigger-happy approach of *Counter Strike*. These directives combine the rule-based Fluxist scores discussed in chapter 2, with digital disobedience techniques (e.g., virtual trespassing and sit-ins) developed by the Critical Art Ensemble and Electronic Disturbance Theater. Like the sprays, suggestions for in-game interventions are authored by the artists and the public and posted on the project's website. One example is the "Recipe for Salvation" by Graphical User Intervention, which reads as follows: "1. Enter a Counter-Strike Server with a hostage scenario as a member of the Terrorist Team; 2. Rescue the Hostages you are supposed to be guarding." Another example is "Recipe for Heart Stand-in" by A.M.S, which contains instructions for a peaceful in-game protest: "1. Ask the members of your Counter-Strike team, (must be at least 14), Counter-Terrorist or Terrorist, to stand in a large, low, flat open area in the game that can be viewed from above. 2. Arrange everyone to stand in the shape of a heart. Do not move or return fire. 3. On all player chat send out the message repeatedly: "Love and Peace." 4. Retain position stoically."[59]

As an intervention, *Velvet-Strike* represents a counter to the hijacking of racist and militaristic video games and gaming culture in the aftermath of 9/11, and also to the claims by industry designers that their games are true to actual situations, as Schleiner notes in her statement of intention on the project's website titled "*Velvet-Strike*: War Times and Reality Games (War Times from a Gamer Perspective)." In it she is openly critical about the regressive implication of realism in mainstream games. She writes:

> Beginning with *Half-life* and continuing with shooter games whose alleged appeal is "realism," a kind of regression took place. In terms of game play, games like *Half-life* are universally seen as advancements. Yet in *Half-life* you are only given one white guy everyman American geek guy to identify with.

And all of the NPC researchers and scientists in the game are male. *Half-life* remaps the original computer game target market back onto itself, excluding all others and reifying gamer culture as a male domain. (Not that I didn't play *Half-life* but I would have enjoyed it more if I could have played a female character).[60]

Schleiner's project is no longer ongoing and now functions mainly as an exemplary intervention inserted into the celebratory media reports about gaming and the war on terror, as news about the project spread. Its preeminent exhibition at the 2004 Whitney Biennial and elsewhere also contributed to the project's prestige, suggesting that games had a role to play as contemporary art. Thus, of the projects discussed so far in this chapter, *Velvet-Strike* has perhaps contributed the most to the visibility and validation of interventionist approaches to digital gaming among video game designers and artists alike. Furthermore, its significance as a project by a woman artist working within a male-dominated context must also be noted. As fellow artist and game designer Mary Flanagan suggests, Schleiner's rearticulations of existing digital games are a form of "subversive play"—actions that appropriate "the cognitive space of public space" with "social and political goals" seeking to "open up dialogue by transgressing the boundaries between art and everyday life." [61] Typifying the utopian currents in play culture, *Velvet-Strike* is also a rearticulation of situationism in the context of cyberfeminist and queer activism in gaming emerging out of TM.

Similarly working in the post-9/11 period in the US, the game-based project by Iraqi-born artist and one-time Yes Men collaborator, Wafaa Bilal, titled *Domestic Tension* (2007) (fig. 4.2), inserts the real into the virtual to speak similarly to the function of mainstream video games as tools of xenophobic and militarist propaganda. Instead of using the spaces of an existing game and turning them into a gallery, as is the case in *Velvet-Strike*, *Domestic Tension* extends the gallery to the internet. The work is conceived as a telematic performance involving the artist and internet audiences via an interactive game-like interface embedded in the project's website.[62] For the event, the artist installed his living quarters in Chicago's Flatfile Gallery, where he resided for thirty days under the voyeuristic gaze of audiences who could peep in via a live webcam, chat, or shoot at him via a rifle-sized paintball gun affixed to the camera. (The gun was modeled on an actual website of a Texas-based ranch that allows online guests to hunt over the internet).[63] Over the course of the game, the gallery room was covered in yellow paint and bits of paint ball shells (yellow references the color used

Figure 4.2. Wafaa Bilal, *Domestic Tension*, 30-day long performance, 2017. © Wafaa Bilal. Courtesy of the Artist.

in paraphernalia sold in the US to show support for the troops). The space was essentially transformed into an environment simulating the conditions of an actual war zone, including the suffocating smell (from the fish-based paint used in the pellets), the sonic disturbance caused by random gun shots, and the artist's performative mimicry of everyday life as a civilian living in a war zone, specifically in Iraq, where Bilal's family lived in similar conditions under US occupation.

The project took off nationally and internationally following a front page feature in the *Chicago Tribune* on the tenth day of the exhibition. The choice of month, May, was timely as it includes Memorial Day, a major US holiday commemorating war veterans. Altogether, the project attracted participants in 128 countries, and Bilal's site received eighty million hits, while sixty thousand paintballs were shot over the course of thirty days. Responses ranged from abusive behaviors like derogatory remarks and attempts at hacking the server to increase the frequency of shots, to encouragement in the form of praise for the project, including a personal donation by a veteran who came to the gallery with a lamp to replace a light previously destroyed by internet shooters, and counteractions by audiences taking turns to divert the gun away from Bilal. Additionally, as part of the performance, Bilal communicated with the public via a chatroom, as well as posted short videos on YouTube, which functioned as a visual diary as the artist spoke about his feelings and experiences in the gallery. Initially, the artist kept his identity and motivations ambiguous to attract public involvement (and possibly because the gallerist feared repercussions). Later, Bilal discussed *Domestic Tension* as an experiment addressing political, personal, and artistic concerns, in response to the Iraq War coverage in US media, as he noted in a subsequent interview: "I was watching the news—in fact, ABC news, when they had an interview with an American soldier sitting in a base in Colorado, and she was [remotely] firing missiles into Iraq after being given information by American soldiers on the ground in Iraq, and when asked if she had any regard for human life, she said 'No, these people are bad, and I'm getting very good intelligence from people on the ground.'"[64]

Bilal set out to mimic the mediated experience of the Iraq War via US media, which, as he states, "consistently excludes images of casualties . . . I want it to be far removed," says Bilal, "I want it to be video game-like. That's how we see this war, as a video game. We don't see the mutilated bodies or the toll on the ground."[65] The absence of sound, as online participants cannot hear the shots in the gallery, focuses the images as ideologically resonant constructs. Purposely degraded, the fuzzy image of Bilal in the gallery seen by online remote shooters functions as a conduit of detachment, constructed, in this case, to position participants in the affective state of the soldier bombing targets in Iraq from a computer terminal in the United States, or the at-home viewer watching the images that result. In effect, this image corresponds not only to the images of the war shown on television but also to the type of image that American drone operators see when targeting people in conflict zones (this is done so as to minimize psychological impact on the drone operators).

Bilal's work posits participation as an antidote for alienation. *Domestic Tension* is intended as a participatory antiwar statement, which he states is conceived "to engage audiences that are otherwise unlikely to actively participate in political or cultural discussions because they feel that these issues do not concern their everyday life."[66] The work's political statement foregrounds the notion that social change is contingent on participation in public life. In interviews and a book about the project, Bilal explicitly states that the project should not be seen as an attempt at martyrdom but as "an artist trying to make a point," and relates the work to his experiences as an artist and conscientious objector under Saddam's rule, as a political refugee in Saudi Arabia, and as an Arab American citizen living in Chicago at the height of anti-Muslim sentiment and post-9/11 paranoia.[67]

Bilal's confinement in a gallery and subjectification as a living target in an artwork brings to mind the legacy of agitational performance (e.g., Chris Burden's 1971 performance, *Shoot*, at the height of protests against the Vietnam War). On a personal level, Bilal responds to trauma (his brother was accidentally killed during an American missile strike in Kufa in 2004, and his father died shortly after the incident) by challenging dehumanizing representations of the Iraq War.[68] Underpinning these views is the exponential turn to automated warfare in military interventions and political discourse, in which drone attacks and terms like *collateral damage* routinely function as sanitizing euphemisms for a systematized use of deadly force where civilians end up as central targets. One of the earliest art projects to address the relationship between gaming and drone warfare, Bilal's intervention hinges on repurposing the tools, spaces, and codes of the dominant culture to create a space for collective dialogue around these issues. Whereas the project's activation of the gallery as a site of protest speaks to a high-art public, its extension onto the internet and its framing in the tropes of entertainment also establishes a semiotic common ground with audiences conversant in mass-media representational modes. As Bilal states, "My work is not didactic or vitriolic, but aims to provoke awareness and dialogue about the toll war takes on all involved."[69] Bilal's celebration as an Iraqi-born digital artist because of *Domestic Tension* (he was ultimately nominated Chicagoan of the Year by the *Chicago Tribune* in 2007) further undermines mass media's spectacular portrayals of "the other," that is, of Iraqis, as either helpless or dangerous, as reified representations (hyperreal signs with no reference to actual people).

While Bilal uses the video game medium as a frame for public dialogue across borders and sociocultural divides, Nevada-based conceptual artist Joseph DeLappe argues that the success of video games designed as training and recruiting tools is an opportunity for the development of nonconfrontational engagement for the purposes of negotiation.[70] DeLappe gained wide artistic recognition for *Dead-in-Iraq* in 2006. The project employs the tactics of electronic civil disobedience, such as virtual trespassing and sit-ins, to create an in-game performance, which he sees as "a new type of street theater," consisting of textual insertions into the messaging function of *America's Army* (US Army and Ubisoft, 2002–ongoing), a freely available online simulation series sponsored by the US government and designed to attract target recruits, young male gamers. Like Schleiner and Bilal's interventions, DeLappe used the multiplayer online game format, in his case, specifically *America's Army*, because of its recruiting function and claim to be a highly realistic rendering of military combat. Entering the game's environments under the code name "dead-in-iraq," the artist typed the name, age, service branch, and date of death of North American military personnel killed in Iraq until he was "killed" or eliminated by other players (he mimics the US military's policy of not accounting for the Iraqi casualties). Upon elimination, DeLappe repeated the process in the next round of the game in imitation of monotonous shooting drills and to make the point that the so-called realism in *America's Army* excludes death (and maiming) as realities of war. By December 11, 2011, the official withdrawal date of US troops in Iraq, the artist completed the input of the names of American soldiers killed, for a total of 4,484 names. During the course of the intervention, the project was highly publicized and public reactions were polarized as to its function as either a meaningful protest against war or as a distasteful invasion of privacy (some expressed objections to the public display of soldiers' names). In interviews, DeLappe referred to these reactions as reflective of the polarized public opinion in the United States about the Iraq War, stating that the project was intended as an activist protest and a memorial to the war's military toll, occupying a space within *America's Army*, which itself was conceived as a tool used by the army to target potential recruits.[71] Less well-known, DeLappe's concept for a role-playing game, titled *America's Diplomat* (2008), elucidates the meaning of *America's Army* and appears to be a tongue-in-cheek commentary on the latter and an argument for the creation of a similar simulation to recruit and train future US diplomats.[72]

America's Diplomat was publicized in 2.1 million paper copies of a fake free edition of the *New York Times*, dated July 4, 2009, which, along with a website version, was distributed in major US cities on November 12, 2008, eight days after the 2008 presidential elections. The article discusses *America's Army* as one of the "top 20 internet-based games . . . initially developed at the cost of $10 million dollars . . . [with] an annual support of

$1.5 million dollars"; its success as a recruiting tool: "40% of army recruits played the game before enlisting"; and its viral marketing in the form of products promoting the game, including "console and cell-phone games, T-shirts, and the 'Real Heroes' program, a section of the *America's Army* website featuring actual soldiers in Iraq and Afghanistan . . . recreated . . . as action figures."[73] The embrace of video games by the US military emerged, as mentioned earlier, in light of its focus on drone-warfare. This type of remote engagement seeks to minimize the number of soldiers on the ground, therefore minimizing American casualties. Because the operation of drones requires similar skills to playing video games, the army is keen on targeting video game consumers, especially players of shooter games, the majority of whom conform to the profile of recruits sought after by the army: young men between the ages of 18 and 35. Given the marked prowar sentiment among the gaming community post-9/11, as exemplified by the explosion of gamer-authored anti-Muslim games on the internet at the time, this move on the part of the US military was quite effective. Amid the hopeful tone of the 2008 American election, the faux *New York Times* announced a utopian future transformed by social policies like national health care, free education, a stop to wars abroad, corporate funding for research into climate change, and so forth, and included links to progressive organizations. The project involved a one-year collaboration between the Yes Men and a network of artists, including DeLappe and Steve Lambert, anonymous *New York Times* employees/saboteurs, several activist groups, and volunteers following a series of instructions distributed through the website set up by the Yes Men, BecauseWeWantIt.org.[74] The spoof challenged the *New York Times*'s support for neoliberal and prowar pundits, among them its regular columnist Tom Friedman, who penned his resignation as an "expert" in the fake edition. The event symbolically corrected the paper's position by appropriating its format to advance the possibility of progressive social change, the title "Because We Want It" being a pun on Barack Obama's campaign chant in 2008, "Yes We Can," itself an appropriation of "Si, se puede," an iconic slogan of the United Farm Workers led by César Chávez and associated with race and class struggles in the 1960s. As kindred interventions into the hyperrealism of video games, the projects of Schleiner, Bilal, and DeLappe also articulate a distinctive situationist view of play as, in Debord's words, "another struggle and representation: the struggle for a life in step with desire, and the concrete representation of such a life."[75]

Taking Back the Streets

Emerging on the miniaturization, portability, mobility, and network integration of digital technologies in the last decade, urban games, or locative games, provide another platform for civil dissent, bringing interventions back into the streets roughly a decade after the Critical Art Ensemble's call for electronic civil disobedience based on the provocation that the streets were no longer useful as sites of protest. Like transnational artists using massively multiplayer online games, their counterparts using urban games exploit the connection between virtual and physical spaces but from the point of view of geographical context and site-specific projects. A prominent concern in these interventions is the impact of containment policies connected with increasing nationalist and xenophobic sentiment globally, which launched a web of surveillance on urban environments, human mobility, and immigrant and Muslim populations worldwide. Hence, play in these projects revolves around synchronizing traditional and electronic forms of protest, melding them to join local and transnational dissent and together amplify their reach and effect.

The continuities between performative virtual disturbances and interventions on the streets and spaces of global urbanity is exemplified by Schleiner's public performance, titled *Operation Urban Terrain* (OUT) (2004), which, to my knowledge, constitutes the first interventionist-themed urban game project using a video game. Distinctively cyberfeminist in concept, OUT was an extension of *Velvet-Strike*, since it engaged the gendered and raced ideologies of so-called reality games by juxtaposing the environment of *America's Army*, a public-funded recruiting game, onto the militarized urban environment of New York City during the protests at the National Republican Convention in August 2004. The performance involved Schleiner and Elke Marhoefer (Germany) as the main protagonists on the street, in collaboration with artists Luis Hernandez (Mexico), Pierre Rahola (France), and Chris Birke (US), in addition to a number of others playing in the electronic environment of *America's Army*. Dressed in Lara Croft's gear and armed with a laptop and a projector, the duo set on a screening dérive through Manhattan, Harlem, and Brooklyn, where they projected live feeds of *America's Army* sent via a wireless connection by players.[76] The project sought to challenge the "convergence of military and civilian space" through the temporary occupation of public spaces in New York City. Schleiner explains: "I matched virtual locations within the

America's Army game servers with physical New York City sites, projecting a live performance of a virtual sit-in inside a tunnel with yellow taxis onto a building in midtown Manhattan, where there were many yellow taxis, and pairing a red brick warehouse in the game with a brick building in Harlem. For the last location I merged a live soldier dancing performance in the popular America's Army map 'Bridge' with projection onto the Manhattan Bridge in Brooklyn."[77]

OUT echoed the protesters' same slogan responding to the propagandist undertones of the US presidential election of 2004, as typified by the Republican Party's symbolic choice to hold its national convention in Madison Square Garden, in Manhattan, a cynical move designed to mobilize xenophobic sentiment around national security in the aftermath of 9/11 events. Militarist imagery from *America's Army* was projected on sites in Manhattan, Brooklyn, and Harlem, respectively, the financial heart of New York City as well as the site of the 9/11 terrorist attacks, and, at the time, two poor and predominantly African American and Hispanic neighborhoods (Brooklyn and Harlem were not gentrified in 2004). This further highlighted the divisive effects of spectacularized politics to which OUT responded by amplifying and synchronizing dissent in real and virtual spaces in New York and transnationally.[78] This modus operandi speaks additionally to the project's historical background, since political activism exploded globally, beginning on February 15, 2003. On this date, according to some estimates, thirty million people demonstrated on the streets across one hundred nations around the globe in opposition to the war on terror. Demonstrations such as the OUT protests were echoes of this global antiwar movement.

Beyond the Global North, urban games emerge as frameworks from which to speak against the controlling and divisive implications of the ongoing reconstitution of global cities as "safe" and "surveilled" environments, as well as a means of concretizing the possibilities of alternative conceptions of urban geographies, mobilities, and citizenship. Additionally, such projects build upon the mass appeal of games and represent the continued transnational development of TM activism.

Cross Coordinates (2010–2011) (figs. 4.3 and 4.4), conceived to be played on the actual spaces of the United States and Mexico's border, speaks to the impact of the increasingly nationalistic policies shaping border regions post-9/11.[79] Created by Iván Abreu Ochoa, a Cuban artist residing in Mexico City, the project consisted of a game of balance played over time

Figure 4.3. Playing *Cross Coordinates* through the border fence between Ciudad Juarez (MX) and El Paso (US). Ivan Abreu Ochoa, *Cross Coordinates*, 2010–2011. © Ivan Abreu Ochoa. Courtesy of the Artist.

in public spaces, in a gallery, and on the internet. The goal of the game was to achieve balance within the context of playful cross-cultural spaces. Playing *Cross Coordinates* required opponents' cooperation in stabilizing a custom-made carpenter's level, which existed both as an analogue and as a wired object. Additionally, the notion of balance in *Cross Coordinates* referenced a key principle in game design: the concept and the practice of managing or adjusting a game's rules, usually with the aim of preventing any of its component systems from being ineffective or otherwise undesirable to players. Commissioned by the curators at the Rubin Center at the University of Texas at El Paso, the game was designed to address the conditions of a historically loaded area, geographically located on the southern border of the United States and northern border of Mexico, dividing El Paso and Ciudad Juarez.

This binational area is presently the largest metropolitan region on the United States/Mexico border. Once a unified city, its present division has its origins in the Mexican-American War (1846–48). This territorial conflict ended in favor of the United States and added an additional 525, 000 square miles to US territory, including the land that makes up present-day

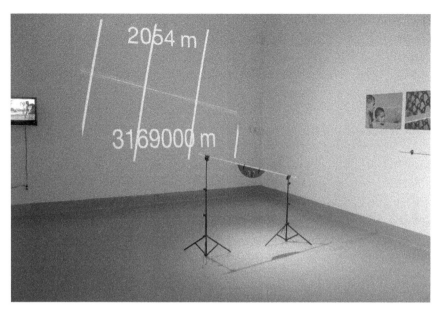

Figure 4.4. Ivan Abreu Ochoa, *Cross Coordinates*, 2010–2011. Installation at the Rubin Center of the University of Texas at El Paso. © Ivan Abreu Ochoa. Courtesy of the Artist.

Arizona, California, Colorado, Nevada, New Mexico, Utah, Wyoming, and Texas, and also recognized the Rio Grande as America's southern boundary (under the 1948 Treaty of Guadalupe Hidalgo). At this time, the city was split in half. The United States annexed the area located on the northern shore, which today is the city of El Paso, located in the US state of Texas. The south shore became Ciudad Juarez, today located in the Mexican state of Chihuahua. Divided by the border, the two populations remain effectively united by shared ethnic and cultural ties. Border crossing, however, is subject to fluctuating immigration policies on the part of the United States. Abreu's project was a response to xenophobic official discourses about Ciudad Juarez's violence used as an excuse to support the buildup of US-government security apparatus at the border. In this context, the game focused the perspectives of the area's residents on the issue.

During his residency at the University of Texas at El Paso (August 26-December 11, 2010), Abreu invited people from each side of the border fence to play *Cross Coordinates* on the streets and public spaces of their cities, including in a church yard located in no-mans-land (an area not divided by the border fence) and attended by residents of both cities, and through the spaces in the fence itself. The videos shot by the artist during these matches show residents coaching each other in an effort to balance the carpenter's level. A metaphor for the delicate balance of border life, the act of successfully balancing the level made concrete the difficulty of negotiating border life as opponents. As a riposte to the US government's rhetoric of safety, the game and its documentation refuted the divisive politicization of migration. This refusal of binaries is embodied in the act of playing the game. The outcome of the game was generally either a win/win or lose/lose situation for both players, but the delicate act of achieving a mutual win reflected the game's (and the residents') message: playgrounds, not borders, are the only spaces with potential to bring about a balanced coexistence for communities.

Abreu's wiring of the carpenter's level for the game's installation at the Rubin Center of the University of Texas at El Paso made this statement even more forcefully.[80] In parallel with street play, gallery visitors played with a different level attached to an electronic device that detected balance and logged the face-to-face play time onto a database and converted it to meters of cooperation. The results were projected on the walls of the space. Thus, the goal of the game was immediately visualized as the numbers on the walls directly referenced the accumulation of meters of cooperation achieved by the players. The goal of play was to exceed the length of the Mexico–US border (3,169,000 m.). The carpenter's level, an instrument ordinarily used to build walls and fences, appeared here again visibly repurposed to construct an aesthetic-political gesture of protest and utopian aspiration, and just like the streets and public spaces of both cities, the gallery space was transformed into a playground. The final score at the gallery, 70,865 meters, however, reflected mostly the El Paso residents' contributions or point of view.

To correct this imbalance, Abreu designed a website that subsequently continued to serve as a platform to extend the goal of surpassing the length of the border wall to global participation. Still functioning at the time of this writing, the website application adds meters under the following rules: (1) the time spent on the website accumulates meters, (2) sharing the URL duplicates the meters accumulated during the visit, and (3) the number of simultaneously connected people adds to the score exponentially.

The deterritorialized space of the internet enabled binational play, which, because of the increasing legal restrictions on border access for Mexican nationals, was not possible in physical space. On March 16, 2011, the gallery score was raised over a four-hour meeting on the website, as 1,500 people in Mexico and the United States gathered on Abreu's call. The end result of this one meeting, fifteen million meters, exceeded the length of the Mexico–US border by more than four times. As the project was exhibited in other countries, the website served to broaden play transnationally, thus linking and amplifying transnational sentiment against borders. Conceived to make a statement against imperialism and in favor of cooperative play, the project affords a glimpse into the latter's potential for liberatory transformation. In this case, playing the games of *Cross Coordinates* produces a symbolic change as the surveilled streets and art spaces of a border city and the virtual spaces on the internet are recoded instead as the playgrounds of civil society.

Overall, *Cross Coordinates* exemplifies Abreu's goal to integrate art, technology, and design to create what he calls a "poetics of demonstration," which manifest in practice as exceptional situations that arise through linking an object, a space, and the historical context of a particular space. These situations are constructed to activate critical thinking and enable the desire of the possible, in this case a decolonized space spanning physical and virtual environments. The online iteration of the project is particularly poignant in this regard, as it recasts a localized issue about borders, immigration, and mobility within the context of an open global space and community. Beyond the spaces of El Paso and Ciudad Juarez, the game affirms the possibility of balance through playful interactions in the transnational spaces of the internet. To this end, its "poetics of demonstration" evoke the utopian tradition and its dream of a ludic, borderless world, and in line with electronic civil disobedience, extends it, opposing the reinscription of old imperialist ideologies, from xenophobia and surveillance to gatekeeping, onto virtual spaces.

Likewise conceived from a transnational perspective, *Gendered Strategies for Loitering* (2008), a video game installation by Shilpa Phadke, Shilpa Ranade, and Sameera Khan, addresses the intersections of nationalism and urban policies in India from the critical vantage point of a three-year research project investigating the relationships between gender norms, gendered access to urban space, and governmental urban policy in Mumbai, India—in particular its focus on safety.[81] *Gendered Strategies for Loitering* consists of two video projections showing footage of public spaces in Mumbai, interwoven with ethnographic and poetic texts and with a video game interface. The footage is manipulated so that audiences are able to note the flow and patterns of human occupancy in the spaces shown, which include parks, railroads, coffee shops, and malls. Projected on the screen as texts are ethnographic observations and fragments of dialogue gathered by the researchers during interviews with women living in Mumbai and Singapore, who provided accounts of their everyday experiences navigating the public spaces of these cities. The women interviewed were randomly approached in a variety of public spaces and represent a pool of subjects that cuts across class, communities, professions, and geographical areas. The design of the game interface proper is based on drawings and sketches representing composites of interviewees and their urban environments.

To play, the player chooses from among four female characters represented by photographic cut-outs. Age, class, and clothing are determinants of each of the characters' access to public space. The goal of the game is to successfully traverse a street in order to meet a particular person or reach a location. Navigation triggers a series of text boxes asking the player to respond to hypothetical scenarios; for instance: "You are standing in the corner waiting for a friend, would you like to stay here, or wait at the bus stop? (a) stay, (b) wait at bus stop"; or "You see a policeman, would you like to ask for directions or continue on? (a) ask for directions, (b) continue on" (this particular question references the rise of women reporting sexual assault by Mumbai policemen). The game ends with a birds-eye-view map of the city block showing the plotted points that the player passed through and a suggestion to continue play as one of the other characters in order to further explore the various strategies employed by the women represented. As one continues to play, it becomes evident that despite their differences, all the women engage the urban space in a similar, goal-oriented way. The texts projected on the screens, which highlight restrictive moral codes equating the height of female respectability with women's segregation and exclusion from public space, further suggest why women might not wish to loiter in the city.

The game is a poignant appropriation of video game tropes like "quests," used by the Partners for Urban Knowledge, Action & Research's Gender and Space Project (2003–2006) to attract particular targets, specifically, youngsters familiar with the medium. As one of the makers stated, the video game medium has proven to be particularly useful "to sensitize" youth in classrooms, the streets, and art festivals "to the issues of gender, the built environment and the city."[82] By encouraging players to experience women's inability to loiter (or drift) in urban spaces, the video game ironically comments on the ideological implications and limitations of the notion of safety currently central to governmental policies on urbanism by city officials (in official discourse, Mumbai is often portrayed as the safest city in India for women; while public safety is similarly one of the biggest draws of Singapore). Video games were only one element of the Space and Gender Project's "participatory research pedagogy," which included workshops and classes taught at colleges, conferences, and public protests and performative interventions in collaboration with women's groups, sex workers' organizations and human rights organizations in India. Like the publications, films, audio documentaries, as well as postcards and photo exhibits produced by the group for and as a result of these activities, the game reflects the group's overall aim to use media for purposes of progressive social change from the perspective of intersectional feminism.

The project builds on Mumbai's current transition from a manufacturing- to a service-oriented city as a spatial context relevant to understanding the concrete impact of safety discourses on the city's built environment and population and on their ideological underpinning of Hindu nationalism. An ongoing process since the 1990s, when the Hindu-led Indian government set the national economy on a neoliberal course, the transformation of Mumbai, historically India's commercial capital, as a global city is tellingly symbolized by the conversion of the city's historic textile mills into luxury shopping malls, a process that has systematically marginalized the city's poor. The parallel rise of Hindu right-wing politics in the country has simultaneously weakened religious tolerance, itself a dynamic exacerbated by the global war on terror (in 2008, Mumbai was the target of a series of attacks by the Islamic group Lashkar-e-Taiba based in Pakistan). This conjunction of neoliberal economics and nationalist politics manifests in a "politics of morality," based on anti-Muslim sentiment and class prejudice spatially inscribed in the city's polarized zoning lines.[83] Along these lines, laws targeting loiterers (the Vagrancy Act), themselves dating to India's period of colonial rule, are today often invoked against "undesirables," in particular, transgender individuals, migrants, and Muslim men. The perception of these groups as loiterers goes hand in hand with their displacement by means of regular slum demolition drives, removal of street vendors, and the closure of dance bars. In turn, "desirables," consisting of middle- and upper-class Hindu women, are confined to the surveilled, "safe" spaces of gated communities and places of consumption, such as malls and coffee shops.[84] As the Partners for Urban Knowledge, Action & Research's Gender Group Project points out, middle-class women, a group in which they are included, "urban, young, Hindu . . . able-bodied, upper-caste, heterosexual, married or marriageable," are historically seen as bearers of moral and cultural values on which the family, community, and nation are structured. These are gendered-, class-, and community-based hierarchies, which are enforced through respectability, sexual choices, and marital alliances (often inscribed on the body through clothing and other markings).[85] As such, Hindu women have been central to India's imagined community. Because of their social construction as "mothers of the nation," the increasing visibility of this group in India's urban spaces as professionals and consumers is highly desirable, as it is seen as a sign of the nation's overall social progress. But it is also a source of anxiety, as these women's mobility and access to the city are contingent on their perceived respectability (and to the nation's ability to safeguard its integrity). Tellingly, Mumbai's zoned urbanism is equally supported by previously segregated groups, such as middle-class Hindu feminist activists, who, along with government planners and the media, call for safety as a primary aim of urban renewal.

By contrast, the Gender Group Project sees this position as a symptom of a failure to address the structural violence underlining the urban fabric in which Indian women live and work. Safety, as their research shows, comes at both the expense of other minoritized bodies, the increased surveillance of women, and the loss of sexual autonomy.[86] They argue that the right to "loiter," that is, to pleasurably and aimlessly occupy public space, ought to be seen as the criterion of a truly progressive urbanity, potentially contributing to erasing social binaries in four ways. First, the oppressive performance of femininity in public spaces would no longer be a requisite to access urban environments; second, the visibility of women as loiterers would render private/public notions of gender and space moot; third, since loitering is here understood as an act geared toward pleasure, as an end in and of itself, the right to loiter would disrupt the consumerist/productivist logic of the global city; and fourth, it would compel a re-visioning of citizenship on more inclusive terms, as the rendering of public space as a shared common space would encourage diversity and difference.[87]

Designed as a direct riposte to the imagined community of Hindu nationalists, the group's project is the more poignant for its recombination of popular media (video games), Western thought and practices, and indigenous feminist utopian visions of space, refuting claims that feminism is a Western idea (this argument is openly invoked by nationalist Hindu groups to discredit feminist culture in India).[88] The group's manifesto, "Imagining

Utopias," reveals *Gendered Strategies for Loitering*, in part, as an homage to Bengali writer and educator Rokeya Hossain, whose science-fiction work, *Sultana's Dream* (1905), describes a feminist utopia, an imagined country where women rule peacefully.[89]

Because the work is not well known outside of India, it is worth a brief description. Written in protest of restrictive gender codes in colonial India, *Sultana's Dream* is structured on a comparative dialogue between two characters, Sultana and her best friend Sara, who turns out to be a strange woman from "Ladyland," a place where women are socially and politically dominant over men, which is seen as part of the natural order.[90] The story, published in a Madras journal, was an ironic commentary on the repressive system of gender-segregated *purdah* imposed on Bengali Muslim women (under this system, girls and women were forbidden from being seen or interacting with men and women other than immediate relatives). As Sultana learns during her visit, in contrast to India, Ladyland knows no violence. Social harmony, as Sara tells her, was only achieved as women took over governance and scientific research from men (their inventions include a pipe-like organ used to regulate the weather, a solar-powered stove, parabolic mirrors used as weapons, and a hydrogen-powered air car). Men are kept in segregated quarters, the *mardana*, where they busy themselves with housework and the care of children (mardana, the equivalent of zenana [the inner part of the house to which women practicing purdah were confined], was Hossain's neologism from the Urdu word "mard," meaning man). Ladyland was imagined as a science-fiction fantasy of a world where science and technology was used (in this case, by women) to change oppressive conditions. Meant as a polemic, the work was conceived as an inversion of the reality in which Hossain lived, to drive home the absurdity of purdah, and is but one of her many contributions as a lifelong educator and activist against the subjugation of Indian women.[91] Her vision of Ladyland echoes today in the Gender Group Project's call to loiter:

> Imagine varied street corners full of women sitting around talking, strolling, feeding children, exchanging recipes and books, planning the neighbourhood festival, or just indulging in some "time pass." Imagine street corners full of young women watching the world go by as they sip tea and discuss politics, soap operas, and the latest financial budget. Imagine street corners full of older women contemplating the state of the world and reminiscing about their lives. Imagine street corners full of female domestic workers planning their next strike for a raise in minimum wage. If one can imagine all of this, one can imagine a radically altered city.[92]

In keeping with the long-standing utopian dream of superseding a world based on oppression by concretizing a life of play and pleasure, the vision underpinning *Gendered Strategies for Loitering* is all the more relevant, not only because it traces historically to Muslim and Indian feminism but because using the internet and social media platforms, it is currently inspiring gendered dissent across India, Pakistan, and Indian diasporas in South Africa. Since 2014, Phadke, Khan, and Renade have been using Tumblr blogs, Twitter, Instagram, and Facebook to organize and report on events involving women (and allies) taking over public spaces in cities in India, Southeast Asia, and South Africa. Under the name *Why Loiter?* these events take the form of games played in the Mumbai subway and on city streets, collective bike rides, group "sleep-ins" and silent reading in city parks, and gatherings at traditionally male-only spaces like *dhabas* (roadside eateries frequented by truck and bus drivers). Additionally, videos, selfies, and stories from these events that are then posted on social media platforms also constitute feminist appropriations of mainstream media, which, like public space, are male-coded environments. Starting in 2015, feminist and transgender communities and groups in India, including Blank Noise, Feminist, and Fear Less (India, Pakistan, and Johannesburg, South Africa, respectively), as well as loose groups of women in urban Pakistan who call themselves Girls at Dhabas, among other names, have joined *Why Loiter?* actions in city spaces and online, presenting a mixture of invisible theater, urban drifts, Fluxus-inspired performances (fig. 4.5), and street games. Representing a cross-section of transgender, Hindu, and Muslim women, these women and groups contribute localized perspectives on gender norms and spaces. Their postings online testify to their shared condition, as one tweet highlights: @whyloiter . . . "The story repeats itself in every city. Women being policed 'for our own good.'"[93] As these interventions make clear, the similitude of feminism and utopian thought between East and West is not an emulation of Western feminism, but a stark reminder that the two emerge from parallel struggles against patriarchal oppression. On the backdrop of a globalized neoliberalist-driven urbanism, they stand against the oppressive discourses of danger. They know that safety by means of enforced segregation, violence, and surveillance cannot constitute the basis of the emancipation of women and their communities; rather the emancipation of women, as utopian thinkers from Fourier to Hossain have remarked, also corresponds to the degree that play and the playful human are understood and valued to be integral to a progressive society.

ATTENTION BLANK NOISE ACTION SHEROES

STEP BY STEP GUIDE TO UNAPOLOGETIC WALKING
is a compilation of very important things to remember while walking. we invite you to walk alone in your city.

walk very very slowly. *walk* without your phone. *walk* without your eyes fixed to the ground. *walk* in the middle of the pavement. *walk* with your chin a little raised. *walk* without your bag. *walk* without your sunglasses. *walk* with your shoulders leaned back. *walk* looking at passersby. *walk* alone. *walk* alone. *walk* at 5 am. 3 am. 2 pm. noon. midnight. 8 pm. 3 pm. *walk* humming a song. *walk* whistling. *walk* day dreaming. *walk* smiling. *walk* swinging your arms. *walk* with a skip. *walk* alone. *walk* wearing clothes you always wanted to but could not because you thought you might be 'asking for it'. *walk* without a duppata. *walk* without your arms folded. *walk* without a clenched fist. *walk* smiling. *walk* smiling. *walk* smiling.

 Try one, try all of the above! Let us know what it felt like! actionhero@blanknoise.org
Blank Noise is a community of 'Action Sheroes' Heroes' Theyroes', citizens and persons united to eradicate sexual and gender based violence.
http://blanknoise.org

Figure 4.5. Blank Noise, *Step by Step Guide to Unapologetic Walking: A Poem for Action Sheroes*, 2008. © Jasmeen Patheja / Blank Noise.

Subversive Mimicry

Tactical media interventions in digital games began as part of a broader set of practices in globalized, postmodern activism aimed at countering the normative underpinnings of techno-scientific capital accompanying the mainstreaming of information technologies, including video games and networks. The inception of tactical interventions in gaming responds to the brand of utopianism surrounding digital technologies and networks, at its height during the introduction of these technologies into public space in the 1990s. As a whole, these discourses construed digital environments as tools of transformation and progress, albeit from the perspective of the entrepreneurs behind the new entertainment markets of the industries of globalization. As one of their most successful products, video games are similarly marketed as spaces that indulge the postmodern self (identity play and the playing out of fantasies), yet as the projects discussed in this chapter show, are in fact highly normative, often reproducing and reinforcing extant privilege and the oppressive power relations of real life (sexism, racism, imperialism, and militarism).

With this backdrop, tactical media practitioners concluded that dissenting interventions in virtual environments and networks should intensify and expand through cross-cultural collaborations. In this sense, TM extends both the digital avant-garde and counterculture's utopian notion of digital technologies as potentially empowering, while also pragmatically responding to these projects' subsequent co-optation and instrumentalization to revitalize capitalism. As a result, this form of playful activism differs from the utopian validation of play and games as inherently desirable by the avant-garde and the digital counterculture; the strategy simply employs concepts and techniques developed within these practices to progressive ends in the globalized spaces of postmodernity.

Conceptually, TM's détournements of video games and gaming culture are conceived to align critiques of existing conditions with social capacities and desire for change in order to challenge and subvert the ways in which dominant ideologies are inscribed in mainstream play. In practice, they use video games and gaming networks to enable the global individual's and collective's rearticulation of the terms of expression and representation, which, however temporary, concretize the possibilities of radically different realities. TM interventions in games take varied forms but, as befitting their memetic model, are generally tactically or subversively mimicking the evolving forms of mainstream games. In the beginning, TM détournements of video games, with a few exceptions, focused on the internet as an environment for creating, playing, and distributing games, or used its capabilities as a communication channel to broadcast or otherwise mobilize distributed infiltrations and subversions of mainstream gaming. Subsequent interventions include projects that counter the claims of verisimilitude within hyperrealist or idealized realist spaces and play of conventional video game environments by both figuratively and literally reinserting othered bodies and alternative visions of reality into these spaces to highlight and subvert the sexist-, xenophobic-, and militaristic-driven desensitizing effects of what are marketed as "realistic" simulations. Interventions that take the form of urban games bring TM disturbances full circle, that is, back to the streets. They connect virtual and physical spheres, thereby further challenging assumed separations between the "reality" of the streets and the "imaginary" of virtual spaces, and demonstrating that their increasingly blurred boundaries can be mobilized as a nexus for contesting exclusivist ideologies and reimagining these spaces otherwise. The criterion of a successful tactical intervention in gaming in any form correlates to the degree to which the project manages to open up these spaces to a multitude of progressive perspectives. If normative simulations merely aim to replicate what *is*, TM correctives reconstruct simulations according to a multitude of visions of what *ought to be*. Because the digital gaming market continues to grow globally, opportunities for intervention are ever imminent, making it likely that electronic disturbances will continue to expand transnationally. Emerging in parallel with tactical media interventions and still developing, persuasive uses of video games represent another set of approaches, the overall focus of which is driven by politicized video game designers working transnationally to create alternatives to the existing scope of aesthetics, forms, and topical range of mainstream video games and the industrial model of the video game industry.

Notes

1. Deleuze, "'Postscript of the Societies of Control," 180.
2. Turkle, *Life on the Screen*.
3. Deleuze, "'Postscript of the Societies of Control," 181.
4. Ibid., 178.
5. Next5Minutes.org, "Archives of Next5Minutes Festivals"; Garcia and Lovink, "The ABC of Tactical Media," 107–114; Lovink, "Tactical Media, the Second Decade."
6. Stalder, "30 Years of Tactical Media," 192. Various theorists relate the term *tactical* to Michel de Certeau's notion of tactics, or unconscious ways that weaker elements engage to counter the strategies of the powerful. For instance, Garcia and Lovink define TM in relation to the "tactical ethics and aesthetics" of popular (mis)appropriations of tools and "styles" of capitalism. Garcia and Lovink, "The ABC of Tactical Media," 107–110. Similarly, McKenzie Wark noted that the tactical prefix defines TM as a stratagem for creating and exploiting opportunities for participation in public discourse. Wark, "On the Tactic of Tactics," 138–140. Joanne Richardson suggests additionally that TM contrasts "to strategic mainstream media." Richardson, "The Language of Tactical Media," 123–124. A recent discussion of tactics by Michael Dieter takes Rita Riley's view of TM as practices that aim to "experientially transform the social and general intellect," and adds that the most relevant aspect of TM is its challenge of humanist ontology. Rita Riley quoted in Dieter, "The Becoming Environmental of Power," 190.
7. Wallis, Weems, and Yenawine, *Art Matters*.
8. Critical Art Ensemble, *The Electronic Disturbance*, 125. CAE's members included Steve Kurtz, Steve Barnes, Dorian Burr, Beverly Schlee, Hope Kurtz, and, at the time, Ricardo Dominguez. CAE's later work focused on the domains of biotechnology, such as genetically engineered foods and animals, and biological warfare. This line of inquiry got CAE founder Stephen Kurtz subpoenaed under the Biological Weapons Anti-Terrorism Act, and then indicted—along with genetics researcher Robert E. Ferrel, CAE's collaborator—for mail fraud by a federal jury in 2004, at the height of terrorism hysteria post-9/11. Charges against Kurtz were dropped in 2008. See "Critical Art Ensemble Defense Fund"; Sholette, "Disciplining the Avant-Garde," 50–59; Pederson and Knouf, "Seized and Displayed," 31–32.

9. Critical Art Ensemble, *Electronic Civil Disobedience & Other Unpopular Ideas*, 26–28. See also Stefan Wray, "Rhizomes, Nomads, and Resistant Internet Use." The term *nomadic capital* refers to capitalist-driven globalization facilitated by the commercialization and expansion of communication networks and informatization technologies, theorized under different concepts by various scholars. See Garcia and Lovink, "The ABC of Tactical Media," 109. British sociologists Kevin Robins and Frank Webster speak of *cybernetic capitalism*, by which they mean the restructuring of both "material" and "psychic reproduction" of "social, political, and cultural relationships" on a local and global scale. Robins and Webster, "Cybernetic Capitalism," 45–75. Felix Guattari's term *integrated world capitalism* is similar to Guy Debord's *integrated spectacle*, a combination of the "concentrated" (authoritarian ideologies) and "diffuse spectacle" (capitalism). See Guattari, *Soft Subversions*, 10–11 and Debord, *Comments on the Society of the Spectacle*. As noted, Gilles Deleuze's concept of "societies of control" designates power backed by informatics that act to simultaneously amplify and disperse control. See Deleuze, "'Postscript of the Societies of Control," 178–179. Lastly, Michael Hardt and Antonio Negri use the term *empire* to refer to economic globalization post-1970s as a "decentered and deterritorializing apparatus" designed to rule "social life in its entirety." Hardt and Negri, *Empire*, xii–xv.

10. Critical Art Ensemble, *Electronic Civil Disobedience & Other Unpopular Ideas*, 77.

11. Ibid., 21.

12. Fusco, "Electronic Disturbance," 100.

13. Bey, *Immediatism*.

14. Fernández and Wilding, "Situating Cyberfeminisms."

15. Ibid.

16. Gere, *Digital Culture*, 113.

17. Deleuze and Guattari, *What is Philosophy?*, 41.

18. Ibid., 99.

19. Bey, "Ontological Anarchy in a Nutshell (Radio Sermonettes)."

20. Lialina, "A Vernacular Web," 19.

21. Galloway and Thacker, *The Exploit*, 81; Mitnick and Simon, *The Art of Deception*.

22. SimEden.com, "An Interview with Jacques Servin: The SimCopter Scandal."

23. Ibid.

24. RTMark came to prominence by claiming involvement in a series of interventions involving spoof websites targeting the brand image of powerful entities, including politicians, corporations, and religious authorities. Likewise it is not at all clear that the *SimCopter* hack happened as Servin claims.

25. See WTO News Releases, "The Simcopter Hack"; Lovejoy, Paul, and Vesna, *Context Providers*, 183.

26. Barry, "The Dilbert Front."

27. Smith, Ollman, and Price, *The Yes Men*; SimEden.com, "An Interview with Jacques Servin: The SimCopter Scandal."

28. The Yes Men, *The Yes Men*, 182.

29. Mongrel is defunct but former members continue to produce work under different groups. Core members included Richard Pierre Davis (Trinidad), Matsuko Yokokoji (Japan), Mervin Jarman (Jamaica), and Graham Hardwood (Britain); other associates of the group included Matthew Fuller, Lisa Haskell, Carole Wrights, and Steve Edgell. The Mongrel network also included groups in India, South Africa, and Surinam communities in Amsterdam, The Netherlands.

30. The Wu-Tang-Clan was a then-popular New York-based group of nine African American MCs known for their strategic use of the collective as a way to insinuate themselves into the music business.

31. Matthew Fuller, "Interview with Mongrel".

32. Ibid.

33. Chun, *Control and Freedom*, 163–164; Fuller, *Behind the Blip*, 69–98. For various perspectives and discussions about the function of gendered and racial stereotyping in digital culture, including online games, see: Nakamura, *Cybertypes*; Kolko, Nakamura, and Rodman, *Race in Cyberspace*; Tu, Nelson, and Hines, *TechniColor*; Everett and Watkins, "The Power of Play," 141–166; Penix-Tadsen, *Cultural Code*; Malkowski and Russworm, *Gaming Representation*; and Murray, *On Video Games*.

34. Memetics refers here to a concept based on the views of British evolutionary biologist Richard Dawkins (*The Selfish Gene*, 1976), who contended that memes (information units) are hosted in the brain and follow replication patterns driven by competition (i.e., similar to genes, or biological units), thereby determining the evolution of human behavior and culture.

35. Wilding, "Where's the Feminism in Cyberfeminism."

36. Waelder, "Interview with Natalie Bookchin."

37. Games referenced included *Pong* (Atari, 1972), *Space Invaders* (Taito, 1978), *Atari Football* (Atari, 1978), *Custer's Revenge* (Mystique, 1982), *Pac-Man* (Namco, 1980).

38. Sargisson, *Contemporary Feminist Utopianism*. Sargisson is referencing the work of French feminist thinkers, including Luce Iragarary, Hélène Cixous, and related strands in 1970s feminist science fiction in the United States.

39. Graham, "New Media."

40. Critical Art Ensemble, *Digital Resistance*, 135–158.

41. Ibid., 137.

42. Ibid., 134.

43. Critical Art Ensemble, "Recombinant Theater and Digital Resistance," 164.

44. Critical Art Ensemble, *Digital Resistance*, 134.

45. Etoy was fashioned as a corporation in much the same way as *RTMark*. The group was the winner of the Prix Ars Electronica in 1996.

46. Etoy, "Toywar."

47. Electronic Disturbance Theater was founded in 1997 by Ricardo Dominguez, Stefan Wray, Brett Stabaum, and Carmin Karasic.

48. See *Info Wars*.

49. Galloway, *Gaming*, 77.

50. Etoy, "Toywar."

51. Wishart and Bochsler, *Leaving Reality Behind*.

52. Etoy, "Toywar."

53. Schleiner, "Dissolving the Magic Circle of Play," 150–151; Schleiner, *The Player's Power to Change the Game*.

54. Schleiner, "Velvet-Strike." See chapter 2 for a description of *Counter Strike*.

55. Skins (or sprays) are visual (and/or audio) files used to change the appearance of the game interface or game characters.

56. Bittanti, "Anne-Marie Schleiner, Brody Condon & Joan Leandre," 413.

57. Schleiner, "Fluidities and Oppositions among Curators."

58. Ibid.; Jansson, "Interview: Julian Oliver's Selectparks.net and QTHOTH (1998–1999)."

59. *Velvet Strike*, http://www.opensorcery.net/velvet-strike/recipes.html.

60. Schleiner, "Velvet-Strike." NPC stands for *nonplaying character* or any character not controlled by a player.

61. Flanagan, *Critical Play*, 11.

62. The original title proposed by the artist was "Shoot an Iraqi." The gallery owner, however, refused to allow the piece to be performed under this title for fear of attacks. See Pederson, "Trauma and Agitation: Video Games in a Time of War."

63. Bilal and Lydersen, *Shoot an Iraqi*, 14.

64. Boyko, "Interview with Wafaa Bilal."

65. Caro, "A Point-and-Shoot Exhibit."

66. Ibid.

67. Bilal and Lydersen, *Shoot an Iraqi*, xviii.

68. Ibid., 10.

69. Personal interview with the artist, June 6, 2009.

70. Winet, "In Conversation Fall 2003: An Interview with Joseph DeLappe," 98. Huntemann and Payne, *Joystick Soldiers*.

71. DeLappe, "Dead-in-Iraq," 2006–2011, http://www.delappe.net/project/dead-in-iraq/.

72. DeLappe, "America's Diplomat," 2009, http://www.delappe.net/intervene/fake-new-york-times/; Sassoon, "Popular 'America's Army' Video Game, Recruiting Tool Cancelled," New York Times, Special Edition, July 4, 2009, A8. http://www.nytimes-se.com/2009/07/04/recruiting-tool-cancelled.

73. See Sassoon, "Popular 'America's Army' Video Game."

74. Activist groups involved included, among others, the Anti-Advertising Agency, CODEPINK, United for Peace and Justice, Not An Alternative, May First/People Link, Improv Everywhere, Evil Twin, and Cultures of Resistance.

75. Debord, "Contribution to a Situationist Definition of Play."

76. Lara Croft is the heroine of the *Tomb Raider* action/adventure video game series (1996–2006), also portrayed by Hollywood actress Angelina Jolie in subsequent films; the character came about on the wave of feminist punk rock music in the 1990s, at the same time that academic discussions about the portrayal of women in video games began emerging. See Schleiner, "Does Lara Croft Wear Fake Polygons"; Cal Jones, "Lara Croft Female Enemy Number One?" 338–339; and Flanagan, "Hyperbodies, Hyperknowledge, 425–455.

77. Schleiner, "Dissolving the Magic Circle of Play: Lessons from Situationist Gaming," 156.

78. See OUT: Operation Urban Terrain. August 28, 2004. http://www.opensorcery.net/OUT/.

79. See https://www.ivanabreu.net/#works/artworks/crosscoordinates.

80. The piece was part of *Contra Flujo: Independence and Revolution*, which opened in August 2010 at the Stanlee and Gerald Rubin Center for the Visual Arts at the University of Texas at El Paso. The exhibit was a joint curatorial project by Kerry Doyle and Karla Jasso.

81. At the time, Phadke, then a social sciences graduate student, Ranade, a practicing architect, and Khan, a freelance journalist and writer, were three associates of Partners for Urban Knowledge, Action & Research (PUKAR), a Mumbai-based, nonprofit, urban research initiative led by anthropologist Arjun Appadurai. PUKAR's Gender and Space Project (2003–2006) was dedicated to researching issues pertaining to gender and urbanity. *Gendered Strategies for Loitering* was realized in collaboration with students at the University Scholars Programme Cyberart Studio of the National University of Singapore, which financed it as part of International Society for the Electronic Arts 2008 in Singapore.

82. Personal communication with Shilpa Phadke, July 15, 2008.

83. Phadke, Ranade, and Khan, "Why Loiter? Radical Possibilities for Gendered Dissent," 187.

84. In colonial India, the British and Portuguese linked vagrancy laws aimed at criminalizing poverty and homelessness with the protection and safety of Hindu women as criteria of the nation's progress and maturity. This view continues to shape gender and class relations in today's India, albeit from the perspective of the neoliberalist-driven modernization promoted by Hindu nationalists. Phadke, Ranade, and Khan, *Why Loiter*, 175.

85. Ibid., 187.

86. For instance, the group notes that the ladies' compartments in Mumbai's trains provide safe spaces to women of all classes but discriminate against other-gendered outsiders, including lesbians, transgendered people, and *hijras* (hijras are considered a third sex in India, neither male nor female, and are recognized as such by the Indian government).

87. Phadke, Ranade, and Khan, "Why Loiter? Radical Possibilities for Gendered Dissent," 175–188.

88. Such a claim was leveled against renowned Indian filmmaker and queer activist Deepa Mehta by Hindu nationalists because of her 2005 film, *Water*, which tells the story of an eight-year-old girl, Chuyia, a child bride who is sent to an ashram (the equivalent of a convent) for widows when her husband dies. She is befriended by a beautiful widow who finds forbidden love with a high-caste Ghandian. The film questions the practice of separating widows from society and addresses other gender issues in India. Hindu nationalists destroyed the set, and the leader of the World Hindu Forum claimed that the "film's script 'smacks of the conspiracy by the votaries of Western culture to tarnish the image of widowhood in India.'" As a result, Mehta was forced to complete the filming of *Water* in Sri Lanka under a false name. Phillips and Alahakoon, "Hindu Chauvinists Block Filming of Deepa Mehta's Water."

89. Hossain, *Sultana's Dream*.

90. Hossain's utopia precedes American author Charlotte Perkins Gilman's *Herland* (1917), similarly an early classic of feminist science fiction/utopia based on the theme of inverted gender segregation.

91. As well as being a writer and chronicler of the everyday conditions of Bengali women of her time, Hossain was also an activist and educator. She founded the Muslim Women's Association as an organization focused on women's education and employment, and a school for girls, which, in the face of hostile criticism from her community, she moved to Calcutta, where it still operates today. Her legacy is honored every year on December 9 in Bangladesh when the country observes Rokeya day, during which selected women are awarded recognition for exceptional intellectual contributions.

92. Phadke, Ranade, and Khan, *Why Loiter*, 180.

93. Sengupta, "Tea and Selfies Driving a Revolution in Pakistan."

5

A DREAMPOLITIK OF PERSUASIVE AND OTHER QUEER GAMES

MARGINALIZED IN MAINSTREAM VIDEO GAMES, TRANSNATIONAL, Indigenous, feminist, and queer perspectives are emerging since the beginning of the twenty-first century through the work of video game designers interested in cultural and social change. Rooted in the belief that marginalization of other perspectives is linked to the commodification of game culture, this project seeks to develop alternatives to the cultural singularity and economic influence of mainstream video games. Associated with a multiplicity of terms, forms, and communities, broadly put, Ian Bogost's notion of *persuasive games* sums up the shared outlooks of this work. Among other things, video games are tools of persuasion and, in this regard, all the more powerful for their participatory nature. This same rhetorical potential makes them a significant means to counter the persuasive games of the mainstream and, by extension, to energize diverse perspectives in video game culture.[1] In this sense, they are part of what media theorist and activist Stephen Duncombe terms a *dreampolitik*, a call for progressive politics that function to compel the public's imagination, activating wonder about what an alternative world and a different life might be. A dreampolitik leverages the utopian imaginary of popular media, including video games, but unlike marketers or reactionary populist fantasists, it uses these spaces to open up the question of alternatives and, most importantly, make room for popular intervention.[2] Designers involved in this project reject the mimetic ideals (the life-like simulations and normative definitions of mainstream games) and commodity models of the video game industry. Their critiques of mainstream games are filtered through a wide range of participatory techniques developed in the historical and parallel avant-garde art and media activism practices that are transnational and transcultural in scope. Conceived in light of these legacies, game narratives are based on or combine real and fictive themes, and span a range of topics, from current and historical events to personal stories. Similarly, visuals and interactions rework these references, both to entice audiences to engage them and, increasingly, to collaborate in their creation. To do this, these games are available for free or a low cost online, often through open-source platforms. Some designers are also interested in divulging and developing technological platforms that enable the public's creation of digital games.

On the whole, and contrary to still-prevalent perceptions of video games as nonhistorical or nonpolitical media forms, this chapter connects persuasive games with the historical legacies from which they draw to situate their sociopolitical importance as both critiques of and alternatives to contemporary mainstream game culture. These affinities are evidenced by their overall diversity in content and form, their stress on democratizing access, and their shared aim: to place games at the service of cultural change, not dominant ideologies. Furthermore, making these connections requires an understanding of the current emergence of persuasive games in relation to their specific cultural milieus. Joining these perspectives, persuasive games are discussed here as arising in affirmation of the utopian imaginaries of a multiplicity of progressive ludic visions in the face of the dominance of mimesis and commodity in mainstream video games to the exclusion of all others.

Persuasive Games

Ian Bogost, a game designer reframing video games on behalf of progressive culture, developed the concept of persuasive games to foreground the rhetorical dimension of the medium both in reference to its mainstream and potential alternative uses. Bogost postulates that the unique aspect of the medium is "procedural rhetoric," a form of communication "particularly devoted to representing, communicating, or persuading the player toward a particular biased point of view."[3] Bogost contends that persuasion functions in video games differently from other media in which words and images are employed, because games convey ideas, relationships, and processes through the encoding of rules and rewards.[4] Thus, the models or simulations that represent the dynamics of complex organizational systems, whether political, commercial, or pedagogical, are always filtered through the point of view or bias of their authors.[5] In highlighting the rhetorical power of video games, Bogost argues for employing them to change players rather than the underlying environment, since, from his perspective, mainstream simulations are "primarily intended to craft new technological constraints that impose conceptual or behavioral change in users."[6] Bogost advocates for a rhetorical approach based on convincing rather than coercing players. In practice, this translates into digital games that, as he puts it, employ persuasion to "disrupt and change fundamental attitudes and beliefs about the world, leading to potentially significant long-term social change."[7]

Rooted in communication scholarship, Bogost's argument for games of progressive persuasion echoes concerns and beliefs developed by German Marxist sociologist Jürgen Habermas, under his notion of the *public sphere*. As Habermas defined it, the public sphere is a conceptual or utopian, rather than a physical, construct; thus, in principle, a virtual or imaginary community that does not necessarily exist in any identifiable space. It is "not a marketplace, nor is it a coffeehouse, a salon, an organisation or a newspaper."[8] Rather, in its ideal form, the public sphere is "made up of private people gathered together as a public and articulating the needs of society with the state." Bogost's view of video games extends the possible forms that the public sphere may take; distinct from the state and the market, they function instead as platforms of pluralistic democratic debate, critical for upholding an open society. Moreover, Bogost's argument on behalf of developing video games in light of this concept is likewise based on reasoned debate. It mirrors Habermas's concept of communicative action, which the latter describes as a type of argumentative communication based on reason in the form of language or speech aimed at persuasion or "understanding."[9]

Similarly, the impetus for Bogost's conceptualization of persuasive games and Habermas's theorizing of the public sphere emerge out of shared concerns about the weakening of democracy, which both link to the commodification of popular culture. Under these conditions, the criteria of rationality are abandoned and with them the media's potential to function as an extended public sphere. Habermas's context is the rise of public relations during the 1950s and 1960s. The work of public relations, as Habermas sees it, goes a step further than a simple sales pitch, since it invades the process of public opinion by systematically creating and exploiting news events that attract attention. He concludes that, in this context, the participation of the masses is only valued in light of media content and cultural products that are bought and sold like any other commodity. The public sphere is delimited to serve as a vehicle for managing consensus and promoting capitalist culture, and consequently, "the world fashioned by the mass media is a public sphere in appearance only."[10] A staged "public opinion" is a semblance of arguments based on the creation and circulation of symbols to which one cannot respond to or engage but only identify with. Habermas's tentative proposals to revitalize the public sphere hinged on *critical publicity* setting "in motion a critical process of public communication through the very organizations that mediatize it."[11] He offered that "a critical publicity brought to life within intraorganizational public spheres" might lead to democratization of the major institutions of civil society, though he stopped short at providing concrete examples, proposing any strategies, or mapping out the features of an oppositional or postbourgeois public sphere.[12] Similarly, Bogost argues for developing the potential of video games to function within the public sphere so as to disrupt their commodification. Like Habermas, Bogost devotes less detail as to how to realize such persuasive games in practice, leaving it as an open-ended project.

Bogost's notion of persuasive games dovetails debates that emerged as a reaction to the earlier work of Habermas, particularly debates about the potential of virtual communities to strengthen civil society. Two opposing strands of arguments about this topic emerged, as the following exemplifies. Early on, skeptics, including communication scholars Jan Fernback and Brad Thompson, cited Habermas's work to highlight the cathartic role of virtual communication, concluding that digital technologies allow the public to feel involved rather than to advance actual participation.[13] Broadly typical of detracting attitudes, Fernback and Thompson's critique furthermore pointed to the dearth of discussions about issues of ownership and control of digital technologies and who benefits from their development. In contrast, rooted in countercultural legacies, a more amiable view of digital technologies in the form of a decentralized network casts their utopian potential as an electronic agora. Exemplary of this position, Howard Rheingold acknowledged the significance of Fernback and Thompson's arguments, yet saw their conclusion as premature. Rheingold argues that digital networks offer the public a unique channel for publishing and communicating, which is fundamental to democratic civic culture. "When we are called to action through the virtual community, we need to keep in mind how much depends on whether we simply 'feel involved' or whether we take the steps to actually participate in the lives of our neighbours, and the civic life of our communities."[14] In *The Virtual Community* (1994), Rheingold pointed out that the digital industry is like any other business, viewing itself primarily as an economic player. In this context, he warned about the dire political implications of corporate-dominated digital technologies and networks. Bogost's notion of persuasive games synthesizes both strands, as is evident in *NewsGames: Journalism at Play* (2010). In it, he further clarifies the impetus of this project in relation to concerns about the demise of the print news as a public sphere, a development that he, just as Fernback and Thompson prior, attributes to processes connecting technological and economic decentralization, with a focus, in his case, on the dominance of digital entertainment such as video games.[15] Echoing Rheingold's emphasis on the democratic potential of virtual communities, and given the cultural resonance of the medium, however, Bogost proposes to use video games to "cultivate the desire for journalistic practice," arguing that journalism ought not be thought of as a medium-specific form but as a practice "in which research combines with a devotion to the public interest, producing materials that help citizens make choices about their private lives and their communities."[16] In sum, inasmuch as Bogost's view of persuasive games reflects critiques about the coevolution of technological transformation and market forces as a source of social disempowerment, it also holds that these conditions can be leveraged to reactivate political engagement, and thus the public sphere (for instance, by using digital technologies and networks as a means of creation and distribution). As such, the concept of persuasive games represents more than a counter to the use of video games as tools of manipulation, or as Habermas puts it, as "manipulative publicity," as it entails belief in their potential to function as "critical publicity."[17]

In this latter sense, the crux of persuasive games parallels contemporaneous practices intersecting art and media activism, which Stephen Duncombe examines in depth in his concepts *dreampolitik* and *ethical spectacle*. Duncombe defines these notions broadly, as an outlook and set of practices working to leverage the persuasive power of "spectacular" culture to build a progressive politics.[18] Recalling Habermas's concept of critical publicity, he elucidates this project as one that revolves around laying claim to "the tools of hidden persuaders in the name of social change." Similarly, Duncombe's proposal builds on the belief that progressives would gain from engaging popular cultural forms, or as he puts it in a nod to the situationists, the *spectacular vernacular* (he cites Las Vegas, video games, advertisement, and celebrity culture as examples). Along the lines of Ernst Bloch's views of ideology, Duncombe argues that it would behoove progressives to approach popular culture as an ideology that works because it contains hints of utopian desires. Accordingly, Duncombe understands *spectacle* as an argument that works because it speaks to popular dreams, or as he writes, it takes "story and myth, fears and desire, imagination and fantasy" and gives them form.[19] Marketers suppress and divert these desires into consumerism, nationalism, or other oppressive ideologies. Without this utopian impulse, however, they could not obtain the consent of their subjects. Duncombe agrees with Habermas in pointing out that under these conditions, Enlightenment and empiricist ideals, particularly of the vision of civil society based on reason, rationality, and self-evident truth, are no longer effective. To ignore the rhetorical power of utopian dreams and fantasies in a "society of the spectacle," Duncombe argues, is politically misguided, "or rather, past fantasy."[20] Invoking Bloch's view of popular culture as a repository of distorted utopian visions of a better world, Duncombe focuses on outlining a dreampolitik as a notion that responds to Habermas's call for critical publicity and, by extension, has implications for Bogost's argument for using video games to persuade for social change. In concept, even if its orientation and forms are different from consumer spectacles, a dreampolitik similarly assumes that fantasy and reality are not separate but rather coexisting and intermingling aspects of human functioning and experience. In practice, dreampolitik's ethical spectacles take ludic forms based on chance, spontaneity, fluidity, and improvisation (Duncombe cites anticorporate activist group the Yes Men, among others).[21] In contrast to manipulative publicity, they are not created by public relations experts to impose normative ideologies but instead require active public realization. They are open-ended, being conceived to set the stage for prompting questions and exploring inquiries. Such spectacles, unlike the deceiving games of marketers, are transparent. Ethical spectacles aim "not to cover over or replace reality and truth but perform and amplify it." In sum, in Duncombe's words, dreampolitik and its practices, ethical spectacles, are "fantasy based on real, truthful intent."[22] Otherwise put, they appeal to utopian dreams for a better life and public commitment for their realization. It is in this sense that I use Bogost's notion of persuasive games in this chapter to refer to a broad range of contemporaneous digital games steeped in the practices and concerns germane to the dreampolitik of historical and parallel utopian currents in culture.

Bogost's concept of persuasive games resonates with kindred notions used by a range of contemporary game designers working in collaboration and in parallel, including Mary Flanagan's *critical play*, Katie Salen and Eric Zimmerman's *transformative play*, Jane McGonigal's *avant-games*, Celia Pierce's *sustainable play*, and Gonzalo Frasca's *forum games*.[23] These designers have discussed and written about the significance of Dada, surrealism, situationism, Fluxus, the New Game movement, and later practices in digital media, including net-art, cyberfeminism, and tactical media, among others. Additionally, some designers, including Frasca and more recently Native American, transgender, and queer designers, highlight among their sources historical precedents, respectively, in Latin American avant-garde currents, Indigenous storytelling, and queer counterculture media forms and expressions. Together, these concepts and practices articulate video games as spaces that go against the dominant set of cultural norms and values for which the video game industry stands. These games are similar to the practices associated with dreampolitik and thus forms of critical publicity or persuasion that, true to progressive ideals, are based on participatory and open-ended frameworks. Therefore, it is not surprising that they share a rejection of the commodified mimesis of mainstream video games and focus on changing gaming culture with richly diverse perspectives on reality as it otherwise could be.

Games of the Oppressed

Among the aforementioned game designers, Bogost's one-time collaborator, Uruguayan video game designer and former CNN en Español reporter Gonzalo Frasca, contributed early and significantly to the conceptual and formal development of persuasive games based on historical practices in participatory dramaturgy. Frasca outlined his ideas in the essay "Video-games of the Oppressed: Critical Thinking, Education, Tolerance, and Other Trivial Issues." Central in this essay are questions such as: "Is it possible to design video games that deal with social and political issues? Do video games offer an alternative way of understanding reality? Could video games be used as a tool for encouraging critical thinking?"[24] Frasca answers these questions affirmatively by proposing forum video games as a feature available inside of a bigger "video games of the oppressed" online community. Forum games are based on the notion that play ought to function as cues designed to prompt players' awareness that they are engaging in simulation (i.e., a constructed or biased representation). The assumption is that if they are aware, players will question the ideologies "hidden" in video games and, ideally, take steps to transform those ideologies in real life.

Conceptually, Frasca envisioned forum video games based on the type of participatory theater developed by Brazilian dramaturg-activist Augusto Boal (1931–2009). Boal himself drew on the work of his friend, Brazilian Paulo Freire, in the field of critical pedagogy. Freire's notion of *critical consciousness* was adapted from the Martinique-born, Algeria-based psychiatrist-philosopher-activist Frantz Fanon (1925–1961), who stressed the decolonization of education as integral to anticolonial processes and struggles. Aesthetically, Boalian theater, which includes games, dovetails with the antinaturalism of epic or dialectical theater developed earlier by German playwright Bertold Brecht (1898–1956).[25] Emerging out of kindred anti-imperialist sentiment on the backdrops of the rise of national socialism in Germany and the military regime in Brazil (1964–1985), respectively, both Boalian and Brechtian dramaturgies translate Marxian theory into theatrical formats. As such, both go against the cathartic realism of classical drama, instead favoring strategies designed to convey the point that reality is a human construct and thus subject to change, depending on one's participation therein.

The participatory model of Boalian theater that most appeals to Frasca consists of short public engagements in which members of the audience are asked to enact a daily-life situation that concerns them in front of the group. For example, a worker might wish to enact an exploitive relation with the boss. As the issue is enacted, audience members can interrupt and engage the person speaking. This process is repeated several times. The point is not to find solutions to the problem proposed but to create communal awareness about its existence and to generate discussion. In this way, forum games create a stage for democratic deliberation and rehearsal for capacitating participation in emancipatory action in society. Boal's concept of the *spect-actor*, his term for the dual role of those involved simultaneously as spectators and actors in forum theater, speaks to this idea. Boal's notion that to partake in performative exchanges is a potentially transformative activity that impacts on real life is re-elaborated in Frasca's concept of a simulated forum in which players engage in analogous actions. In practice, this consists of simulations that both allow players to share their stories and to make modifications independent of designers. In this sense, forum video games resemble the *open games systems* discussed by Katie Salen and Eric Zimmerman, which like open-source software, are "designed to be evolutionary, not static, and to be expressed in multiple forms." They involve "players [operating] as a community of developers, transforming elements of the game system, playtesting them, sharing them with other players, and submitting them to further modification."²⁶ Frasca's concept of forum games, however, is not open-source but more similar to conventional customizable games, although designed with a pedagogical function in mind. As he envisions it, "publishers would sell software that allow players to construct characters that would have different behaviors . . . [to] help players realize that the concept of behavior—and particularly deviant behavior—is not a fixed entity but rather a social construction."²⁷ In this manner, he argues, forum games would function to promote "the development of a tolerant attitude that accepts multiplicity as the rule and not the exception."²⁸

Whereas forum games were conceived as a conceptual exercise, Frasca did develop digital games under the heading Play the News in collaboration with other designers, including Bogost (Frasca later renamed the project newsgames).²⁹ The design strategies employed in these games are based on Brecht's dialectical methods, which he applied to both technologically mediated and theatrical forms. Brecht's notion of radio as a two-way rather than a one-way medium and his concept of epic theater both emerge out of his concern with human alienation and how to overcome it. To this end, Brecht made the *Verfremdungseffekt* (alienating effect) central to his epic theater, dramas about contemporary political and social issues. Including techniques such as fragmentation, interruption, juxtaposition, and contrast and contradiction, Brecht's alienating effects were designed to disrupt the audience's immersion in the spectacle. For example, actors would address the public directly, or speak out loud stage instructions, use songs to interrupt the action, or rearrange the set in full view of the audiences. Disruptive uses of props, including explanatory placards, or elements of the set, such as lighting flooding the theater (illuminating the audience as well as the actors), would be similarly employed to alienate spectators and prevent their identification with the actions and characters. Brecht believed that the absence of cathartic resolution would create an emotional gap that could only be resolved through the audience's involvement in political action in the real world.

Newsgames draw attention to mainstream simulations' artifice by way of similar strategies, since the ultimate aim is likewise to provoke reflection about a particular issue. Like Brechtian epic theater, and as the title indicates, newsgames engage players with views on current social and political events. According to Frasca, newsgames emerged out of antiwar sentiment, in protest of the United States' call for war on terror subsequent the 9/11 events: "For political video games, September 11 was the trigger. If it had happened in the sixties, people would have grabbed their guitar and written a song about it. Now they're making games."[30] Just as Brecht's and Boal's participatory theaters were rooted in personal experiences with authoritarian politics, newsgames are similarly rooted in Frasca's personal background growing up during the military dictatorship in Uruguay (1973–1985) modeled on the Brazilian military regime (1964–1985). In some of his writings, he references this background by recounting a childhood memory of witnessing his family burning banned literature in their backyard. Boal was kidnapped, tortured, and exiled because his teachings were seen as a threat by the Brazilian regime. Both regimes emerged in the context of a US-backed period of similar dictatorships in Latin America.

Reflecting Frasca's antiwar stance, *September 12th* (2003) (fig. 5.1) was the first newsgame simulation designed by him and the team at Powerful Robot Games, Frasca's then video game studio in Uruguay.[31] The studio created a variety of web-based games for American entertainment corporations, including the Cartoon Network, Disney, Pixar, Warner Bros., and Lucasfilm. This work, in turn, financed the creation of games like *September 12th*, a freely available short simulation designed in a cartoonish style evocative of popular video games at the time, such as the *Sims* franchise. *September 12th* takes the realist model of *The Sims* but rejects the latter's consumerist ideology. The *Sims* franchise is a significant moment in video game history because of its representation of everyday life. *Sims*'s characters are common civilians rather than trolls, aliens, monsters, or soldiers. Nevertheless, the *Sims* games represent a "Disneyfied" version of life. *Sims* characters are suburbanites, and the game has no space for ideological conflict. Additionally, *September 12th* plays with the mechanics and alleged realism of mainstream games, in particular, first-person shooter video games, to convey an antiwar message.

September 12th's opening image, showing an Arab woman holding a dead child in her arms, evokes the iconic antiwar depictions of German expressionist Käthe Kollwitz, and in the context of Latin America, the mothers of Plaza de Mayo, who campaigned for their children disappeared at the hands of the military dictatorship in Argentina. A follow-up image shows a clichéd visual stereotype of a "terrorist," recognizable by a white *kafayeh* and a gun, next to a similarly stereotypical family of Muslim "civilians," the woman fully covered and the man and child wearing *dishdashas*. The accompanying text reads: "This is not a game. You can't win and you

Figure 5.1. Screenshot of *September 12th, A Toy World* (Gonzalo Frasca / Newsgaming, 2003).
© Gonzalo Frasca / Newsgaming.

can't lose. This is a simulation. It has no ending. It has already begun. The rules are deadly simple. You can shoot. Or not. This is a simple model you can use to explore some aspects of the war on terror." The scenario is set in a crowded market square of a Middle Eastern town where terrorists mingle with dogs and civilians. An obvious reference to Pablo Picasso's *Guernica* (1937), this setting further drives the message of the game.[32] Picasso's painting not only documents a war crime (the bombing of Guernica's women and children by Nazi Germany and Italian fascist war planes at the behest of Franco) but does so with specific symbolism. The destruction of the market square, the first forum to which we trace democracy, has a clear message. The fascists knew it, as did Picasso. *Guernica* is considered by many to be one of the most moving and powerful antiwar statements by a twentieth-century artist. A full-size tapestry replicating the painting hangs at the entrance of the Security Council room at the United Nations headquarters in New York. This reference is all the more poignant because of *Guernica*'s role in the public relations fiasco involving US general Colin Powell and other

US diplomats arguing for the war on Iraq against the background of this full-sized tapestry, concealed by a blue curtain, during televised conferences on February 5, 2003. This cover-up, as some journalists pointed out at the time, spoke volumes about the US government's contempt for global civic appeals against war, as Frasca explores in a follow-up game, *Madrid*.

September 12th reflects similar concern about the intensification of terrorism as a likely outcome of the war on terror to that of protesters on the streets opposing the Iraq War. The player controls a side-scrolling sniper window juxtaposed onto the scene. Despite the visual suggestion of a gun, it soon becomes obvious that it is not a bullet that is fired but a missile. The player is cast in the role of a drone operator. Because of the impact, it is impossible to strike accurately, and when a passerby is hit, others gathering around the casualty transform into terrorists. Repetitive shooting causes the square to become entirely populated by terrorists amid the rubble. A reference to the disproportionate firepower of the US military, the message of *September 12th* is evident: violence elicits violence. The game conveys the circularity of the war on terror as a vicious feedback loop with no ending.

In contrast, *Madrid* (2004) (fig. 5.2), the second simulation designed by Frasca's studio, again highlights the forum, in this case, as previously mentioned, in the form of the global, antiwar protests emerging after 9/11. Released two days after the Madrid train bombings on March 11, 2004, the game commemorates the victims of the attacks. *Madrid* consists of a single vignette styled on political cartoons in newspapers and shows a group of people, both young and old, holding candles amid darkness.[33] Each character wears a T-shirt that reads: "I love" and the name of a world city that has been the target of terrorist acts, including New York City, Oklahoma City, Paris, Madrid, Tokyo, and Beirut. The goal is to synchronize the candle flames by clicking on one at a time, though the futility of this task soon becomes clear, because by the time the player is through with clicking on all the flames, the candles first clicked on have already died out. In absence of action, a screen appears that reads, "You must keep trying," urging the player to keep clicking.

In contrast to *September 12th*, the frustrating repetitiveness of *Madrid* does not at first seem to correspond to an evident takeaway message beyond its overall suggestion of collective mourning and remembrance. Bogost noted that players mistook the difficulty of the game as making an argument for "the futility of remembrance rather than its necessity."[34] The game can be seen as a follow-up comment on *September 12th*. As well as a memorial,

Figure 5.2. Screenshot of *Madrid* (Gonzalo Frasca / Newsgaming, 2004). © Gonzalo Frasca / Newsgaming.

it functions in this regard to clarify Frasca and his team's position, which, conceived in the spirit of Brechtian and Boalian theater, reaffirms belief in the possibility of change through active civic participation. Made in the image of the massive global dissent and movement against the war on terror, *Madrid* uses a global platform—video games—not only to show and amplify antiwar sentiment but also to ask the player to join in, "to keep trying."[35] *September 12th* and *Madrid* encapsulate Frasca's view of video games as a forum, a means of creating a culture of conviviality that works against the melancholia of empire.[36] This project is most poignant in the context of the regressive realism of mainstream video games, exemplified by their use post-9/11, their support of xenophobia (anti-Muslim sentiment), and their use to recruit and train soldiers for drone warfare in the war on terror. As such, the work of Frasca and his team was recognized by the Knight Foundation with a Lifetime Achievement Award (the Knight Foundation's mission, and by extension this award, acknowledges its founders' belief [the brothers' John S. and James L. Knight] in journalism's, arts', and technology's central roles in fostering "informed and engaged communities, essential for a healthy democracy").[37]

In the United States, Bogost developed newsgames subsumed under the heading of persuasive games, which he similarly made freely available online. In 2006, he began creating short role-playing games on current events in the format of news editorials. Reflecting a North American perspective on life post-9/11, the series includes *Airport Insecurity*, a game in which the player takes the role of a Transportation Security Agency agent attempting to enforce rapidly changing and increasingly zany security rules. Another game, *Bacteria Salad*, gives the player managerial control over agribusiness food production in the face of the continuing risk of E. coli contamination, a nearly impossible task as made obvious by the increasingly frantic pace of the game, ultimately bringing the would-be manager to face bowel-upset consumers. A third game, *Oil God*, is a God's-eye view simulation that lets the player manipulate civil unrest and natural disaster variables to influence the future of the oil market.[38] Like Frasca's, Bogost's games draw on political cartoons, a genre of political discourse emerging with newspapers, to similarly comment on real-world topics. Additionally, Bogost collaborated with Frasca on designing the first official game commissioned for a US presidential campaign. Called *The Howard Dean for Iowa Game* (2003), it was designed as part of the Howard Dean campaign's grassroots outreach encouraging participation in precaucus campaigning in Iowa or the players' local areas. Modeled on a viral network, the game allowed players to send instant messages via any of the four major networks (AOL IM, Yahoo! Messenger, MSN Messenger, and ICQ) to online contacts so as to spread the word about the game and Dean's political platform. Frasca and his team subsequently designed a similar game, *Cambiemos* (*Let Us Change*) (Frente Amplio 2004), for the leftist coalition Frente Amplio's political campaign, that went on to win the 2004 presidential election in Uruguay.

By 2008, designers working along the lines of newsgames began looking to the rising popularity of casual games using apps (mobile applications) and social-network platforms like Facebook, rather than to the internet, as another opportunity for viral intervention. Game designer and theorist Jesper Juul even deemed the emergence of casual games "revolutionary," since such games, which are designed to be user-friendly and short in duration, brought new audiences into the fold (women and older people, traditionally seen as nongamers). In view of these new audiences, designers could potentially provide another opportunity to break away, as Juul said, from "goal-oriented play styles."[39] Taking this view to heart and conceived from a feminist perspective, Mary Flanagan's *Layoff!* (Tiltfactor Lab, 2009) is an example of a newsgame that utilizes the format of a casual game to make a point about the dynamics of the 2008–2009 economic recession. The game is a simulation that uses the aesthetics and mechanics of *Bejeweled* (PopCap Games, 2001), a multiplatform, match-three puzzle game featuring colorful diamond-shaped jewels, to comment on corporate immunity. The player plays on the side of management, laying off workers and replacing them with financiers and bankers. Starting with a grid of workers, the goal is to match them by the same type. When the workers are matched, they disappear, and in their stead a text appears announcing the savings gained by eliminating so-called redundancies. To emphasize the game's prolabor message, Flanagan provided biographies of each of the disappearing workers as reminders that these people are real. In contrast to the workers, in the game bankers are fixed and cannot be eliminated.[40] In addition, economic data about the recession appears along the bottom of the game while a sad musical score plays in the background. *Layoff!* stands as both a feminist and an anticorporate statement, as it simultaneously shines a light on workers and subverts the stereotypically gendered coding of *Bejeweled*, designed to appeal to women and girls. To this end, Flanagan subverts the game's consumerist appeal with commentary on the dehumanizing effects of predatory capitalism in order to highlight the plight of workers treated as disposable objects in the face of corporate-driven financial collapse.

Similarly, *Phone Story* (2012) by Molleindustria (the alias of Italian game designer Paolo Pedercini) is like Flanagan's *Layoff!*, an anticorporate statement, but it is also combined with a fundraising goal that allows the player to participate in supporting workers. *Phone Story* was designed in collaboration with the art-activist duo, the Yes Men, to benefit SACOM (Students and Scholars Against Corporate Misbehavior), a grassroots activist group active on American campuses. In addition, the project was conceived as a rebuttal of gamification, as it reroutes the popularity of casual games in the interest of creating grassroots, innovative forms of activism.[41] Hailed as the cutting edge in online marketing techniques, *gamification* refers to the application of games and elements typical of game-playing, such as action, fun, point-scoring, and so forth, to build loyalty to a product or a brand. *Phone Story* was created as an app for the Android and iPhone, both popular platforms for casual games, to educate about the exploitative processes of production, consumption, and disposal of these products, by involving the player (i.e., the consumer of these phones) in four scenarios that satirize these dynamics. The "coltan" and "suicides" levels highlight labor exploitation, respectively, of children in Congolese coltan mines and Chinese assembly workers (the goal is to save workers from committing suicide by jumping off the Foxconn factory roof).[42] The "obsolescence" and "waste" levels focus on marketing strategies fueling the rapid cycles of consumption of mobile phones in the West and the resulting problem of disposing highly toxic electronic waste (in this case, in Pakistan).

Additionally, the game effectively uses Apple's and Google's platforms (i.e., their app stores, where the game could be purchased) to reroute revenue (the $1.00 paid by players) to SACOM (with Pedercini pledging to donate artist's fees).[43] However, the real game began as Apple removed *Phone Story* from its app store shortly after the game was posted (as of this writing it is still available on Android). According to Pedercini, an Apple public relations representative cited objections to the game's depiction of child labor as the basis for this decision. This decision placed Apple in a bad light, as it propelled the project to public prominence on the heels of already widely circulating media reports detailing the sweatshop conditions of Foxconn factories, in which the company's products are assembled. Subsequent to the game's removal by Apple, the total revenue it brought in while in store, $6,047, was donated to a young woman worker at Foxconn then recovering from a suicide attempt. Similar to the Yes Men's tactical use of media for purposes of "corporate identity correction," in an interview Pedercini cited his long-standing involvement in the "alterglobalization" media movement as the main inspiration for *Phone Story*. As part and parcel of these practices, the game is also exemplary of their goal, as Pedercini puts it, to effect "the radicalization of popular culture."[44] From this perspective, *Phone Story* is gamification conceived at the behest of changing corporate behavior: to educate consumers about the exploitative underside of the digital industry and allow them to contribute (in this case, monetarily) toward rectifying these conditions.[45]

Since Frasca first began developing newsgames in 2003, they have, just as mainstream games, spread transnationally. In *NewsGames: Journalism at Play*, Bogost had already noted the resonance of Frasca's work in transnational game designer circles. For instance, he points out that *Madrid* inspired *Huys* (Hope) (2009), the first Turkish political game, by Yavuz Kerem Demirbaş. Similarly conceived as a newsgame, *Huys* pays homage to the then recently assassinated Turkish-Armenian journalist Hrant Dink. Dink was killed by a Turkish nationalist in 2007 because of his outspoken critiques of the Turkish government's denial of the 1915 Armenian genocide by the Ottoman Empire.[46] Like *Madrid, Huys* portrays and implicates the player in civic protest; in this case, the peaceful demonstrations in Turkey in response to Dink's assassination. By extension, like Frasca, Demirbaş uses the medium to eulogize conditions that typify a robust forum or public sphere: freedom of the press and freedom of speech.

The ongoing, transnational expansion of newsgames is centrally show-cased in Games and Politics, a touring international exhibition sponsored by the Goethe-Institute and the Center for Art and Media Karlsruhe. Still unfolding at the time of this writing, in 2020, this exhibition's world tour started in November 2016 in Mexico and Korea and continued to the United States, and after, to subsequently tour nineteen countries, including Brazil, Turkey, Russia, Iran, Palestine, Nigeria, India, and Vietnam. Games and Politics features both Frasca's *Madrid* and Molleindustria's *Phone Story*, and more recent newsgames including *Yellow Umbrella* (2014), a game designed by Chinese game designer Fung Kam-Keung in support of prodemocracy protests in Hong Kong, which were themselves inspired by the worldwide Occupy movement. Other games in the exhibition speak similarly to current and relevant social issues and include *Sunset* (2015), by African American artist and game designer Auriea Harvey, about the precarious working conditions of an African immigrant woman; *This War Is Mine* (2014), developed by the Polish independent company 11 Bit Studios, which addressed wartime atrocities endured by Bosnian civilians during the 1992–1996 Siege of Sarajevo; as well as older games, such as *Escape from Woomera* (2004), a game designed by a group of Australian programmers in collaboration with an investigative journalist, about the plight of the mandatory incarceration of asylum seekers in Australia, an issue that continues to play out at present, among others. Exhibitions like Games and Politics are significant for showcasing such work and featuring the significance of video games as a political medium globally. Addressing this concern, the exhibit also functions as a platform for the discussion, exchange, and development of newsgames, including presentations by invited game designers and theorists, as well as providing workshops geared toward practice that are open to public participation in each location.

Decolonizing Games

Although it is incidental to newsgames, public participation is central to video game projects used foremost as pedagogical tools designed to encourage marginalized people and communities in mainstream gaming culture to represent themselves. The following two video games, *Tropical America* (OnRamp Arts, 2002) and *Never Alone / Kisima Inŋitchuŋa* (Upper One Games, 2014), are exemplary of this conception in both their formal aspects and their production mode. Both projects are collaborations among game designers, artists, community organizations, educators, and students. Both are created to counter stereotypical depictions, respectively, of Hispanic and Native Americans in mainstream video games and to address the lack of diversity in the industry by capacitating young, nonwhite audiences to create their own games based on their own personal histories and experiences.

By no means an exception in mainstream games, Sid Meyer's *Civilization IV: Colonization* (Firaxis Games, 2008) demonstrates the significance and enduring need for projects like *Tropical America* and *Never Alone*. A remake of a 1994 strategy game titled *Colonization* (Microprose), *Civilization IV* puts the player in control of colonizing forces (all men) from four European nations: Spain, England, France, or the Netherlands. The goal is to settle all of the Americas and win independence from Europe. In contrast, Native American characters (from North, Central, and South America, and also all male) are not playable. They can be used to win the game, however, providing conversion. This entails pursuing a strategy of amicable relations with Indigenous groups, so as to generate "converted native" units. These units can graduate from schools in colonist settlements. Upon graduation they literally convert into "free colonists" (with European features and clothing) and can be added to the units rebelling against Europe and thus win the game. (There is no option for Europeans to convert into Native Americans, however).[47] Faced with criticism about the game's offensive racism or conversely sanitizing of the ugly realities of colonization, the game's developer claimed no ideological position or strategy, while fans of the game stated on forums that it simply depicts "reality." In contrast, *Tropical America* and *Never Alone* depict the colonial experience from the point of view of Native American peoples, as a historical encounter that continues to negatively impact Indigenous lives and environments. Additionally, these projects can be understood as emerging out of resistance to colonization, which includes a long history of using art and technologies, and in these cases from within educational frameworks, to confront the dominant power relationships mediating conditions of representation. In this way, the use of video games speaks both to the students' familiarity with the medium as consumers and to their empowerment as designers instead.

They stormed into town early in the morning.
There were 30 or 40 of them. They had machetes and guns.
They were asking questions.
I didn't know who they were, or why they came.

We were all forced to line-up in the main plaza.
My mom and I were taken into the church.
They closed the door and everything was dark.
When I opened my eyes, I was the only one left.

Figure 5.3. Opening screenshot of *Tropical America*, a project of OnRamp Arts © 2002. This work is licensed under a Creative Commons License, CC BY-NC-ND 2.0 (https://creativecommons.org/licenses/by-nc-nd/2.0/).

In this context, *Tropical America* (fig. 5.3) should be noted as one of the first examples of a video game created within a project that resonates Freire's critical pedagogy's aim at critical consciousness.[48] The project emerged out of a collaboration between Los Angeles–based OnRamp Arts, an organization dedicated to developing new media projects led by Steven Metts and Jessica Irish, Colombian media artist Juan Devis, Mexican visual artist Artemio Rodriguez, and teachers and students at a predominantly Hispanic high school where the student population consisted primarily of first- and second-generation immigrants from El Salvador and elsewhere in Central America. Created in the context of an after-school violence-prevention program, the game was designed to engage students with historical and contemporary processes pertinent to their own experiences as newly arrived immigrants fleeing widespread violence in their home countries. Many of the students involved in the project fled their countries to escape the notoriously brutal gang *mara salvatrucha*, or *mara*. The mara originated among Salvadoran immigrants who arrived in Los Angeles after the Central American civil wars of the 1980s and subsequently spread to other

Central American countries due to the deportation of mara members from the United States. This deportation policy created a feedback loop, as it displaced mara gang activity in the United States and led the group to re-create itself into a transnational network spanning the United States, Canada, and Central America. *Tropical America* speaks to the students' continued vulnerability to the violence and forcible recruitment by the mara and, conversely, to education as a means to break this cycle.

The title of the game, *Tropical America*, references the mural painted by the Mexican muralist David Alfaro Siqueiros in Los Angeles, *América Tropical: Oprimida y Destrozada por los Imperialismos*, or *Tropical America: Oppressed and Destroyed by Imperialism* (1932). The mural was whitewashed shortly after it was painted because of its anti-imperialist message, but it was rediscovered in the 1960s by Chicano activists at a time when the Chicano mural movement in Los Angeles was emerging alongside their struggles for civil rights. Conceived in the spirit of Siqueiros's and the Chicano muralist movement's participatory ethos, *Tropical America* is exemplary of how video game design can provide a collaborative frame to continue the work of giving voice to marginalized histories and cultures from their own perspective.[49] Rodriguez based the game's graphics on the woodcut prints produced in Mexico from the 1930s through the 1960s by the Taller de Gráfica Popular, or People's Graphic Workshop, which used this medium for sociopolitical critique. The game's narrative, both in English and Spanish, was culled from materials previously compiled by Devis for a play about key episodes in Latin American history. *Tropical America* uses a familiar video game trope, the quest, to set the player out in search of evidence of the 1981 massacre at a small village in El Salvador, El Mozote. It begins as the player takes on the role of the sole survivor of the massacre, either as a female or a male avatar, and unfolds as a complex tapestry of historical and cultural references to Latin America's precolonial, colonial, and postcolonial periods. Each section is represented by crops (sugar, melon, corn, or grapes) and transports the player to different times and spaces where various figures, fictional and historical, including Aztec gods to Subcomandante Marcos of the Zapatista National Liberation Army, each provide pieces of evidence. Rufina Amaya, the real-life sole survivor of the El Mozote massacre, provides the last testimony. Together, these testimonies, which are bequeathed to the player, contextualize the roots of contemporary violence in Latin America within the histories of Western colonization and imperialism, while simultaneously highlighting historical and contemporary resistance to these processes by Indigenous populations. The project functions on several levels: as a means for educating students about the roots of their own displacement; as a rebuttal of xenophobic views on immigrants, since it represents the students and their communities in light of creative collaboration; and, finally, as an open call to redress the crimes detailed in the gathered evidence (the evidence is accessible to any-one on the internet and consists of an extensive database of the source texts and imagery used in the creation of the game). Ultimately, *Tropical America* carries the implication that the quest for decolonization is long-standing and ongoing and that video games and gaming culture have a role to play in its realization.

In this context, *Tropical America* goes beyond a counter to the ste-reotyped representations of Latinos in mainstream video games, either as passive characters, such as in *Civilization IV: Colonization*, or as mara like gangsters, as is the case in urban shooter games. This is part of the use of video games by a host of Latin American artists and designers, who have similarly engaged the medium in opposition to the tired politics of race in the United States post-9/11. The impact of this dynamic is expressed both in the normalization of xenophobia (e.g., the Patriot Act) and in the invis-ibility and devaluation of the conviviality characteristic of border culture. Oppositional games include *La Migra* (2001), by Rafael Fajardo, and *Turista Fronterizo* (2005), by Coco Fusco and Ricardo Dominguez, both of which document and mirror the complexities of the sociocultural space of the US–Mexico border, in contrast to its mainstream depiction as a container of violence and lawlessness. Just as *Tropical America* was created partly in homage to Siqueiros's cross-border, anti-imperialist muralism, these games emphasize the shared histories of the United States and Mexico that do not fit neatly into national borders nor, by extension, in clash-of-civilizations narratives.

On the northern border of the United States, First Nations artists and designers have used video games similarly as forums to relate their histo-ries, lives, challenges, and visions to younger generations and to the world. Though this motivation drives a variety of video games by Indigenous American designers, it was *Never Alone / Kisima Inɲitchuɲa* (Upper One Games, 2014) (fig. 5.4) that first garnered widespread attention in the main-stream media and among media scholars.[50] The game was created from the point of view of an Iñupiaq community in Alaska and emerged from a collaboration between E-line Media, a publisher of educational games,

Figure 5.4. Screenshot of *Never Alone/ Kisima Iŋitchuŋa* (Upper One Games / E-Line Media, 2014). © E-Line Media.

and the Cook Inlet Tribal Council, a community group including Iñupiaq and other Alaska Natives.[51] Together, E-line Media and the Cook Inlet Tribal Council founded Upper One Games, the first Indigenous-owned video game company in the United States. Iñupiaq artists, storytellers, and residents, including elders and high school students, from various towns served by the council contributed to *Never Alone*. Combining narration in Iñupiaq with scrimshaw-inspired graphics, native myth, 3D animation, and documentary, the game was conceived to revitalize the Iñupiaq language, which has been in decline since English colonization and its legacy of boarding schools (where forcibly removed Iñupiaq children were forbidden to speak their own language). Proceeds from the game go toward funding the council's education programs, and just like *Tropical America*, the video game format is used to attract youngsters to learning about and sharing their community's culture and to become involved in its ongoing struggles against colonization. In addition, the game amplifies the community's long-standing appeals to the international community regarding the devastating ecological impact of resource extraction in the area, most recently intensive oil-drilling and mining, beginning with the 1970s energy crisis (at the time of oil embargo against the United States).[52]

   In light of these concerns, the traditional story of Kunuuksaayuka, on which the game's narrative is partly based, makes an apt parable for the

United States' present position on climate change from the perspective of the contemporary Inuit community. In the story, a boy named Kunuuksaayuka goes on a journey to identify the source of a world-destroying blizzard, which eventually leads him, in the calm eye of the storm, to a man heaving shovelfuls of snow into the air, unmindful that they gather and grow into the storm battering Kunuuksaayuka's home downstream. *Never Alone* adapts this tale to speak of ecological interdependence. This point is conveyed by allowing the player to play the roles of two different species: a young Iñupiaq girl named Nuna and her companion, an arctic fox. As each character is given a different set of skills, the player must pair them to successfully complete their joint goal, which mirrors that of Kunuuksaayuka: to save the village. *Never Alone* integrates documentary as part of the game throughout, as collectible rewards in the form of video testimonies by Alaska Natives sharing personal stories and knowledge about the Arctic environment. In her discussions of the game, Donna Haraway sums up its motivation aptly, as an argument about "ongoing worlding" and its hinging on learning to play differently.[53]

Additionally, like *Tropical America*, *Never Alone* pays homage to and is an extension of the collaborative spirit of much of Indigenous-based media, itself tracing as far back as *Nanook of the North* (Robert J. Flaherty, 1922). As it transpires, far from the idealized, naive primitives depicted in Flaherty's docudrama, the Inuit were Flaherty's collaborators; they fixed his camera, developed his film, and participated in the filmmaking process. From this vantage point, the use of video games for purposes of self-representation evidences how creative readaptation of global media technologies can work to sustain and amplify the cultural outlooks of Indigenous peoples.

Never Alone is but one of various video games conveying the urgency of ecological redress from the point of view of local Indigenous communities.[54] *Thunderbird Strike* (2017) by Elizabeth LaPensée, an Anishinaabe and Métis game designer, ought to be noted for its provocative approach to ecological concerns. In this game, the player takes on the role of a thunderbird flying from the tar sands in Canada to the Great Lakes on the US–Canada border. The goal is to protect Turtle Island from the snake threatening to swallow the land and waters. The player gains points by either letting the thunderbird take lightning strikes at oil-industry machinery, vehicles, buildings, and pipelines, or strike at the bones of caribou, wolves, buffalo, and people to restore them back to life. In the final scene, players battle a pipeline snake that represents the oil pipeline running underneath the

Mackinac Bridge in the Great Lakes, home to LaPensée's community, who contributed the stories for the game. The game won the Best Digital Media Work Award at the ImagineNATIVE festival, the world's largest Indigenous film and media arts festival, held annually in Toronto. At the same time, further south, the Standing Rock protests against the Dakota access pipeline captured worldwide attention both for their urgency in the context of the 2016 United Nations Climate Conference (the United States withdrew from the accords signed there in 2017) and the subsequent brutal suppression of protesters by the North Dakota state government and the federal government. In light of this, it is ironic that *Thunderbird Strike* drew the ire of Republican senator of Minnesota David Osmek, who objected to its funding by a Minnesota public arts fund since, according to him, the game promotes ecoterrorism. In contrast, Anishinaabe and Indigenous studies scholar Grace Dillon's concept of *Indigenous futurisms* provides the central gist of these projects' concerns: to aid processes of decolonization. From this perspective, *Never Alone* and *Thunderbird Strike* are extensions of long-standing uses of media, spanning art, literature, film, comics, and now video games, by Native American creators and communities to construct self-determined representations and alternative narratives about the future, past, and present. As expressions of Indigenous futurisms, *Never Alone* and *Thunderbird Strike* speak back to the tropes of colonialism in gaming culture, those that celebrate rugged individualism, the conquest of foreign worlds, and the taming of the frontier. They are more than rejections of colonialism (and the playgrounds made in its image); they are celebrations of Indigenous perspectives in their own right. In these two cases, they involve video games as spaces that celebrate relationships and connection to human and nonhuman communities, coexistence, the sharing of technology and the land, and the honoring of ongoing anticolonial struggles. They create spaces to dare imagining that Indigenous knowledge offers the larger world something that might contribute to its survival.

Beyond including the public as collaborator in developing games, designers have also enabled the public to create their own games via testing the potential of free software as game tools and making them accessible online. Working in this vein from within an academic context, in 2013, Ulises A. Mejias at SUNY Oswego created and released an "alternate reality game engine" (SOAP) using the open-source narrative-based platforms WordPress and BuddyPress. The project grew out of Mejias's use of *alternate reality* games, or as he calls them, SOAP simulations, in his classes to engage students in participatory research on current social justice issues. Classes were structured around narrative-based games, with students participating by contributing stories, documentation, and responses to prompts and to each other's posts, to create a collective narrative at the end.[55] These games spanned diverse topics impacting students and their immediate communities, including hydro fracking (a prevalent and contentious practice in upstate New York), Islamophobia, immigration, the war on drugs, and issues related to education and the university, such as cuts to public education and racism on campus. First conceived as a tool of critical pedagogy, SOAP was later released online. It fits Frasca's notion of forum games but was open-source, unlike a publisher-authored product. SOAP is no longer functional (due to WordPress updates), but similarly conceived game-making platforms are currently emerging as significant tools for democratizing video game production and distribution and, by extension, for changing game culture from a variety of perspectives routinely excluded in mainstream video games. In retrospect, Frasca's forum games appear the more prescient, since along with the increasing availability of free tools for the creation and distribution of games, personal narratives are becoming a prominent part of the transformation of gaming culture at present. In this context, feminist and queer gaming culture is at the foreground of the development of forum games in practice.

Queer Games

Among designers of queer games, Twine, an open-source hypertext software, has recently been thrust into the limelight as a platform for feminist and queer do-it-yourself (DIY) game culture. Twine was released by developer Chris Klimas in 2009, who conceived it as an easy-to-use tool requiring no programming skills. Though not primarily intended to function as a game design tool, in the hands of Anna Antrophy, Charity Heartscape Porpentine, and Zoë Quinn, among others, Twine became synonymous with the anticommodity, DIY ethos of feminist and queer designers responding to their marginalization in mainstream video game culture. On a broader level, this project is also an open invitation to participate in transforming video games and game culture based on open-access forms of production and distribution.

Contemporary queer and feminist Twine games are rooted in various cultural forms spanning analog and digital formats. From the perspective of video game history, Twine games are an extension of early interactive fiction games distributed as open-source software, of which *Colossal Game Adventure* (William Crowther, 1976) is the best-known example, and, more precisely, of queer games similarly conceived as free games at the height of the AIDS crisis in the 1980s, which are currently just resurfacing through the efforts of queer-game historians. This hacker ethos is shared by DIY feminist and queer subcultural communities growing out of frustrations with their marginalized roles in subcultures such as 1980s punk. Contemporary queer and feminist Twine games echo these communities' use of fanzines, music, and art to counter the dominant, exclusionary impulses (sexism and commodity culture) in mainstream gaming spaces. In art, these games have historical precedents in net-art and cyberfeminist projects in the 1990s, including hypertext literature and digital games.[56] In concept, these practices share feminists' and queer people's rejection of hierarchical culture, and in practice, they work through similar appropriations of digital technologies and mass media culture forms, in this case Twine, to develop alternative visions and models to those of mainstream games. Their shared penchant for hypertext reflects these concerns. As theorized by Katherine Hayles, hypertext is a hybrid formation, as it combines traditional forms of media, "letter forms, print conventions, and print literary modes," with digital media forms, including "computer games, films, animations, digital arts, graphic design, and electronic visual culture."[57] Hayles understood hypertext as a form of nonbinary expression, in her case, associated with the concept of the cyborg, a hybrid of machine and organism invoked by Donna Haraway in her essay "A Cyborg Manifesto" (1985), in which she called for the appropriation of digital technologies for feminist ends. The cyborg became as such synonymous with 1990s cyberfeminist activism online. From this vantage point, Hayles theorized hypertext literature as a "hopeful monster" or a "trading zone" in which disparate traditions, media forms, and knowledges come together, not necessarily harmoniously but nonetheless in defiance of conventional gender and media hierarchies.[58] In regard to the latter, Hayles pointed to the significance of "the structure and specificity of the underlying code" or the software, as a central component of the meaning of hypertext literature. Historical feminist hypertext projects and contemporary feminist and queer Twine games are kindred responses to the use of digital media to uphold the norms and values of patriarchal culture. They are simultaneously also explorations of media for opposite ends, to project alternative visions in the public domain. In this latter sense, Twine surpasses the tools available to feminist and queer media practitioners in the 1990s, as it affords broadened access to the creation and distribution of digital games.

Additionally, though queer games—as it is becoming increasingly evident through ongoing historical research—are not new, the emergence of Twine games are also emblematic of the dynamics and concerns of queer culture at the present moment.[59] In this regard, this project both stands in rejection of assimilation into the mainstream and in commitment to queerness as a synonym with struggle for cultural change. The late Latinx queer theorist José Esteban Muñoz best summed up this stance as *queer utopianism*. Muñoz theorized this outlook against the "normalization" of queerness, as typified by the movement's recent focus on marriage equality; rather, it is a call for defining queerness as a platform of "transformative political imagination."[60] Counter to normative identification, Muñoz argues that it is "disentification," or the belief in the possibility of "queer futurity," that best characterizes the crux of "queer counterpublics." In this context, Muñoz looks to aesthetics to map the inklings of queer utopianism and, more specifically, its traces in the works of queer artists, including literature, visual art, dance, and performance. For Muñoz, the significance of these works is in their contributions to catalyze actions toward progressive cultural transformation. In this sense, the mobilization of Twine by feminist and queer game designers befits Muñoz's understanding of cultural production as a significant locus for the performance of disentification. These games are similarly conceived in light of queer utopianism: as subversions of heteronormative video games and as a means to empower gender-progressive change. Along these lines, this project resonates with ongoing parallel practices that revolve around what artist and queer activist Zach Blas calls *queer technology*. Inspired by tactical media projects in the 1990s, Blas developed the term in reference to technologies that are conceptually and materially constructed to interrogate binary logics. Blas's notion of queer technology aptly focuses on the stakes of Twine games as a feminist and queer project, as according to him, queer technologies "resist heteronormative formations of technological control," and provide "the queer community with discursive/practical tools for activism, resistance, and empowerment."[61] In their anthology on queer games, Adrienne Shaw and Bonnie Ruberg define this project similarly, as making "a commitment to seeing differently, to finding the marginalized between the lines," by way of "unlocking the non-normative potential that has been waiting in video games all along."[62]

In practice, as previously mentioned, Twine games conceived from feminist and queer perspectives are based on autobiographical narratives, a focus that signals facetious commentary on the "realism" of conventional games and kinship with feminist and queer aesthetics, since personal perspectives have historically been centrally featured in these practices in response to their marginalization in dominant culture. In video games, *Casper in the Castro* (1989), which was designed by CM Ralph as "charityware," to solicit donations for AIDS-related programs at the height of the epidemic, may be a first instance of this focus on personal, living experience by a queer woman game designer. In the present context, this personal focus, to paraphrase Anthropy, rejects what she deems "the single perspective of engineering and venture capitalism," manifesting a realism of "orcs, elves, and wish-fulfillment power fantasies."[63] In contrast, Twine games by feminist and queer designers use personal narratives to explore the fluidity of lived experience, often relating trauma, loss, love, and pleasure, blurring fact and fiction, past, present, and future, virtual and real spaces, and reality and the imaginary. Conceived as nonlinear narratives, these games reflect intersectional feminist and queer perspectives, and, in particular they focus on exploring how our overlapping identities, including race, religion, ethnicity, class, sexual orientation, and physical disability impact experiences of oppression and discrimination. In the words of Shaw and Ruberg, they explore the intersections of feminism and queerness with "interrelated concerns of access, visibility, subjecthood, agency, and voice."[64] Shifting the focus from dominant to marginalized populations in gaming results, as one would expect, in games that are not only representationally but also formally distinct from the norm. As it turns out, inadvertently, they would also show the continued relevance of calls to appropriate technologies by feminists and queer people, including historical strands of feminist utopianism, to the present time.

In this light, *Depression Quest* (2013) (fig. 5.5), by game developer Zoë Quinn in collaboration with writer Patrick Lindsey, was the first project that became paradigmatic of the significance of Twine as a gaming platform at the behest of a feminist project. Quinn and Lindsey based it on their shared life-long personal struggles with depression.[65] The project was conceived both to increase awareness of depression and as a fundraising tool benefiting the national suicide prevention hotline (a percentage of proceeds from the game, when players choose to buy it, are donated to the organization). Structured as a diary, *Depression Quest* consists of a series of

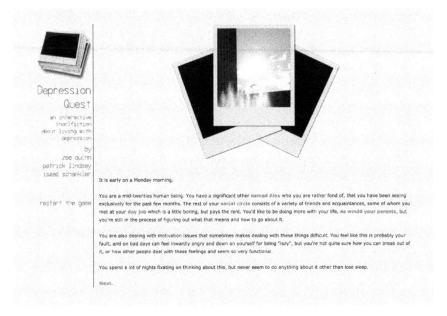

Figure 5.5. Screenshot of *Depression Quest* (Zoë Quinn, 2013). © Zoë Quinn.

entries or scenarios in which the player takes on the persona of a depressed person (a composite of Quinn and Lindsey) attempting to manage illness and possible treatment while navigating the maelstrom of quotidian life. Entries offer narratives about interpersonal relationships, work, and school. The mood of depression is conveyed through the game's sparse aesthetic, combining black text and toned-down images against a grainy, gray background with a repetitive and eerie score. Like conventional role-playing games, *Depression Quest* unfolds based on the choices made by the player. The possibility of linear cause-and-effect clicking, used in mainstream games to signal mastery and control, is here denied, however, to further emphasize the limitations arising from depression. The player is presented instead with both available and nonavailable options: available choices are displayed in gold letters, while non-clickable sentences, which stand for the limitations of chronic depression, appear as crossed-out sentences in blue lettering. Additionally, statements about the character, including data indicating their level of depression, whether or not they are in therapy, and whether or not they are currently on medication, appear underneath the selection of choices available to the player. By using the diary format, atmospheric sound, and through simple manipulations of Twine's hyper-text form, *Depression Quest* allows an intimate glimpse into the designers' struggle with debilitating depression. Given the fun-focused and male-dominated gaming industry, this game is exceptional both for its choice of topic, mental illness, and for its vantage point, that of a woman game designer. Additionally, *Depression Quest* is also important for its promi-nent role in the GamerGate controversy, when the game became the first target of anonymous attacks on women developers and critics. As we will see later, GamerGate inadvertently propelled Quinn to public notoriety and with her, other game designers using Twine in similar ways. Although her attackers certainly did not intend it, targeting Quinn ultimately drew atten-tion to the marginalization of women and queer people in video games and the video game industry, as well as to their shared projects aimed at creat-ing women- and queer-centric alternatives.

The work of Porpentine Charity Heartscape (known as Porpentine), which predates GamerGate, would emerge prominently profiled in the con-text of this controversy in the mainstream press as emblematic of the flour-ishing queer gaming scene around Twine. Like Quinn, Porpentine uses Twine to explore themes relating to personal experiences, in her case, as a transgender woman. In contrast to Quinn's, however, Porpentine's games are not as obviously autobiographical at first sight, since they interweave the fictional and the biographical. Exemplary of this distinctive design sen-sibility, *Howling Dogs* (2012, US) (fig. 5.6), is a Twine game that first brought attention to Porpentine's work.[66] The game was created in a week, shortly after Porpentine started hormone replacement therapy in 2012 while stay-ing at a friend's remodeled barn. In *Howling Dogs*, she interweaves this context with professional interests and, specifically, a focus on expanding the formal vocabularies of games. In this light, Porpentine rejects the reli-ance of conventional video games on challenges, such as fighting battles and completing puzzles, in favor of a different challenge: to create games as a jump-off point for envisioning alternative realities.

Vision is implicitly invoked in *Howling Dogs* in reference to liter-ary sources. The opening quote in the game is from *The Day He Himself Shall Wipe My Tears Away* (1972), by Japanese writer and Noble Prize win-ner Kenzaburo Oe. The closing quote of the game is by Australian theo-logian John Hull (1935–2015).[67] Both authors are interested in vision as a literary topic and as a metaphor to address private and public conditions. (An ambivalent meditation on his coming-of-age experiences in defeated,

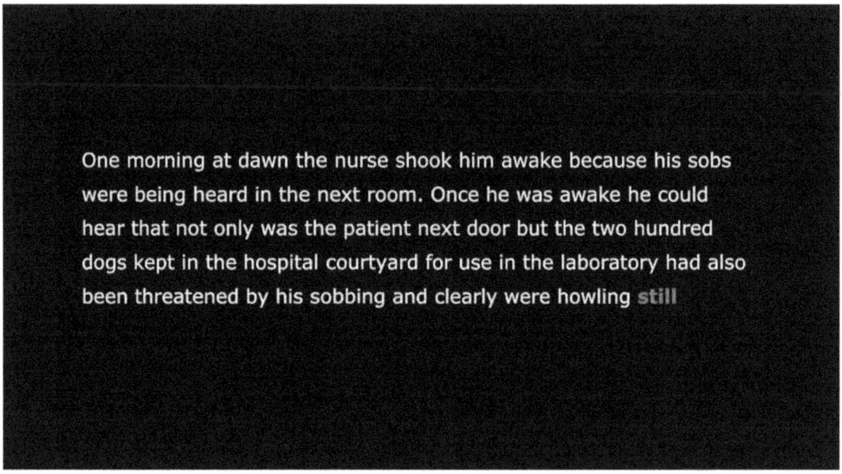

One morning at dawn the nurse shook him awake because his sobs were being heard in the next room. Once he was awake he could hear that not only was the patient next door but the two hundred dogs kept in the hospital courtyard for use in the laboratory had also been threatened by his sobbing and clearly were howling still

Figure 5.6. Screenshot of *Howling Dogs* (Porpentine Charity Heartscape, 2012). Quote by Kenzaburo Oe. © Porpentine Charity Heartscape.

post–WWII Japan, Kenzaburo's book parodies the nationalism of his literary antithesis, Yukio Mishima, which led the latter to commit *seppuku* [ritual suicide] in 1970 after a failed coup).[68] The novel draws parallels between nationalism and restricted vision by portraying Mishima wearing goggles and headphones while spiraling into a nihilistic withdrawal from life. In contrast, Hull is notable for his meditations on going blind. Hull documented the progression of his blindness in audio recordings that interweave personal accounts of his condition and analysis of the negative attitudes toward blindness harbored by sighted culture. A passionate antiwar activist before going blind, Hull subsequently became a prominent voice within the disability rights movements in the West and Asia, and subsequently came to consider his blindness a "dark, paradoxical gift." While offering contrasting views about vision, Kenzaburo's and Hull's works are similarly rooted in autobiographical writing and, by extension, in the belief that the personal is political. Working with this insight, Porpentine adapts it to the format of video games. Unlike mainstream games, *Howling Dogs* does not aim at escaping reality; rather, it engages escapism as an impetus for change, for seeing differently.

The narrative and aesthetic of *Howling Dogs* are even more sparse than those of *Depression Quest*. The screen consists simply of white text with blue hyperlinks leading to more text and occasionally to pixelated images on a black background. Evocative of Kenzaburo's narrative and style, which is characterized by circular structure and loose employment of punctuation, the narrative projects the player into a confined metallic space in an unspecified location, bathed in fluorescent lights. The space provides its resident with a food dispenser, a trash disposal, a toilet, a shower, and a virtual reality station. Play involves repeated rounds of caring for the body: eating, drinking, cleaning, grooming, and sleeping, interspersed with sessions of virtual reality viewing. The tasks are interrelated by way of requiring the player to repeat routine self-care in order to unlock the virtual reality visor. This conceit is familiar in video games under the term *grinding*, a process of engaging in repetitive tasks often used to signal eventual reward. This expectation is thwarted in *Howling Dogs*, however, as all the virtual reality scenarios lead to repeated ejection from the station. Indeed, all the various virtual reality personae inhabited by the player face death in some form—cannibalism, execution, murder, and ritual sacrifice—in various places and times: as a collaborator in the murder of an abuser, as a cannibal in a war on Mars, as a daughter attending her mother's funeral, as an infant empress training for ritual self-sacrifice, and as a witch about to be burned at the stake. Similarly, upon each return to the cell, the player finds it increasingly deteriorated—as the trash disposal and the shower break down, one wonders whether access to virtual reality will, in time, also become impossible. It soon becomes clear that escape (or escapism) is not one of *Howling Dogs*'s options. Rather, through chronological and spatial disjunctions, the game evokes a sense of repetition and, by extension, entrapment.

In contrast to mainstream games, *Howling Dogs* offers no closure. Like its literary sources, it defines narrative, and specifically autobiographical games, as a process of discovery and transformation rather than a resolved or closed story. Porpentine's video games are literal puns on their native environment, the "digital," a term originally referring to fingers—the word "digit" is from the Latin *digitus*, meaning a finger (or toe). It is from this standpoint that in referencing her interest in autobiographical approaches to games, Porpentine characterizes her work in relation to "touch . . . so there can be as little separation as possible."[69] Similarly, contrasting Twine games to the hyperrealistic, kinetic, and generally violent representations of the commercial mainstream, game critic Carla Ellison suggested that Twine mainly works as a "mechanics of intimacy." This approach certainly reflects Porpentine's games, for as Ellison contends, the focus emerges through explorations of issues concerning "consciousness, personal and interpersonal relationships, and other matters related to intimacy."[70] Matters of intimacy have long been the staples of autobiography, including numerous feminist and queer authors, and it is in this vein that *Howling Dogs* resonates Muñoz's call to "strive, in the face of the here and now's totalizing rendering of reality, to think and feel a *then and there*."[71] In sum, Twine games like Porpentine's extend queer autobiography, making it culturally and politically relevant to the present moment by linking it with gaming culture.

In more obvious ways, touch and intimacy are central to Anna Anthropy's games, most often in reference to the queer BDSM community, to which she belongs. A ten-second game, *Queers in Love at the End of the World* (2013, US), aptly illustrates the developer's knack for irreverent, often humorous Twine design.[72] Carrying subversive commentary on mainstream games' investment in mastery, the game employs short sentences and terms referencing erotic exchanges with a lover, as a timer in the upper left of the browser window counts down, urging the player to rush before "everything is wiped away." The game's postscript reads: "When we have each other, we have everything." Anthropy wrote about the game: "If you only had ten seconds left with your partner, what would you do with them? What would you say?" adding that *Queers in Love at the End of the World* is "a game about the transformative, transcendent power of queer love, and is dedicated to every queer I've loved, no matter how briefly, or for how long."[73] Similar to Porpentine, Anthropy plays with hypertext, but more forcefully. In *Queers in Love at the End of the World*, she uses the imperative mood playfully, urging the play to carry out demands, instructions, and requests related to BDSM-infused roleplay. Exemplary of her overall work, this game subverts video games' heteronormative identity and re-creates it in light of queer intimacy. *Queers in Love at the End of the World* literally mimics BDSM play, as the player clicking on the highlighted words submits to Anthropy.

Additionally, *Queers in Love at the End of the World* is exemplary of Anthropy's notion of games as *zines*, a term that evokes the DIY ethos of 1980s queer fanzine culture, used here to reference games that are short in duration and based on personal experiences. Following this, Anthropy reimagines gaming in light of the anticonsumerist ethos of zine culture, calling on players to likewise create a gaming culture of their own. In this way, rather than a singular point of view, video games and game culture would be more intersectional, including, according to Anthropy, "a plurality of voices . . . a wider set of experiences . . . a wider range of perspectives."[74] In practice, as envisioned by Quinn, Porpentine, and Anthropy, game culture would be reconceived, like their games, as an open-ended and playful exchange, which is best characterized by its (literal) personal touch. As their work suggests, games like theirs would be based on sharing autobiographical hypertext fiction and poetry. Considered historically, this vision of games is not new, since its precedents go from historical playful exchanges of textual and visual materials in both analog and digital avant-garde art and digital counterculture to later practices, including net-art and cyberfeminist interventions, gaming culture such as Salen and Zimmerman's open games systems and Frasca's forum games, as well as DIY queer culture, which as we will see, goes beyond fanzines to video games. As extensions of these historical currents, these games challenge dominant norms and assumptions about what games are, how they should be played, and whose realities they represent. Incidentally, these new games have been criticized by some gamers for rejecting normative assumptions that games should be fun, challenging, or masterable. For instance, *Depression Quest* was critiqued for being a nonlinear narrative rather than "a real game" because it lacks a core challenge or rules that can be mastered. As it happens, the recent emergence of queer gaming culture in the public eye is, in part, inadvertently linked to such critiques, as *Depression Quest* became the first target of what has been framed in mainstream media reporting as queer gaming's cultural nemesis, GamerGate.

While experiences of harassment have a long history in gaming culture, GamerGate refers to a recent escalation involving a loosely organized and anonymous group identifying themselves by the Twitter hashtag #Gamer-Gate. During its height in 2014, GamerGate-related incidents included doxing (researching and broadcasting personally identifiable information about an individual), hacking the targets' various social media and digital accounts, swatting (making a prank call to emergency services in an attempt to bring about the dispatch of a large number of armed police officers to a particular address), and online posts and calls threatening assault, rape, and murder.

In the mainstream media, GamerGate was chiefly portrayed as an antifeminist crusade of sorts, with Quinn singled out as an example. Such reports focused on Quinn's targeting after a former disgruntled partner publicly denounced *Depression Quest*'s recognition in video game online review sites as the result of her romantic involvement with a journalist. He later retracted the claim, but by then the harassment had spread virulently online. The case of Anita Sarkeesian, media critic and founder of Feminist Frequency, an online educational nonprofit dedicated to gender equity in media, illustrates that, in addition, GamerGate was also underpinned by antimedia sentiment. In 2011, Sarkeesian began hosting a YouTube video series, *Tropes versus Women in Video Games*, that focused on the pervasive objectifying portrayals of women in mainstream video games. Although the series had always been singled out for hateful commentary online, in 2014 the kind of anonymous harassment associated with GamerGate intensified. Like Quinn, Sarkeesian received rape and death threats, and her private information, including her home address, was leaked. The harassment culminated with callers identifying as GamerGaters threatening mass shootings on the eve of Sarkeesian's invited lecture at the University of Utah. Anonymous callers threatened a "Montreal-style massacre" involving her, her audiences, and the staff and students of the nearby Women's Center, which led to her canceling the event because of concerns for her audience's safety. Additionally, at the height of GamerGate, both Quinn and Sarkeesian, among other women and sympathizers who were targeted, felt compelled to flee their homes. Subsequently, many of those targeted whose work addressed issues concerning gender, sexuality, and video games, opted either for working outside of the public eye or for leaving the field.[75] In the aftermath of GamerGate, Quinn, Sarkeesian, and several other women joined forces to develop crowd-funded and female-led initiatives focused on researching and countering online harassment. Quinn created the Crash Override network as a crisis helpline, advocacy group, and resource center for people experiencing online abuse, supported by individual donors, including Sarkeesian. Similarly, other women-led nonprofits focused on expanding research on online harassment beyond simplistic understandings of digital technologies, spaces, and communities as being either emancipatory or oppressive.[76] In this regard, Jamia Wilson, executive director of Women, Action, and the Media, cited the ahistoricism of media reporting on GamerGate as a factor that plays a central role in perpetuating public perception of online harassment as a new phenomenon. From this perspective, Wilson cited the hate mail received by Martin Luther King Jr. as an example of pre-internet harassment and intimidation that was likewise designed to enforce the status quo (of racial segregation).[77] Wilson's perspective is the more poignant as some journalists and queer game designers point out that GamerGate became, in retrospect, a model for the culture-war-styled, white nationalist campaigns online, as exemplified by Breitbart News, a Far Right syndicated American news, opinion, and commentary website (among its founders, Steve Bannon was executive chair, a position he relinquished in 2016 to become chief executive of Donald Trump's presidential campaign). Most notably, Breitbart's queer polemicist, Milo Yiannopoulos, was among those who self-styled as a GamerGate supporter to leverage the misogynistic and antimedia sentiment of sympathizers for Far Right radicalization. As of this writing, similar polarizing rhetoric and strategies, including attacks on the rights of women, queer people, African Americans, and journalists, are the norm for many conservative politicians in the United States, including President Donald Trump, and allies in the Republican Far Right. Seen from this perspective, GamerGate represents another instance of leveraging media culture, in this case video games, for divisive ends and yet again in the name of cultural gatekeeping.

In contrast to the negative light in which the GamerGate controversy has been portrayed in mainstream media, voices in the queer gaming community, while similarly noting connections with hate groups, refuse nonetheless to equate GamerGate with either video game culture or the self-styled gamer community in toto. Most recently, in their joint anthology on queer gaming, Bonnie Ruberg and Adrienne Shaw characterize Gamer-Gate as a phenomenon that is "diverse in both its stakeholders and targets," including self-styed defenders of gaming culture, which they perceive to be under threat from outsiders, to others insisting that video games are sufficiently inclusive spaces and that arguments to the contrary unfairly mischaracterize it.[78] Quinn is more specific, indicating that GamerGate is best thought of as a loose coalition of "online white supremacist movements, misogynist nerds, conspiracy theorists, and dispassionate hoaxers."[79] In the end, feminist and queer perspectives on GamerGate tend to discuss it as an event that represents a singular perspective among the multiplicity of other outlooks currently shaping gaming culture.[80] In this light, Shaw concludes that video game communities are "multiple and overlapping . . . intersectional and coalitional" formations and, in this vein, points out that contrary to the view of some GamerGate supporters, feminist and queer communities are similarly diverse and fragmented, sometimes overlapping and sometimes in tension.[81] This position not only refutes the exclusionary rhetoric of GamerGate but also, in contrast, is a reminder that ambiguity can be a significant touchpoint for progressive voices in gaming. The diversity of gaming communities reminds us that video games simultaneously hold oppressive and emancipatory potentials and that, as the Far Right recognizes, engaging them is politically significant. To reconfigure video games as spaces welcoming to diverse formal and representational elements, and by extension multiple perspectives, is intrinsically an important contribution to progressive public life. GamerGate proves this point clearly, for as Ruberg and Shaw note, it provided a rallying point for progressive voices in gaming culture, although not by design. As such, it ultimately served not only to publicly highlight feminist and queer lives and visions in mass media but also to generate connections with and support from individuals and communities who do not necessarily identify as gamers but are similarly interested in the potential of digital technologies for progressive cultural change.

Among them, some in the mainstream cultural and educational spaces lend significant support to feminist and queer Twine developers. It is in this context that since 2016, alongside the independent game scene, the work of Quinn, Porpentine, and Anthropy has gained increasing recognition from established museums and art venues in the United States and their extensions online.[82] Both *Queers in Love at the End of the World* and *Howling Dogs* are now included in Rhizome's Net Art Anthology, an online archive of net-art launched in 2016.[83] In the same year, Rhizome, the digital-art branch of the New Museum in New York City, also commissioned Porpentine and two other Twine developers, Brenda Neotenomie and Sloane, to create a new game for the museum's collection series First Look: New Art Online. The resulting project, *Psycho Nymph Asylum*, consists of a Twine game, a booklet, and stickers designed to be applied on the player's skin. The project is conceived as another experiment in tactile-oriented game design, in this case, with a focus on post-traumatic stress disorder experiences.[84] Porpentine also received Rhizome's annual Prix Net Art of 2017 for her collaborative game with Neotenomie, titled *With Those We Love Alive* (2014). Similarly based on autobiographical themes, in this game the player is trapped in an alien and violent empire. As the game progresses, players are prompted to transform their physical appearance by inscribing some form of sigils on their body with a marker, according to their responses to others' demands and violence. Understood as a trans-allegory of game communities, the game highlights ways in which the participatory contexts of video games can be channeled into systematic oppression and violence but also how they can lead to creative collaboration, in this case, between Porpentine and the player.[85] *With Those We Love Alive* was included in the prestigious Whitney biennial of 2017.[86] In 2019, Adrienne Shaw curated *Rainbow Arcade: Queer Gaming History 1985–2018* at the invitation of the Schwules Museum (Gay Museum) and the Computerspiele Museum (Computer Game Museum), both located in Berlin, Germany. A first of its kind, the materials in the exhibition come out of Shaw's ongoing research into queer gaming contained in the LGBTQ Gaming Archive, which she funded at Temple University. *Rainbow Arcade* includes one hundred games and a crowd-funded catalog focused on histories of queer gaming, which altogether challenge assumptions about queer gaming as either being chiefly Western in cultural outlook or of recent date. The exhibition's transcultural scope documents three decades of work by queer game designers, working both in digital and nondigital forms, in Europe, North America, South America, Asia, Africa, and Australia, and includes *Casper in the Castro* (1989), which, as aforementioned, may be one of the first queer games in digital form in the United States.

Although institutional support for progressive voices in game design and research is not new, as previously mentioned game designers, including Frasca, Bogost, Molleindustria, and others have similarly exhibited in art and design venues, worked in academia, or collaborated with artists, the inclusion of queer gaming, including Twine games, has further consolidated these ties. Regarding these connections, it is useful to recall that Hayles's notion of hypertext as "hopeful monster" reflects the activist conceptualization of practices associated with net-art and cyberfeminism in the 1990s, which included a strong DIY ethos. As previously noted, net-artists took to the internet for artistic creation and distribution in order to circumvent the commodity model associated with art institutions. Some cyberfeminist, antiracist, and queer artists additionally focused on disrupting misogynistic, racist, and homophobic representations in digital entertainment and networks, including the internet and video games. It is out of this context that the current interest and support of Rhizome for queer and feminist game developers can be understood, since this organization emerged from artist-led cultural activism embedded in such networks. Like historical art- and activist-based interventions in digital culture, feminist and queer Twine games constitute a pluralistic rather than unified project. Their common ground resides in a shared rejection of dominant definitions, identities, and structures. Similarly, their affinities for the *monstrous* and the *queer* speak of their shared condition as historically marginalized voices in popular culture, and conversely, to their commitment to disrupt and recode it with a multitude of personal, deeply intimate accounts and perspectives. It bears repetition: the resurgence of feminist and queer Twine games in the context of recent gaming controversies shows the continued relevance of this project. As for the future, they leave visions of alternatives open-ended to encourage players to imagine and create their own.

Whose Games

Overall, designers using the video game for cultural and social change do so in recognition of the persuasive power of the medium, which is based on its appeal to fantasy and imagination. In contrast to the immersive realism of mainstream entertainment and rigid definitions of what a "real game" is, their project claims the medium to empower dreams of change and the possibility of an emancipated world. The concept and forms of these games point to paths leading to change: diversity, participation, open-endedness, transparency, and grounding in reality and truthful intent. These principles link this project to the utopian spirit of historical cultural currents that take many names and forms, among them avant-garde media arts, Indigenous myth, participatory theater and pedagogy, and revolutionary printmaking and murals. Their kindred conception as practices aiming at cultural and political transformation shapes them along similar formations, as decentered, multiple, and participatory. As such, their appropriation, cannibalization, and rearticulation by contemporary video game designers using video games to counter dominant ideologies is consistent with their conception, for such games function to reactivate the transformative aim of the practices from which they draw in the games' media environment. Following these precedents, contemporary designers expanded on them to create games in a wide range of participatory and open-ended forms, designed to speak to and intervene in contemporaneous conditions.

In the first instance, many socially engaged game designers began using the medium to comment on current social, political, and cultural processes. Taking the form of self-published, freely available games online, these projects aimed to not only highlight the role of games as ideological tools but also to persuade on behalf of progressive views. In contrast, other designers, choosing to create video games as collaborative projects, sought to stress the participation of players as active makers. These projects' persuasive goal was a symbolic demonstration of players' capacity to effect change. As open-source game software is increasingly available, designers envision video games as a DIY practice involving anyone interested in actively creating video games in the image of their own perspectives.

It is in this context of extending the use of Twine so that players can create games, that queer designers see it as a participatory game-design tool with the potential to change the commodified frame of gaming culture. As a highly publicized intervention, in the hands of feminist and queer designers Twine has proved to be an effective tool for contesting the exclusionary culture of mainstream gaming. In this regard, GamerGate manifested the challenges that progressive designers face, illustrating the extent to which video games can be an emancipatory practice. Broad support for targeted feminist and queer designers of Twine games, sources of which include cultural institutions, mainstream media, critics, and some in the video game industry, indicates widespread appreciation for their project. Yet, beyond this context, the Twine project issues a broader challenge. Anna Anthropy, who has been particularly active in promoting and teaching game design using Twine and other open-source platforms, says that this work is conceived as an invitation to imagine "a world in which digital games are not manufactured by publishers for the same small audience, but one in which games are authored by you and me for the benefit of our peers."[87] Other game designers, including Quinn and Brianna Wu, a Boston-based game designer and entrepreneur, have published similar tutorials and spoken about the significance of developing easy-to-use software as a means of democratizing gaming culture. Other designers associated with queer games, including Merrit Kopas, pointed out that Twine's potential is still underdeveloped, citing the dominance of English in Twine games as an example. In this interest, Porpentine, who alongside creating also curates Twine games online, recently highlighted Josue Monchan's *Oh Diosa!*, a Twine game named after a pun on the Spanish word for "goddess" (Oh Goddess!) and *odiosa*, the Spanish word for an odious, or monstrous, woman, a transphobic slur often used against transgender women.[88] In the spirit of intersectionality, feminist and queer Twine designers propose approaching video games as a form of a global DIY culture wherein the aggregate of individual or small-scale contributions would ultimately become an evolving repository of collective visions of progressive alternatives to the market-driven games of global capitalism. Referring to this utopian outlook, Bonnie Ruberg succinctly echoes what others in the queer games community have similarly stressed, that the attitude most essential to the development of this project is openness to change. As Ruberg sums up: "We may never find our utopia, and that is how it should be. There is no perfection, only change—in games, in our communities, and in ourselves. That is what I hope for."[89]

As practices aimed to challenge the reactionary cultural outlooks of global video game consumers and reconfigure games as progressive spaces, the work of these designers testifies to its roots in the historical avant-garde's and counterculture's utopian pursuit of play and games. Similarly, the appropriation and refashioning of these utopian legacies for commercial ends was fundamental to the development of video games as a global cultural commodity and entertainment market. Ironically, in this context, these projects bring these dynamics full circle and beyond, expanding on them, as they infuse digital culture with marginalized points of view. In the end, they offer expanded visions of the forum as it could be, a worldly game shaped by as many dreams and imaginaries as there are gamers.

Notes

1. Bogost, *Persuasive Games.*
2. Duncombe, *Dream.*
3. Bogost, *Persuasive Games*, 29.
4. Ibid.
5. Bogost, *Unit Operations*, 135.
6. Ibid., 29.
7. Ibid., ix.
8. Hinton, "The Potential of the Latent Public Sphere."
9. Habermas, *Theory of Communicative Action*, vol. 1, 275–287.
10. Habermas, *Structural Transformation of the Public Sphere*, 170.
11. Ibid., 232.
12. Ibid.
13. Fernback and Thompson, "Virtual Communities."
14. Rheingold, "Virtual Communities, Phony Civil Society?"
15. Bogost, Ferrari, and Schweizer, *NewsGames*, 177.
16. Bogost, *Persuasive Games*, 180.
17. Habermas, *The Structural Transformation of the Public Sphere*, 178.
18. Duncombe, *Dream*, 17.
19. Ibid., 30.
20. Ibid., 5.
21. Ibid., 27.
22. Ibid., 18.

23. See Flanagan, *Critical Play*; Salen and Zimmerman, *Rules of Play*, 305; Frasca, "Videogames of the Oppressed"; McGonigal, *Reality Is Broken*; Pearce, Fullerton, and Morie, "Sustainable Play."

24. Frasca, "Videogames of the Oppressed," 85.

25. See Boal, *Games for Actor and Non-Actors*.

26. Salen and Zimmerman, *Rules of Play*, 545.

27. Frasca, "Rethinking Agency and Immersion."

28. Frasca, "Videogames of the Oppressed," 93.

29. Personal communication with Gonzalo Frasca.

30. McClellan, "The Role of Play."

31. Powerful Robot Games was cofounded with Sofia Battegazzore in 2002, and closed down in 2012. Part of PR's profits were donated to various progressive causes.

32. *Guernica* was first displayed at the 1937 World's Fair in Paris and subsequently toured around the world to raise funds for Spanish war relief. It was used again as a background by anti-Vietnam War protesters in the United States, including at the Museum of Modern Art in New York City in the 1970s.

33. Powerful Robot Games, "Madrid," 2004, http://www.newsgaming.com. See Bogost, Ferrari, and Schweizer, *NewsGames*, 22.

34. Bogost, Ferrari, and Schweizer, *NewsGames*, 28.

35. Estimates quote thirty-six million people across the globe taking part in almost three thousand protests against the Iraq War between January 3 and April 12, 2003.

36. Gilroy, *Postcolonial Melancholia*. As Gilroy explains, conviviality is distinct from multiculturalism, which is a top-down co-option and repackaging of the spontaneous, unruly, and bottom-up characteristics of convivial culture.

37. Available at https://knightfoundation.org/about/.

38. All games are available at Ian Bogost, "Persuasive Games," http://www .persuasivegames.com/games/. Bogost, Ferrari, and Schweizer, *NewsGames*, 175.

39. Juul, *A Casual Revolution*.

40. Available at http://www.tiltfactor.org/layoff/.

41. Molleindustria's games are available at http://www.molleindustria.org/. Bogost, Ferrari, and Schweizer, *NewsGames*, 26–31.

42. Coltan is a mineral used in the manufacture of tantalum capacitors, which are found in consumer electronics such as mobile phones, video game systems, and computers.

43. Ciociola, "Phone Story behind Apple Allure."

44. Ramos, "Leaky World Creators Interview."

45. In this sense, *Phone Story* can also be characterized by Nick Dyer-Witheford's and Greig de Peuter's notion of "games of multitude," as opposed to the "games of empire" (*empire* and *multitude* are concepts developed by Antonio Negri and Michael Hardt to denote, respectively, the new form of globalization emerging post-1989 and new forms of resistance to it). Mainstream video games designed in reflection of empire mirror its global reach, exploitive conditions, and retrograde ideologies based on militarist and capitalist expansion, precarious labor, and control over all aspects of life. Dyer-Witheford and de Peuter describe how video games exemplify one of the integral features of empire— bio-power, or control over biological processes, in this case, playful interactions. The interactive capabilities of video games are used toward this purpose to harness the creative contributions of consumers in order to reinforce their emotional investment in products

as cocreators (this is similar to the notion of gamification). Because Dyer-Witheford's and de Peuter's focus is on empire, their discussion of games reflective of the multitude is less developed. I cite it here as an example of academic acknowledgement of the significance of video games as a means to both resist and foster other visions of a world beyond empire. The games of multitude represent the conjunction of individual and collective creative capabilities, a social movement, and a political project. Like the games of empire, the games of the multitude are global, as they intersect with emancipatory social and political projects, working in parallel and in collaboration worldwide. Dyer-Witheford and de Peuter, *Games of Empire*; Dyer-Witheford and de Peuter, "Games of Multitude"; Hardt and Negri, *Empire*.

46. Sezen, *"Huys"/"Hope"–Turkey's First Political Game*; Bogost, Ferrari, and Schweizer, *NewsGames*, 32.

47. Mir and Owens, "Modelling Indigenous Peoples," 91–106. See also, Chapman, *Digital Games as History*.

48. *Tropical America* is now archived in the Rhizome Net Art Anthology database (Rhizome is affiliated with the New Museum in New York City), https://rhizome.org/art /artbase/artwork/tropical-america/. See also, Penix-Tadsen, *Cultural Code*, 83–86.

49. Siqueiros conceived *La América Tropical* as an anti-imperialist statement, and as such it was rejected by the downtown Los Angeles business and political establishment.

50. LaPensée, *Survivance*; Dillon, "Indigenous Futurisms"; Baudemann, "Indigenous Futurisms," 117–150.

51. The game is available in PC, PlayStation 4, and Xbox One formats.

52. In connecting the erosion of Iñupiaq culture with the destruction of the community's environment, *Never Alone* reiterates the gist of a previous joint petition in 2005 seeking relief from the violations of Inuit human rights resulting from global warming caused by greenhouse gas emissions from the United States.

53. Haraway, "Symbiogenesis, Sympoiesis, and Art Science," 44.

54. Also, ecological issues are increasingly a topic prominent in independent video games as a whole. See, Chang, *Playing Nature*.

55. SOAP stands for SUNY Oswego ARG Package. The project is archived at http://blog .ulisesmejias.com/soap-2/. Clark et al., "Interactive Social Media," 171–185.

56. Coming at different angles to mainstream cyberculture then, net-artists sought to simultaneously circumvent control from art institutions and reclaim virtual spaces for artistic purposes. Similarly, cyberfeminist artists also focused on intervening into the male-coding of digital technologies. For instance, *The Intruder* (1997) by Natalie Bookchin, discussed in chapter 4, is an example of such an intervention, in this case, into game culture. Other projects, such as *doll yoko* (1997) and *FleshMeat* (1998) by Francesca da Rimini, a former member of the Australian cyberfeminist collective VNS Matrix can similarly be seen as significant precursors to today's feminist and queer Twine games. *doll yoko* is a hypertext work conceived to comment on femicide in China. The piece combines haunting, distorted imagery, recalling collage. It includes a spectral face of a woman that appears intermittently on the background of texts evocative of misogynistic erasure, such as the following sentence, "All women are ghosts and should rightly be feared." *FleshMeat* takes the form of an online diary, with similar references to the erasure of women in online culture: "I am Gash Girl . . . /Puppet Mistress . . . /Voice Idol . . . /Doll Yoko/Exquisite Aberrant/Intelligence. Ghost AI. / These are my stories. /I will not remain silent. /They are all true. /I am not mad. /I have wept enough/ (Lies/Lies)." Additionally, *The Patchwork Girl* (1995), by American author Shelley

Jackson, is perhaps the best known example of cyberfeminist fiction in hypertext form. An homage to Mary Shelley's *Frankenstein*, this work pivots on rejection of systems of property and ownership underpinning the historical objectification of women, as this resounding text indicates: "I belong nowhere. This is not bizarre for my sex however, nor is it uncomfortable for us, to whom belonging has generally meant, belonging TO." In this spirit, Jackson invites the reader to construct a global "rebellious" and "modern" femininity from various female body parts by way of reading, an action that ultimately stitches together texts and images to resurrect the monster (a cyborg feminist, as theorized by Donna Haraway in her famous essay "A Cyborg Manifesto," in 1985). Additionally, the figure of Frankenstein is significant in transgender history in the United States, through the work of the historian, filmmaker, and transgender activist Susan Stryker. Stryker's groundbreaking essay titled "My Words to Victor Frankenstein boave the Village of Chamounix: Performing Transgender Rage" (1994) reclaimed monstrosity (embodied by Frankenstein's monster) as an empowering metaphor for transness, which in the essay emerges as such synonymous with the capacity to remake ourselves and the world into a more sustainable reality. Stryker, "My Words to Victor Frankenstein above the Village of Chamounix: Performing Transgender Rage."

57. Hayles, "Electronic Literature: What Is It?"
58. Ibid.
59. Shaw and Ruberg, *Queer Game Studies*, xx.
60. Muñoz, *Cruising Utopia*, 3.
61. Blas, "Queer Technologies." In addition, see Bagnall, "Queer(ing) Gaming Technologies," 135–143.
62. Shaw and Ruberg, *Queer Game Studies*, xxii.
63. Anthropy, *Rise of the Videogame Zinesters*, 160.
64. Shaw and Ruberg, *Queer Game Studies*, xviii.
65. *Depression Quest* available at http://www.depressionquest.com/.
66. *Howling Dogs* available at http://slimedaughter.com/games/twine/howlingdogs/.
67. The opening quote, which references howling dogs, lends the game its title. It reads: "One morning at dawn the nurse shook him awake because his sobs were being heard in the next room. Once he was awake he could hear that not only was the patient next door but the two hundred dogs kept in the hospital courtyard for use in the laboratory had also been threatened by his sobbing and clearly were howling still; nonetheless, he thought to himself, I am only dreaming; besides, I'm already fully conscious of the significance of those howling dogs because I've written about them, this is no time for howling dogs." The closing quote of the game is as follows: "And they are indefatigable in their bad work: They never are faint or weary. Indeed, it seems no spirits are capable of weariness but those that inhabit flesh and blood."
68. Yukio Mishima (1925–1970) is considered to be the foremost postwar Japanese avant-garde writer, leaving behind an oeuvre characterized by a futurist aesthetic that is closely related to Italian futurism's embrace of hypermasculinity, misogyny, militarism, war, and nationalism. A prolific writer, actor, filmmaker, and queer icon (he was himself a closeted queer man), Mishima was also a leader of an extreme nationalist group. Alongside other members, he was involved in a coup in 1970 aimed at retracting Western-imposed values, which he saw as spreading and weakening Japan like a cancer (he called for reestablishing Japan's honor, that is, restoring the divinity of the emperor, strengthening Japan's army, and repealing the country's pacifist constitution). The coup failed, ending with Mishima's ritual

suicide, or *seppuku*, at Japan's military headquarters. The affair was a media sensation at the time.

69. Short, "Interview with Porpentine."

70. Hudson, "Twine, the Video-Game Technology for All."

71. Muñoz, *Cruising Utopia*, 1.

72. *Queers in Love at the End of the World* is available at http://webenact.rhizome.org /queers-in-love-at-the-end-of-the-world/http:/auntiepixelante.com/endoftheworld/#2t.1y.10 .2c.q.1e.

73. Ibid.

74. Anthropy, *Rise of the Videogame Zinesters*, 8.

75. Shaw and Ruberg, *Queer Game Studies*, xxi.

76. Because lack of research on online harassment is seen as a main factor of officials' inadequate responses, the United Nations Broadband Commission's report on gendered cyberviolence, "Cyber Violence against Women and Girls: A World-Wide Wake-Up Call," was expected to make a significant contribution to further understanding of the issue. However, as it stands, the report falls short of such expectations. Major pitfalls include the writers' framing of GamerGate on unfounded correlations between video games and violence and sweepingly broad definitions of cyberviolence against women and girls that include, in addition to online abuse, sex-trafficking and pornography. Equally troublesome are the writers' recommendations, which hinge on making nation-states responsible for "monitoring" and enforcing "accountability," presumably through discretionary surveillance and censorship of citizens' online activity. Thus, the report does little but endorse a paternalistic view of the nation-state as custodian of girls and women. Tellingly, while women targeted in GamerGate, including Quinn and Sarkeesian, were written about in the report and, in both cases, invited to testify at the panel held at the United Nations on the occasion of its release, they were not consulted on its contents and recommendations. Quinn has published a book on her experiences with GamerGate. Quinn, *Crash Override*.

77. Alexander, "Online Abuse."

78. Shaw and Ruberg, *Queer Game Studies*, xx–xxi, xx.

79. Quinn, *Crash Override*, 4.

80. This view echoes Nancy Fraser's notion of the public sphere as an arena that includes multiple, competing publics, rather than one public. Similarly, Fraser indicates that inasmuch as subaltern counterpublics emerge as a response to exclusions by the dominant publics, their field of discursive contestation can be antiegalitarian and antidemocratic. Fraser, "Rethinking the Public Sphere."

81. Shaw and Ruberg, *Queer Game Studies*, 155.

82. For instance, *Depression Quest* received awards and honorary mentions at several competitions, including Indiecade 2013, MassDiGi, and Boston Fig. *Howling Dogs* was awarded the 2012 XYZZY Awards in the Best Story and Best Writing categories, and listed by *Boston Phoenix* among the top five indie games of 2012.

83. Available at https://anthology.rhizome.org/.

84. Available at http://slimedaughter.com/games/twine/wtwla/.

85. The game is reminiscent of Shelley Jackson's *Skin* project in 2011, a story published on the skin of 2,095 volunteers, each allotted a word tattooed on their body. Available at https:// ineradicablestain.com/skindex.html. The game's Frankensteinian aesthetic evokes as well homage to Stryker, as referenced in note 56.

86. Available at http://aliendovecote.com/uploads/twine/empress/empress.html.

87. Anthropy, *Rise of the Videogame Zinesters*, 8. The book also contains information about other platforms and games. See also, Quinn, "A Beginner's Guide to Making Your First Video Game."

88. Available at http://sillyberrys.net/works/201612/OhDiosa/OhDiosa.html.

89. Shaw and Ruberg, *Queer Game Studies*, 274.

CONCLUSION
Unfinished Processes

THE STUDIES IN THIS BOOK DEMONSTRATE THAT RADICAL gaming emerges from avant-garde currents that remake technologies and media and repositions them for utopian politics with multiple strategies.

First defining this strategy as a game, the Dadaists in Zurich brought pre–WWI avant-garde art and the language of mass media together in performative and participatory theatrical events. Designed as sensory assaults on audiences, they mirrored and subverted the jingoism of mass media and marketing. In effect, they tricked audiences, presumably expecting artistic novelty or entertainment, into participating in raucous or Dionysian mockeries of nationalist, militarist, and consumerist sloganeering in Europe amidst World War I and the industrial age. This was done, in part, to create and agentivize disturbances in the face of Swiss complacency.

Similarly, the Berlin Dadaists played on the sensationalism of mass media to spread agitation. Their integration of art and technology extended Zurich Dada's reach and techniques via public scandals, media hoaxes, and mock institutions. Dadaist collage in Berlin repositioned the detritus of mass media in support of dissent against the restricted media sphere of the Weimar Republic. John Heartfield's collages are examples of antifascist propaganda. Hannah Höch's, in contrast, illustrate subtle critiques of the objectification of women's bodies in media. Dadaist collages, publications, and revolutionary literature were designed to reach a wide audience, to create the perception of ubiquitous resistance, and to create an international network of Dadaists similarly engaged. In the hands of the Berlin Dadaists, visual and print media served to demoralize the existing order and to precipitate the revolutionary process on a global scale.

The games of the surrealists integrated art and psychoanalytic language and techniques as a similar strategy to compel transformation. In contrast to the goal of psychoanalysis, to restore the patient to reason, the surrealists employed automatism and paranoia (paranoid criticism) to discredit the supremacy of reason and provoke a crisis of consciousness.

The surrealist quest to free the repressed utopian imagination and, by extension, the ludic human—homo ludens—is concretely illustrated by Claude Cahun and Marcel Moore's campaign against Nazi occupation of their home, the island of Jersey. Inspired by surrealist games, their strategies in this campaign involved the use of transcripts of radio broadcasts; altered comic books and magazines; modified gambling tokens; painting of slogans on walls, cemeteries, and churches; and masquerading. Like the Dadaists before, these strategies were intended to demoralize the enemy by creating the perception of a vast inside (among Nazi troops) and international network of antifascist resisters and, moreover, empower those already inclined to stand on the side of freedom and concrete action. In short, as the surrealists saw it, the quest for a better world required the integration of reason and imagination.

Working in parallel, Xul Solar's modified chess game, *panajadrez*, fused his interests in art, science, and technology in support of the emerging Latin American avant-garde, independent of European models. *Panajadrez* disrupts the imperialist (colonizing) logic of chess, originally a game of war strategy, to instead model a world where the ludic underlines the notion that reality can be incessantly bettered and reimagined through participatory and collective processes.

The games of the digital avant-gardes, including situationist and Fluxus networks, merge the legacies of Dada and surrealism with cybernetic concepts against the rising tide of Cold War technocracy. Their games model decentralized concepts and forms, incipient in the emerging information age and implicit in notions of multimedia, networking, telecommunications, and information. Designed to involve the public in playful, participatory interactions, situationist and Fluxus games were similarly conceived to decondition and activate individual and collective creativity and free will in a bid to stymie control culture.

New Babylon exemplifies a concept for a situationist city that integrated art, science (cybernetics), and technologies in service of the life of homo ludens. As conceived by Constant, this cybernetic utopia détourned (rerouted) Le Corbusier's centralized, technocratic urbanism, which was similarly conceived as a synthesis of art and technology and was positioned, as Le Corbusier proclaimed, to prevent revolution. In contrast, spanning a global network of environments, *New Babylon* modeled a global playground designed to be continuously changed at the ludic pleasure of its inhabitants.

Fluxus games were embedded in the group's subversive parody of international corporatization and quest for alternatives to institutionalized/

commodified culture. On the one hand, these games were democratically accessible through Fluxus mail-order catalogs and Fluxshops in Europe, Asia, and the United States. On the other hand, Fluxus games illustrate the concept of intermedia as a strategy to jettison the object in favor of fusing genres, forms, and media to create open-ended interactions. Some games involve play that destroys the object. Others point to the notion that play itself is what determines the game's structure. Yet, others stress the cultivation of sensory pleasure as a political position against rationalism. All extend Dada's provocations, as they challenge the audience/player to decide how to play, to invent the rules of participation for themselves.

Cold War research into new technologies, and in particular computers and computer networks, provided inadvertently for extraordinary, even if brief, synergy between utopian currents in the arts, sciences, and counterculture. In one regard, against the centralist and zero-sum logic of Cold War game theory, the games emerging out of this synergy illustrated new notions of ecology, which, reconceived as the study and practice concerning the symbiosis/interdependence between human, machine, and their environment, became a shared focus for concretizing a more peaceful and sustainable world. Conversely, as a rerouting of militarized technologies and networks toward the creation of a framework for global, civic, and creative participation and reciprocal interactions, these games elaborated and projected avant-garde strategies of détournment cross-culturally and ultimately into digital culture.

At the time, the digital avant-gardes engaged computers ambivalently. Some artists, such as Charles Csuri and others involved in the *9 Evenings* events, mobilized computers and other technologies to create games intended as antiwar statements. Others, such as Roy Ascott, repositioned computers and computer networks as global playgrounds, where remote artists and audiences literally participated in creating an imaginary, fairytale-like world, a telematics of utopia.

Ascott's notion of computer networks as spaces of utopian globality, as an open, participatory, borderless, interconnected, and emergent ecology, resonated if not in the art world, then with countercultural designers and entrepreneurs. R. Buckminster Fuller's *World Game* championed this idea as science-based design intent on enabling popular participation in matters of communal stewardship so as to circumvent centralized government altogether. In the proximity of Cold War labs, and in today's Silicon Valley, countercultural entrepreneurs like Stewart Brand promoted this decentralist ethos via the *Whole Earth Catalogue*, a publication reminiscent of Fluxus catalogs but much more successful in its wide reach of a cross-cultural audience captivated by its message, namely that cybernetics and cybernetic technologies in the hands of citizens empowered utopian change; that is, their capacity to independently and individually participate in creating an environmentally and socially sustainable world. Among others, Brand promoted, in revolutionary terms, the hacker as a countercultural engineer working toward this goal by furthering democratic access to computers, and hacker games as tools that could be mobilized toward sharing technological expertise so as to empower civic agency and networks.

Tactical media (TM) emerged post–Cold War in the early 1990s, alongside control societies postmodernity, as a global informational corporatism built on the enclosure of modernist utopian currents as hackers turned entrepreneurs in the 1980s. TM included transnational networks of artists, designers, hackers, technologists, professionals, and civic society, in collaborations aimed at developing new modes of resistance appropriate to this context. Spanning exploits of digital technologies and networks, which they deemed electronic civil disobedience, TM strategies merged techniques developed in avant-garde art and counterculture, from détournement to hacking, in order to slow down and disrupt information flows vital to the informational economy.

TM interventions into games were but a subset of the domains identified as relevant to this form of playful activism. As corporate, white, heteronormative-coded spaces, video games, as TM practitioners concluded, were emblematic of the overall regressive ideologies behind the utopian rhetoric accompanying the marketing of digital technologies, including video games, as tools of individual empowerment and transformation. Conversely, video games provided TM practitioners the ability to reach a broad, transnational, and already captive audience, yet disconnected from art and activism. The malleable forms of video games, that is, their built-in capabilities for modification, was additionally attractive. TM interventions into video games include media stunts, provocations, covert infiltrations, and overt implications of the player, either through direct participation or by way of projects designed to impart skills and knowledge such as to allow replication.

Early interventions, such as RTMark's *SimCopter*, Mongrel's *Blacklash*, Natalie Bookchin's *The Intruder*, and Critical Art Ensemble's *KidFighter*, each test different approaches to electronic civil disobedience, respectively, as an insider sabotage of a video game, as two hijackings of search engines online, and as an instructional hack of a game console involving the public. Toywar represents both a combination of all of these strategies and concrete proof of the relevance of electronic civil disobedience as a form of resistance, as it successfully mobilized transnational and cross-cultural players against a corporation (e-commerce).

Subsequent TM-inspired interventions in multiplayer online games emerge post-9/11 as mainstream gaming culture takes a realist turn, entrenching digital play in militarization and xenophobia. Anne-Marie Schleiner's *Velvet-Strike* and Joseph DeLappe's *Dead-in-Iraq* represent highly publicized antiwar interventions into militarized game spaces. Two shooter games are themed on the war on terror, one of which, *America's Army*, is publically financed and designed on behest of the United States Army to recruit gamers for drone warfare. The other, Wafaa Bilal's *Domestic Tension*, where the Iraq-born artist inserts himself as a living target in simulation of the circumstances of civilians under drone war, evidences most concretely the relevance of video games for utopian politics, as beyond attracting national and international media attention, the project involved participants in 128 countries, with Bilal's site receiving eighty million hits.

The emergence of urban games, enabled through miniaturization, mobility, and technological integration, provide yet another focus of TM-inspired interventions designed to counter global urbanism as spaces shaped by rising nationalism, surveillance, and xenophobic sentiment post-9/11. An early project, Schleiner's *Operation Urban Terrain*, repurposed mobile technologies to synchronize dissent in *America's Army* and on the ground, on the streets of New York, to amplify antiwar protests. Iván Abréu Ochoa's *Cross Coordinates* integrated art, technology, and design against the militarization of the Mexico–US border in El Paso, through playful and symbolic collaborations involving local and global citizens. *Gendered Strategies for Loitering* used a video game to promote access to urban space as a form of pleasure and right of all citizens of India, regardless of gender, class, or religious affiliations. In 2020, it still serves as inspiration to ongoing and similarly conceived playful interventions into urban spaces by coalitions of cisgender, trans, and queer women in India, Pakistan, and South Africa, organizing and coordinating them through social media and mobile platforms.

Developing in parallel to TM interventions in games and the mainstream gaming industry, game designers are today at the forefront of the creation of a vibrant and still emerging gaming culture attuned to transnational, Indigenous, feminist, and queer perspectives and altogether sharing in intent: to transform gaming into a democratic platform.

Conceived as an intervention into the commodification of the public sphere, and working to leverage the allure of video games on behalf of progressive change, these games go against the dominance of mimesis and commodity in mainstream games. They integrate gaming with Western and non-Western avant-garde art, countercultural currents, Indigenous art and storytelling, and feminist and queer media forms and expressions, among others, and are distributed for free or at low cost via digital networks and platforms. These games are not only designed to insert and circulate marginalized points of view into gaming culture (and, in practice, the global spaces of digital media) but also to open them up to the public. Hence, the focus of some of these designers is on readapting open-source platforms, so as to enable broad participation in repositioning gaming as a decentered, multiple, and participatory process.

As an early example, Gonzalo Frasca's concept of video games of the oppressed juxtaposes Latin American and European forms of participatory theater into short simulations designed to create collective awareness about the political dynamics of the war on terror and to persuade the player to join in to change them. Inspired by TM, Molleindustria's *Phone Story* hijacks Apple's and Google's platforms (app stores) to not only educate about the labor and environmental exploitation behind these companies' products but, additionally, to allow players to participate in supporting labor struggles via monetary donations to activist organizations. Yet, other designers collaborate with artists, community organizations, educators, and student populations from marginalized communities to capacitate their creation of games reflective of these communities' experiences and histories. Games like *Tropical America* and *Never Alone* mobilize video games as tools of radical pedagogy, invoking and expanding the anticolonial legacy of Freirean pedagogy.

Most recently, feminist, queer, and transgender game designers have seized on open-source, easy-to-use software, like Twine, to create and invite global creation of games alternative to mainstream models. In the hands of Zoë Quinn, Charity Heartscape Porpentine, and Anna Anthropy, among others, gaming becomes a framework for sharing intimate, personal stories. Taking the open forms of poetic exchanges, and ranging in topics marginalized in mainstream gaming, such as depression, transitioning, and BDSM role-play, their work altogether challenges heteronormative notions of these technologies as tools of mastery and control. Combined with tutorials and invitations to join in, they suggest that gaming is a technology that can potentialize processes of discovery and transformation, rather than offer resolved and closed stories. The backlash against these designers and allies, GamerGate, is then not just an attempt at enforcing cultural gatekeeping but, most significantly, concrete evidence of the continued relevance of games as spaces of utopian politics.

As it emerges in this book, radical gaming repurposes and extends modernist avant-garde strategies through the spaces of technology and mass media, and in so doing, elaborates on the utopian ethos of these currents as a transformative cultural expression that resists fitting the confines of linear historicism of or in modernity. Operationalized through media and technological networks, radical gaming has expanded the utopian tradition of modernist avant-garde art cross-culturally, both as an inter- and transdisciplinary practice and domain, and as a current not restricted to the Global North but rather a global phenomenon relevant to the contexts of contemporary digital culture. Repositioned in the transnational spaces of technology, subversions of games as an exclusively corporate, male, white, heteronormative-coded domain are then not only an expression of an emerging politicized culture in contemporary gaming but also of ongoing and evolving reimaginations of the utopian tradition of modernism as yet unfinished processes.

REFERENCES

Aceti, Lanfranco, Tihomir Milovac, and Ozden Sahin, eds. *Dislocations, Leonardo Electronic Almanac* 2, vol. 18. 2012. https://www.leoalmanac.org/vol18-no2-dislocations/.

Ades, Dawn, ed. *The Dada Reader: A Critical Anthology*. London: Tate Publishing, 2006.

Ahl, David H., ed. "BASIC Computer Games." Atari Archives. 1978. http://www.atariarchives.org/basicgames/showpage.php?page=cover.

———. "Basic Computer Games: Small Basic 2010." 2010. https://www.kidwaresoftware.com/DavidAhlsBasicComputerAdventures/.

Albrecht, Robert. *What to Do after You Hit Return or P.C.C.'s First Book of Computer Games.* Menlo Park, CA: People's Computer, 1975.

Albright, Thomas. "New Art School: Correspondence Art." *Rolling Stone* 106, April 13, 1972, 32.

———. "Correspondence Art." *Rolling Stone* 107, April 27, 1972, 28–29.

Alexander, Leight. "Online Abuse: How Women Are Fighting Back." *Guardian*, April 13, 2016. https://www.theguardian.com/technology/2016/apr/13/online-abuse-how-women-are-fighting-back.

Andreotti, Libero, and Internationale Situationniste. *Theory of the Dérive and Other Situationist Writings on the City.* Barcelona: Museu d'Art Contemporani de Barcelona, 1996.

Anthropy, Anna. *Rise of the Videogame Zinesters: How Freaks, Normals, Amateurs, Artists, Dreamers, Dropouts, Queers, Housewives, and People Like You Are Taking Back an Art Form.* New York: Seven Stories, 2012.

Artundo, Patricia M., ed. *Alexandro Xul Solar: Entrevistas, Artículos y Textos Inéditos.* Buenos Aires: Corregidor, 2006.

Ascott, Roy. "Distance Makes the Art Grow Further: Distributed Authorship and Telematic Textuality in *La Plissure Du Texte.*" In *At a Distance: Precursors to Art and Activism on the Internet,* edited by Annmarie Chandler and Norie Neumark, 282–296. Cambridge, MA: MIT Press, 2005.

Association des amis de Benjamin Péret (website). Accessed April 6, 2020. http://www.benjamin-peret.org/.

Baer, Ralph H. *Videogames: In the Beginning.* Springfield, NJ: Rolenta, 2005.

Bagnall, Gregory L. "Queer(ing) Gaming Technologies: Thinking on Constructions of Normativity Inscribed in Digital Gaming Hardware." In *Queer Game Studies,* edited by Adrienne Shaw and Bonnie Ruberg, 135–143. Minneapolis: University of Minnesota Press, 2017.

Bakhtin, Mikhail. *Rabelais and His World.* Translated by Hélène Iswolsky. Bloomington: Indiana University Press, 1984.

Ball, Hugo. *Flight Out of Time: A Dada Diary.* Translated by Ann Raimes. Berkeley: University of California Press, 1996.

Barry, Ellen. "The Dilbert Front." *Boston Phoenix*, January 1998.

Bateson, Gregory. *Steps to an Ecology of Mind.* Chicago: The University of Chicago Press, 1972.

Baudemann, Kristina. "Indigenous Futurisms in North American Indigenous Art." *Extrapolation* 57, no. 1–2 (2016): 117–150.

Baudrillard, Jean. *Seduction.* Translated by Brian Singer. New York: St. Martin's, 1990.

———. *Simulacra and Simulation.* Translated by Sharia Faria Glazer. Ann Arbor, MI: University of Michigan Press, 1994.

———. *Simulations.* Translated by Paul Foss, Paul Patton and Philip Beitchman. Los Angeles: Semiotext(e), 1983.

Becker-Ho, Alice, and Guy Debord. *A Game of War.* Translated by Donald Nicholson-Smith. London: Atlas, 2007.

Benhabib, Seyla. "Models of Public Space: Hannah Arendt, the Liberal Tradition, and Jürgen Habermas." In *Habermas and the Public Sphere*, edited by Craig Calhoun, 73–98. Cambridge, MA: MIT Press, 1999.

Benjamin, Walter. "Surrealism: The Last Snapshot of the European Intelligentsia." In *Selected Writings 1927–1930*, edited by Michael William Jennings, Howard Eiland, and Gary Smith, 2:207–221. Cambridge, MA: Harvard University Press, 1999.

Benson, Timothy O. "Mysticism, Materialism, and the Machine in Berlin Dada." *Art Journal* 46, no. 1 (Spring 1987): 46–55.

Bergson, Henry. *Creative Evolution.* Translated by Arthur Mitchell. New York: Henry Holt, 1911.

———. *Laughter: An Essay on the Meaning of the Comic.* Translated by Cloudesley Shovell and Fred Rothwell. New York: Macmillan, 1914.

Berréby, Gérard, ed. *Documents Relatifs `a la Fondation de l'Internationale Situationniste: 1948–1957.* Paris: Allia, 1985.

Bey, Hakim, and Moorish Orthodox Radio Crusade Collective. *Immediatism.* San Francisco, CA: AK Press, 2001.

Bey, Hakim. "Ontological Anarchy in a Nutshell." 1993. https://users.aalto.fi/~saarit2/deoxy /hakim/ontologicalanarchy.htm.

Bilal, Wafaa, and Kari Lydersen. *Shoot an Iraqi: Art, Life and Resistance Under the Gun.* San Francisco: City Lights, 2008.

Bilton, Nick. "One on One: Jack Tretton, Sony C.E.O. America." *New York Times*, July 13, 2011. http://bits.blogs.nytimes.com/2011/06/13/one-on-one-jack-tretton-sony-c-e-o-america/.

Biro, Matthew. *Dada Cyborg: Visions of the New Human in Weimar Berlin.* Minneapolis: University of Minnesota Press, 2009.

Bishop, Claire. *Artificial Hells: Participatory Art and the Politics of Spectatorship.* New York: Verso Books, 2012.

Bittanti, Matteo. "Anne-Marie Schleiner, Brody Condon & Joan Leandre: Velvet-Strike, 2002." In *GameScenes: Art in the Age of Videogames*, edited by Matteo Bittanti and Domenico Quaranta, 413–414. Milano: Johan & Levi Editore, 2006.

Blas, Zach. "Queer Technologies." Artist presentation at ISEA 2008, Singapore. http://www .isea2008singapore.org/abstract/s-z/p217.html.

Blauvelt, Andrew. *Hippie Modernism: The Struggle for Utopia.* New York: Art Publishers and Minneapolis: Walker Art Center, 2015. Exhibition catalogue.

Bloch, Ernst. *The Principle of Hope.* Translated by Neville Plaice, Stephen Plaice, and Paul Knight. 3 vols. Cambridge, MA: MIT Press, 1995.

Boal, Augusto. *Games for Actors and Non-Actors.* Translated by Adrian Jackson. London: Routledge, 1992.

Bogost, Ian. *Persuasive Games: The Expressive Power of Videogames.* Cambridge, MA: MIT Press, 2007.

———. *Unit Operations: An Approach to Videogame Criticism.* Cambridge, MA: MIT Press, 2006.

Bogost, Ian, Simon Ferrari, and Bobby Schweizer. *NewsGames: Journalism at Play.* Cambridge, MA: MIT Press, 2010.

Borges, Jorge Luis, and María Kodama. *Atlas.* Buenos Aires: Editorial Sudamericana, 1984.

———. *Collected Fictions.* Translated by Andrew Hurley. New York: Viking, 1998.

Boyko, Brian. "Interview with Wafaa Bilal: Lessons about Dehumanization and Technology from a Man Living under the Gun." In *Network Performance Daily* (May 18, 2007).

Boyle, Michael Shane. "Aura of the Archive: Confronting the Incendiary Fliers of Kommune 1." *Performing Arts Resources*, no. 28 (2011): 297–303.

Brand, Stewart. "*Spacewar:* Fanatic Life and Symbolic Death among the Computer Bums." *Rolling Stone*, December 1972. http://wheels.org/spacewar/stone/rolling _stone.html.

Brecht, Bertolt. "The Radio as an Apparatus of Communication." Telematic Connections. Accessed April 6, 2020. http://telematic.walkerart.org/telereal/bit_brecht.html.

Breton, André. *Anthology of Black Humor.* Translated by Mark Polizzotti. San Francisco, CA: City Lights, 1997.

———. "Le Jeux de Marseille." Edited by David Hare. *VVV* 4 (1944): 89–90.

———. "The Lighthouse." *Le Libertaire*, November 1, 1952. http://raforum.info/spip.php ?article2408&lang=fr.

———. *L'un Dans L'autre.* Paris: Eric Losfeld, 1970.

———. "Manifesto of Surrealism (1924)." In *Manifestoes of Surrealism.* Translated by Richard Seaver and Helen R. Lane. Ann Arbor: University of Michigan Press, 1972.

———. "To the Light House." In *Drunken Boat: Art, Rebellion, Anarchy*, edited by Max Blechman and translated by Doug Imrie and Michale William, 159–161. New York: Autonomedia, 1994.

Breton, André, and Leon Trotsky. "For an Independent Revolution in Art (1938)." Generation Online. Accessed April 6, 2020. http://www.generation-online.org/c/fcsurrealism1 .htm.

Brotchie, Alastair, and Mel Gooding. *A Book of Surrealist Games.* London: Shambhala, 1995.

Broue, Pierre. *The German Revolution, 1917–1923.* Chicago: Haymarket Books, 2006.

Buck-Morss, Susan. *Hegel, Haiti, and Universal History.* Pittsburgh: University of Pittsburgh Press, 2009.

Bürger, Peter. *Theory of the Avant-Garde.* Translated by Michael Snow. Minneapolis: University of Minnesota Press, 1992.

Burnham, Jack. *Beyond Modern Sculpture.* New York: George Braziller, 1968.

———. "Systems Esthetics." In *Great Western Salt Works—Essay on Meaning of Post-Formalist Art*, edited by Jack Burnham, 15–26. New York: Braziller, 1974.

Bush, Vannevar. "As We May Think." In *The New Media Reader*, edited by Noah Wardrip-Fruin and Nick Montfort, 35–47. Cambridge, MA: MIT Press, 2003.

Cage, John. "Experimental Music." In *Silence: Lectures and Writings*, edited by John Cage, 7–12. Middletown, CT: Wesleyan University Press, 1961.

Cahun, Claude. *Disavowals: Or Cancelled Confessions.* Translated by Susan de Muth. Cambridge, MA: MIT Press, 2008.

Caro, Mark. "A Point-and-Shoot Exhibit Display's Creator Lives under the Gun Controlled by Web Viewers." *Chicago Tribune*, May 10, 2007. http://www.chicagotribune.com /news/nationworld/chi0705091398may10,1,6307515.story?ctrack=2&cset=true.

Certeau, Michel de. *The Practice of Everyday Life*. Translated by Steven Rendall. Berkeley: University of California Press, 1984.

Chang, Alenda Y. *Playing Nature: Ecology in Videogames*. Minneapolis: University of Minnesota Press, 2019.

Chapman, Adam. *Digital Games as History: How Videogames Represent the Past and Offer Access to Historical Practice*. New York: Routledge, 2016.

Chun, Wendy Hui Kyong. *Control and Freedom: Power and Paranoia in the Age of Fiber Optics*. Cambridge, MA: MIT Press, 2006.

———. *Programmed Visions: Software and Memory*. Cambridge, MA: MIT Press, 2011.

Ciociola, Chiara. "Phone Story behind Apple Allure." *Neural* 41 (Winter 2012). http://www .neural.it/art/2012/04/phone_story_behind_apple_allur. phtml.

Clark, Patricia E., Ulises A. Mejias, Peter Cavana, Daniel Herson, and Sharon M. Strong. "Interactive Social Media and the Art of Telling Stories: Strategies for Social Justice through Oswego.net 2010: Racism on Campus." In *Activist Art in Social Justice Pedagogy*, edited by Barbara Beyerbach and R. Deborah Davis, 171–185. New York: Peter Lang, 2011.

Clarke, Andy, and Grethe Mitchel, eds. *Videogames and Art*. Chicago: Intellect, 2007.

Clynes, Manfred E., and Nathan S. Kline. "Cyborgs and Space." *Astronautics*, September 1960, 26–28, 75–76. http://cyberneticzoo.com/wp-content/uploads/2012/01 /cyborgs-Astronautics-sep1960.pdf.

Codrescu, Andrei. *The Posthuman Dada Guide: Tzara and Lenin Play Chess*. Princeton, NJ: Princeton University Press, 2009.

Colebrook, Claire. *Deleuze and the Meaning of Life*. New York: Continuum International, 2010.

Conzen, Ina, Staatsgalerie Stuttgart, and Karl-Ernst-Osthaus-Museum. *Art Games: Die Schachteln Der Fluxusku"nstler*. Sohm Dossier 1. Stuttgart: Staatsgalerie, 1997.

Crandall, Jordan. "Anything That Moves: Armed Vision." *CTheory*, June 15, 1999. http:// ctheory.net/articles.aspx?id=115.

Critical Art Ensemble. Accessed April 20, 2020. http://www.critical-art.net/.

———. "Critical Art Ensemble Defense Fund." 2004. http://critical-art.net/defense/overview .html.

———. *Digital Resistance: Explorations in Tactical Media*. New York: Autonomedia, 2001.

———. *Electronic Civil Disobedience & Other Unpopular Ideas*. New York: Autonomedia, 1996.

———. *The Electronic Disturbance*. Brooklyn: Autonomedia, 1994.

———. "Recombinant Theater and Digital Resistance." *Drama Review* 44, no. 4 (Winter 2000): 151–166.

Critical Art Ensemble and Carbon Defense League. "Super Kid Fighter." 1999. Selectparks. Added on July 6, 2004. http://ljudmila.org/~selectparks/modules.php?name= Downloads&d_op=search&query=super%20kid%20fighter.

Couchot, Edmond. *Images. De l'optique au numérique*. Paris: Hermès, 1988.

Crogan, Patrick. *Gameplay Mode: War, Simulation and Technoculture*. Minneapolis: University of Minnesota Press, 2011.

Csuri, Charles. Charles A. Csuri Project. Ohio State University, 2007. https://csuriproject .osu.edu/.

Dali, Salvador. *The Collected Writings of Salvador Dali.* Translated by Haim Finkelstein. Cambridge, UK: Cambridge University Press, 1998.

———. "The Object as Revealed in Surrealist Experiment." In *Surrealists on Art,* edited by Lucy R. Lippard, 87–97. New Jersey: Prentice-Hall, 1970.

———. "The Stinking Ass." In *Surrealists on Art,* edited by Lucy R. Lippard, 97–100. New Jersey: Prentice-Hall, 1970.

Davis, Erik. *TechGnosis: Myth, Magic, and Mysticism in the Age of Information.* New York: Harmony, 1998.

Debord, Guy. *Comments on the Society of the Spectacle.* Translated by Malcolm Imrie. London: Verso, 1998.

———. "Contribution to a Situationist Definition of Play." Situationist International Online. Accessed April 6, 2020. http://www.cddc.vt.edu/sionline/si/play.html.

———. *Correspondence: The Foundation of the Situationist International (June 1957–August 1960).* Translated by Stuart Kendall and John McHale. Los Angeles: Semiotext(e), 2009.

———. "Correspondence avec un Cyberneticien." *Internationalle Situationiste* 9 (Paris, August 1964), 4, reprinted in *Internationale Situationiste 1958–1969*, 44–48. Accessed April 6, 2020. http://www.mai68.org/textes/IS_Revue-Internationale-Situationniste/IS /i-situationniste.blogspot.com/2007/04/correspondance-avec-un-cyberneticien.html.

———. "L'avant-garde de la presence." In *Internationalle Situationiste* 8 (January1963). http://www.mai68.org/textes/IS_Revue-Internationale-Situationniste/IS /i-situationniste.blogspot.com/2007/04/avant-garde-de-la-presence.html.

———. "The Situationists and the New Action Forms in Politics and Art." In *Situationist International Anthology,* edited and translated by Ken Knabb, 402–407. Berkeley: Bureau of Public Secrets, 2006.

———. *The Society of the Spectacle.* Translated by Donald Nicholson-Smith. Cambridge, MA: Zone Books, 1994.

———. "Theory of the Dérive." In *Situationist International Anthology,* edited and translated by Ken Knabb, 62–66. Berkeley: Bureau of Public Secrets, 2006.

———. "Untitled Text." In *Situationist International Anthology,* edited and translated(by Ken Knabb, 476–478. Berkeley: Bureau of Public Secrets, 2006.

Debord, Guy, Gianfranco Sanguinetti, and Internationale Situationniste. *The Real Split in the International: Theses on the Situationist International and Its Time, 1972.* Translated by John McHale. London: Pluto, 2003.

Debord, Guy, and Gil Wolman. "A User's Guide to Détournement." In *Situationist International Anthology,* edited and translated by Ken Knabb, 14–20. Berkeley: Bureau of Public Secrets, 2006.

DeLappe, Joseph. "Dead-in-Iraq," 2006–2011. http://www.delappe.net/project/dead-in-iraq/.

———. "America's Diplomat." 2009. http://www.delappe.net/intervene/fake-new-york-times/.

Deleuze, Gilles. "'Postscript of the Societies of Control." In *Negotiations,* translated by Martin Joughin, 177–182. New York: Columbia University Press, 1995.

Deleuze, Gilles, and Felix Guattari. *Anti-Oedipus: Capitalism and Schizophrenia.* Translated by Robert Hurley, Mark Seem, and Helen R. Lane. London: Continuum, 2004.

———. *What is Philosophy?* Translated by Hugh Tomlinson. New York: Columbia University Press, 1994.

Dery, Mark. *Escape Velocity: Cyberculture at the End of the Century.* New York: Grove, 1996.

Dieter, Michael. "The Becoming Environmental of Power: Tactical Media after Control." *The Fibreculture Journal* 18 (2011): 177–205.

Dillon, Grace. "Indigenous Futurisms, Bimaashi Biidaas Mose, Flying and Walking towards You." *Extrapolation* 57, no. 1–2 (2016): 1–6.

Dosse, François. *Gilles Deleuze and Felix Guattari: Intersecting Lives.* Translated by Deborah Glassman. New York: Colombia University Press, 2010.

Downie, Louise, ed. *Don't Kiss Me: The Art of Claude Cahun and Marcel Moore.* London: Aperture/Tate, 2006.

Duchamp, Marcel, and Vitaly Halberstadt. *Opposition et Cases Conjugu'ees sont Reconcili'ees/Opposition und Schwesterfelder sind durch Vers'ohnt/Opposition and Sister Squares Are Reconciled.* Paris: L'Editions l'Echiquier, 1932.

Duncombe, Stephen. *Dream: Re-imagining Progressive Politics in an Age of Fantasy.* New York: New Press, 2007.

Dyer-Witheford, Nick, and Greig de Peuter. *Games of Empire: Global Capitalism and Video Games.* Minneapolis: University of Minnesota Press, 2009.

———. "Games of Multitude." In *Fibreculture Journal* 16 (2010). http://sixteen.fibre culturejournal.org/games-of-multitude/.

Dyson, Frances. "Art and Technology." In *Then It Was Now.* 2006. https://www .fondation-langlois.org/html/e/page.php?NumPage=2156.

Edwards, Paul N. *The Closed World: Computers and the Politics of Discourse in Cold War America.* Cambridge, MA: MIT Press, 1996.

Efland, Arthur. "An Interview with Charles Csuri." In *Cybernetic Serendipity: The Computer and the Arts*, edited by Jasia Reichardt, 81–84. New York: Frederick A. Praeger, 1968.

Einstein, Carl. "On Primitive Art." Translated by Charles W. Haxthausen. In *October* 105 (Summer 2003): 124.

Enzensberger, Ulrich. *Die Jahre der Kommune I. Berlin 1967–1969.* Köln: Kiepenheuer & Witsch, 2004.

Etoy.com. "Toywar." 1999. http://toywar.etoy.com/.

Everett, Anna. *Digital Diaspora: A Race for Cyberspace.* New York: SUNY Press, 2009.

Everett, Anna, and Craig Watkins. "The Power of Play: The Portrayal and Performance of Race in Videogames." In *The Ecology of Games: Connecting Youth, Games, and Learning*, edited by Katie Salen, 141–166. Cambridge, MA: MIT Press, 2008.

Experiments in Art and Technology. *Pavilion.* New York: E. P. Dutton, 1972.

Feldman, Hannah. "National Negotiations: Art, Historical Experience, and the Public in Paris, 1945–1962." PhD diss., Columbia University, 2004.

Fernández, María, and Faith Wilding, "Situating Cyberfeminisms." In *Domain Errors! Cyberfeminist Practices*, edited by María Fernández, Faith Wilding, and Michelle M. Wright, 17–28. New York: Autonomedia, 2002.

Fernández, María. "'Aesthetically Potent Environments,' or How Gordon Pask Detourned Instrumental Cybernetics." In *White Heat, Cold Logic: British Computer Art 1960–1980*, edited by Paul Brown, Charlie Gere, Nicholas Lambert, and Catherine Mason, 53–70. Cambridge, MA: MIT Press, 2008.

———. "Cyberfeminism, Racism, Embodiment." In *Domain Errors!: Cyberfeminist Practices*, edited by María Fernández, Faith Wilding, and Michelle M. Wright, 29–44. New York: Autonomedia, 2002.

———. "Life-Like: Historicizing Process and Responsiveness in Digital Art." In *The Art of Art History*, edited by Donald Preziosi, 468–487. Oxford, UK: Oxford University Press, 2009.

Fernback, Jan, and Brad Thompson. "Virtual Communities: Abort, Retry, Failure?" 1995. http://www.well.com/user/hlr/texts/VCcivil.html.

Filipovic, Elena. "Surrealism in 1938: The Exhibition at War." In *Surrealism, Politics and Culture*, edited by Raymond Spiteri and Donald LaCoss, 179–203. London: Ashgate, 2003.

Filliou, Robert. "La Cedille Qui Sourit." In *Lehren und Lernen als Auffuehrungskuen ste/ Teaching and Learning as Performance Arts*, edited by Kasper König, 198–204. New York: Verlag Gebr. Koenig, 1970.

Flanagan, Mary. *Critical Play: Radical Game Design*. Cambridge, MA: MIT Press, 2009.

———. "Hyperbodies, Hyperknowledge: Women in Games, Women in Cyberpunk, and Strategies of Resistance." In *Reload: Rethinking Women + Cyberculture*, edited by Mary Flanagan and Austin Booth, 425–455. Cambridge, MA: MIT Press, 2002.

Flanagan, Mary, and Austin Booth, eds. *Reload: Rethinking Women + Cyberculture*. Cambridge, MA: MIT Press, 2002.

Fluegelman, Andrew, and New Games Foundation. *The New Games Book*. New York: Dolphin Books/Doubleday, 1976.

———. *More New Games! And Playful Ideas from the New Games Foundation*. New York: Dolphin Books/Doubleday, 1981.

Fogg, B. J. *Persuasive Technology: Using Computers to Change What We Think and Do*. San Francisco: Morgan Kaufmann, 2003.

Foster, Hal. *The Return of the Real: Art and Theory at the End of the Century*. Cambridge, MA: MIT Press, 1996.

Foster, Stephen C. "The Mortality of Roles: Johannes Baader and Spiritual Materialism." In *Dada Culture: Critical Texts on the Avantgarde*, edited by Dafydd Jones, 187–199. New York: Rodopi, 2006.

Foster, Stephen C., and Hanne Benguis. *The History of Dada: Dada Triumphs! Berlin Dada 1917–1923*. Vol. 5, *Crisis and the Arts*. Farmington Hills, MI: G K Hall, 2003.

Frasca, Gonzalo. "Rethinking Agency and Immersion: Videogames as a Means of Consciousness-Raising." Presentation at SIGGRAPH 2001, August 12–17, Los Angeles, CA, 2001. http://www. ludology.com.

———. "Videogames of the Oppressed: Critical Thinking, Education, Tolerance, and Other Trivial Issues." In *First Person, New Media as Story, Performance, and Game*, edited by Noah Wardrip-Fruin and Pat Harrigan, 85–94. Cambridge, MA: MIT Press, 2004.

Fraser, Nancy. "Rethinking the Public Sphere: A Contribution to the Critique of Actually Existing Democracy." In *Habermas and the Public Sphere*, edited by Craig Calhoun, 109–142. Cambridge, MA: MIT Press, 1992.

Freiberger, Paul, and Michael Swaine. *Fire in the Valley: The Making of the Personal Computer*. Berkeley, CA: Osborne/McGraw-Hill, 1984.

Friedman, Ken. "Forty Years of Fluxus." 1989. http://www.mostowa2.net/angelpastor /kfriedman40yearsoffluxus.html.

———. "The Early Days of Mail Art." In *Eternal Network: A Mail Art Anthology*, edited by Chuck Welch, 3–16. Calgary, Alberta, Canada: University of Calgary Press, 1995.

Fuller, Matthew. *Behind the Blip: Essays on the Culture of Software*. New York: Autonomedia, 2003.

———. "Interview with Mongrel." http://www.nettime.org/Lists-Archives/nettime-l-9902 /msg00077.html.

Fuller, R. Buckminster. "Everything I Know" (televised lecture). Open Culture. 1975. http:// www.openculture.com/2012/08/ieverything_i_knowi_42_hours_of_visionary _buckminster_fuller_lectures_1975.html.

———. *Operating Manual for Spaceship Earth.* Carbondale, IL: Southern Illinois University Press, 1969.

———. *Synergetics: Explorations in the Geometry of Thinking.* 1979. http://www.rwgray projects.com/synergetics/synergetics.html.

———. *Utopia or Oblivion: The Prospects for Humanity.* New York: Bantam Books, 1969.

———. *The World Game: Integrative Resource Utilization Planning Tool.* World Game Series: Document 1. Carbondale, IL: Southern Illinois University, 1971.

Fusco, Coco. "Electronic Disturbance." In *Anarchitexts, Voices from the Global Digital Resistance,* edited by Joanne Richardson, 98–106. New York: Autonomedia, 2003.

Galloway, Alexander. "Debord's Nostalgic Algorithm." *Culture Machine* 10 (2009): 131–156.

———. *Gaming: Essays on Algorithmic Culture.* Minneapolis: University of Minnesota Press, 2006.

Galloway, Alexander, and Eugene Thacker. *The Exploit.* Minneapolis: University of Minnesota Press, 2007.

Gammel, Irene. *Baroness Elsa: Gender, Dada, and Everyday Modernity.* Cambridge, MA: MIT Press, 2002.

Garcia, David, and Geert Lovink. "The ABC of Tactical Media." In *Anarchitexts: Voices from the Global Digital Resistance,* edited by Joanne Richardson, 107–114. New York: Autonomedia, 2003.

Garrigues, Emmanuel, ed. *Archives du Surrealisme, Les Jeux Surréalistes Mars 1921–Septembre 1962.* Paris: Gallimard, 1995.

Gates, Bill. "An Open Letter to Hobbyists." *Homebrew Computer Club Newsletter* 2, no. 1 (January 31, 1976). http://www.digibarn.com/collections/newsletters/homebrew/V2_01 /index.html.

Gere, Charlie. *Digital Culture.* London: Reaktion Books, 2002.

Getsy, David, ed. *From Diversion to Subversion: Games, Play, and Twentieth-Century Art.* University Park: Pennsylvania State University Press, 2011.

Gibson, William. *Neuromancer.* New York: Ace Books, 1984.

Gilman, Claire. "Asger Jorn's Avant-Garde Archives." In *Guy Debord and the Situationist International,* edited by Tom McDonough, 189–212. Cambridge, MA: MIT Press, 2001.

Gilroy, Paul. *Postcolonial Melancholia.* New York: Colombia University Press, 2006.

Giraudy, Daniéle, and Musée Cantini. *Le jeu de Marseille: Autour d'André Breton et des Surréalistes á Marseille en 1940–1941.* Marseille: Alors Hors Du Temps, 2003.

Glass, Liz. "Stirring the Intermix: An Interview with Tony Martin." In *Hippie Modernism: The Struggle for Utopia,* edited by Andrew Blauvelt, 403–410. New York: Art Publishers and Minneapolis: Walker Art Center, 2015. Exhibition catalogue.

Glowski, Janice M., ed. *Charles A. Csuri: Beyond Boundaries, 1963–Present.* Columbus: Ohio State University College of Arts, 2006. Exhibition catalogue.

Gradowczyk, Mario Horacio. *Alexandro Xul Solar.* Buenos Aires: Ediciones Alba, 1994.

Graetz, J. M. "The Origin of Spacewar." *Creative Computing,* August 1981, 56–57.

Gradowczyk, Mario Horacio. *Alexandro Xul Solar.* Buenos Aires: Ediciones Alba, 1994.

Graham, Beryl. "New Media, 'Community Art,' and Net.Art Activism. Interviews with Natalie Bookchin and Brendan Jackson." *Crumb*. 2001. http://www.crumbweb.org /getInterviewDetail.php?id=3&op=3.

Greenberg, Clement. "Avant-Garde and Kitsch." *The Partisan Review*, Fall 1939, 34–49.

Guattari, Félix. *Chaosmosis: An Ethico-Aesthetic Paradigm*. Translated by Paul Bains and Julian Pefanis. Bloomington: Indiana University Press, 1995.

———. *Soft Subversions*. Edited by Sylvere Lotringer. Translated by David L. Sweet and Chet Wiener. New York: Semiotext(e)/Autonomedia, 1996.

Habermas, Jürgen. *The Structural Transformation of the Public Sphere: An Inquiry into a Category of Bourgeois Society*. Translated by Thomas Burger and Frederick Lawrence. Cambridge, MA: MIT Press, 1991.

———. *Theory of Communicative Action*. Vol. 1, *Reason and the Rationalization of Society*. Translated by Thomas McCarthy. Boston: Beacon Press, 1984.

Haftmann, Werner. Postscript to *Dada: Art and Anti-Art*, by Hans Richter, 215–222. New York: Thames & Hudson, 1997.

Haraway, Donna J. "A Cyborg Manifesto: Science, Technology, and Socialist-Feminism in the Late Twentieth Century." In *Simians, Cyborgs and Women: The Reinvention of Nature,* edited by Donna J. Haraway, 149–181. New York: Routledge, 1991.

———. "Symbiogenesis, Sympoiesis, and Art Science Activisms for Staying with the Trouble." In *Arts of Living on a Damaged Planet*, edited by Anna Tsing, Heather Swason, Elaine Gan, Nils Bubandt, M25–M50. Minneapolis: University of Minnesota Press, 2017.

Hardt, Michael, and Antonio Negri. *Empire*. Cambridge, MA: Harvard University Press, 2000.

Hausmann, Raoul. "Dadaism and Today's Avant-Garde [1964]." In *Dada,* edited by Rudolf Kuenzli, 280. New York: Phaidon Press, 2006.

Hayles, N. Katherine. "Electronic Literature: What Is It?" Electronic Literature Organization. January 2, 2007. https://eliterature.org/pad/elp.html.

———. *How We Became Posthuman: Virtual Bodies in Cybernetics, Literature, and Informatics*. Chicago: Chicago University Press, 1999.

Hendricks, Jon, Gilbert and Lila Silverman Fluxus Collection. *Fluxus Codex*. New York: Gilbert/Lila Silverman Fluxus Collection in association with H. N. Abrams, 1988.

Higgins, Dick. *The Poetics and Theory of the Intermedia*. Carbondale: Southern Illinois University Press, 1984.

Higgins, Dick, Wolf Vostell, and Claes Oldenburg. *Fantastic Architecture*. London: Something Else Press, 1969.

Higgins, Hannah. "Fluxus Fortuna." In *The Fluxus Reader*, edited by Ken Friedman, 31–62. Chicester, UK: Academy Editions, 1998.

Hinton, Sam. "The Potential of the Latent Public Sphere." Australian National University. 1998. Unpublished essay.

Hockensmith, Amanda L. "Hugo Ball." In *Dada: Zurich, Berlin, Hannover, Cologne, New York, Paris*, edited by Leah Dickerman, 462–463. Washington DC: National Gallery of Art, 2005.

Home, Stewart. *The Assault on Culture: Utopian Currents from Lettrisme to Class War*. London: Aporia Press & Unpopular Books, 1988.

———. *What Is Situationism: A Reader*. Oakland, CA: AK Press, 1996.

Hossain, Rokeya Sakhawat. *Sultana's Dream: A Feminist Utopia and Selections from the Secluded Ones*. Edited and translated by Roushan Jahan. New York: Feminist Press, 1988.

Hudson, Laura. "Twine, the Video-Game Technology for All." *New York Times Magazine,* November 19, 2014. https://www.nytimes.com/2014/11/23/magazine /Twine-the-video-game-technology-for-all.html?_r=0.

Huelsenbeck, Richard. "Avant Dada: A History of Dadaism (1920)." In *Dada Painters and Poets: An Anthology,* edited by Robert Motherwell, 21–48. Boston: G. K. Hall, 1981.

———. "Der Neue Mensch." *Neue Jugend,* May 1917, 2–3.

———. "First Dada Speech in Germany (1918)." In *Dada Almanac,* edited by Richard Huelsenbeck. Translated by Malcolm Green. London: Atlas Press, 1994.

———. *Reise bis ans Ende der Freiheit: Autobiographische Fragmente (Veroffentlichungen der Deutschen Akademie fur Sprache und Dichtung Darmstadt).* Heidelberg: Verlag Lambert Schneider, 1984.

Huelsenbeck, Richard, and Malcolm Green. *The Dada Almanac.* London: Atlas Press, 1994.

Huizinga, Johan. *Homo Ludens: A Study of the Play Element in Culture.* Boston: Beacon Press, 1955.

Huntemann, Nina B., and Matthew Thomas Payne, eds. *Joystick Soldiers: The Politics of Play in Military Video Games.* New York: Routledge, 2010.

Info Wars. Directed by J. F. Sebastian. DVD. Austria: Parallel Universe, 2004.

Internationale Situationniste. "Contribution a une Definition Situationniste du Jeu." In *Internationale Situationniste 1958–1969.* Edited by Patrick Mosconi. Paris, France: Librairie Arth'eme Fayard, 1997.

———. "Definitions." In *Situationist International Anthology,* edited and translated by Ken Knabb, 51–52. Berkeley: Bureau of Public Secrets, 2006.

———. "Questionnaire." In *Situationist International Anthology,* edited and translated by Ken Knabb, 178–183. Berkeley: Bureau of Public Secrets, 2006.

———. *Internationale Situationniste 1958–69.* Amsterdam: Van Gennep, 1972.

Jameson, Fredric. *Postmodernism, or, The Cultural Logic of Late Capitalism.* Durham, NC: Duke University Press, 2003.

Jansson, Mathias. "Interview: Julian Oliver's Selectparks.net and QTHOTH (1998–1999)." May 14, 2010. https://www.gamescenes.org/2010/05/interview-julian-olivers -selectparksnet-and-qthoth-19981999.html.

Jones, Cal. "Lara Croft Female Enemy Number One?" In *From Barbie to Mortal Kombat,* edited by Justine Cassell and Henry Jenkins, 338–339. Cambridge, MA: MIT Press, 1991.

Jones, Jonathan. "Sorry MOMA, Videogames Are Not Art." *Guardian,* November 30, 2012. https://www.theguardian.com/artanddesign/jonathanjonesblog/2012/nov/30 /moma-video-games-art.

Jones, Steven Edward. *Against Technology: From the Luddites to Neo-Luddism.* New York: Routledge, 2006.

Jorn, Asger. "Notes on the Formation of an Imaginist Bauhaus." In *Situationist International Anthology,* edited and translated by Ken Knabb, 23–24. Berkeley: Bureau of Public Secrets, 2006.

Juul, Jesper. *A Casual Revolution: Reinventing Video Games and Their Players.* Cambridge, MA: MIT Press, 2010.

Kepes, György. *Arts of the Environment.* New York: George Braziller, 1972.

Khayati, Mustapha. "On the Poverty of Student Life." In *Situationist International Anthology,* edited and translated by Ken Knabb, 408–429. Berkeley: Bureau of Public Secrets, 2006.

Klüver, Billy. "Four Difficult Pieces." *Art in America* 79, no.7 (July 1991): 81–138.

Knabb, Ken. *Situationist International Anthology.* Berkeley: Bureau of Public Secrets, 2006.
———. "The Society of Situationism." 1976. http://www.bopsecrets.org/PS/situationism.htm.
Kolko, Beth, Lisa Nakamura, and Gilbert Rodman. *Race in Cyberspace.* London: Routledge, 2000.
Krauss, Rosalind E. *The Originality of the Avant-Garde and Other Modernist Myths.* Cambridge, MA: MIT Press, 1986.
Kuo, Michelle. "9 Evenings in Reverse." In *9 Evenings Reconsidered: Art, Theater, and Engineering, 1966,* edited by Catherine Morris, 31–44. Cambridge, MA: MIT List Visual Arts Center, 2006. Exhibition catalogue.
Kuenzli, Rudolf, ed. *Dada.* London: Phaidon, 2006.
Kurczynski, Karen. "A Maximum of Openness: Jacqueline de Jong in Conversation with Karen Kurczynski." In *Expect Nothing Fear Nothing: The Situationist Movement in Scandinavia and Elsewhere,* edited by Mikkel Bolt Rasmussen and Jakob Jakobsen, 183–204. Copenhagen: Nebula/Autonomedia, 2011.
Lacerte, Sylvie. "9 Evenings and Experiments in Art and Technology: A Gap to Fill in Art History's Recent Chronicles." La Fondation Daniel Langlois. 2005. https://www.fondation-langlois.org/html/f/page.php?NumPage=1716.
LaPensée, Elizabeth. "*Survivance:* An Indigenous Social Impact Game." PhD diss., Simon Fraser University, 2014.
Lazzarato, Maurizio. "Immaterial Labour." In *Radical Thought in Italy: A Potential Politics,* edited by Paolo Virno and Michael Hardt, 133–150. Minneapolis: University of Minnesota Press, 2006.
Léger, Marc James. "A Filliou for the Game: From Political Economy to Poetical Economy and Fluxus." *Racar: revue d'art canadienne / Canadian Art Review* 37, no. 1 (2012): 64–74.
Leighten, Patricia. *Re-Ordering the Universe: Picasso and Anarchism 1897–1914.* Princeton, NJ: Princeton University Press, 1989.
Leperlier, François. *Claude Cahun: L'écart et la métamorphose: Essai.* Paris: Jean-Michel Place, 1992.
Lettrist International. "Proposals for Rationally Improving the City of Paris (1955)." In *Situationist International Anthology,* edited by Ken Knabb, 12–14. Berkeley: Bureau of Public Secrets, 2006.
Levy, Steven. *Hackers: Heroes of the Computer Revolution.* Sebastopol, CA: O'Reilly Media, 2010.
Lewer, Debbie. "From the Cabaret to the Kaufleutensaal: Mapping Zurich Dada." In *Dada Zurich: A Clown's Game from Nothing,* edited by Brigitte Pichon and Karl Riha, 45–49. New York: G. K. Hall, 1996.
Lewis, Helena. *The Politics of Surrealism.* New York: Paragon House, 1988.
Lialina, Olia. "A Vernacular Web." In *Digital Folklore,* edited by Olia Lialina and Dragan Espenschied, 19–33. Stuttgart: Merz & Solitude, 2009.
Licklider, J. C. R. "Man-Computer Symbiosis." In *New Media Reader,* edited by Noah Wardrip-Fruin and Nick Montfort, 74–82. Cambridge, MA: MIT Press, 2003.
Lippard, Lucy R., ed. "The Abridged Dictionary of Surrealism." In *Surrealists on Art,* 207–211. New Jersey: Prentice-Hall, 1970.
———. *Six Years: The dematerialization of the art object from 1966 to 1972 . . .* Berkeley: University of California Press, 1997.

List, Larry. "The Imagery of Chess Revisited." In *The Imagery of Chess Revisited*, edited by Larry List, 15–136. New York: George Braziller, 2005.

Livezeanu, Irina. "'From Dada to Gaga': The Peripatetic Romanian Avant-Garde Confronts Communism." In *Littératures et Pouvoir Symbolique*, edited by Mihai Dinu Gheorghiu with Lucia Dragomir, 239–253. Bucharest: Paralela 45, 2005.

Lovejoy, Margot, Christiane Paul, and Victoria Vesna, eds. *Context Providers: Conditions of Meaning in Media Arts*. Bristol: Intellect, 2011.

Lovink, Geert. "Tactical Media, the Second Decade (Preface to the Brazilian Submidialogia publication)." São Paulo, October 2005. http://www.tacticalmediafiles.net/articles/3410 /Tactical-Media-the-Second-Decade;jsessionid=02ECA580BC711D79A05D03D372A5B15E.

Lubar, Steven. "'Do Not Fold, Spindle or Mutilate': A Cultural History of the Punch Card." *Journal of American Culture* 15, no. 4 (1992): 43–55.

Maciunas, George, Emmett Williams, Ay-o, and Ann Noël. *Mr. Fluxus: A Collective Portrait of George Maciunas 1931–1978: Based upon Personal Reminiscences*. London: Thames & Hudson, 1997.

Maciunas, George, and Robert Watts, "Proposal for the Greene Street Precinct, Inc. (ca. December 1967)." In *Fluxus Codex*, edited by Jon Hendricks. New York: Gilbert/Lila Silverman Fluxus Collection in association with H. N. Abrams, 1988, 44.

Mahon, Alyce. *Surrealism and the Politics of Eros, 1938–1968*. London: Thames & Hudson, 2005.

Malkowski, Jennifer, and TreaAndrea M. Russworm, eds. *Gaming Representation: Race, Gender, and Sexuality in Video Games*. Bloomington: University of Indiana Press, 2017.

Mallen, George. "Bridging Computing in the Arts and Software Development." In *White Heat, Cold Logic: British Computer Art 1960–1980*, edited by Paul Brown, Charlie Gere, Nicholas Lambert, and Catherine Mason, 190–202. Cambridge, MA: MIT Press, 2008.

Marcuse, Herbert. *Eros and Civilization: A Philosophical Inquiry into Freud*. Boston, MA: Beacon Press, 1974.

Markoff, John. *What the Dormouse Said: How the Sixties Counterculture Shaped the Personal Computer Industry*. New York: Penguin Books, 2005.

Marshall, Dave. "History of the Internet: Timeline." NetValley. Accessed May 5, 2020. http:// www.netvalley.com/archives/mirrors/davemarsh-timeline-1.htm.

Martin, J. V., Jan Strijbosh, Raoul Vaneigem, and Rene Viegnet. "Response to a Questionnaire from the Center for Socio-Experimental Art, (1963)." In *Situationist International Anthology*, edited by Ken Knabb, 183–188. Berkeley: Bureau of Public Secrets, 2006.

McClellan, Jim. "The Role of Play." *Guardian*, May, 13, 2004. http://www.guardian.co.uk /technology/2004/may/13/games.onlinesupplement.

McDonough, Thomas F. "Situationist Space." *October* 67 (Winter 1994): 58–77.

McDowel, Tara. "Fluxus Games." In *Game Show*, edited by Laura Steward Heon, 68–75. Cambridge, MA: MASS MoCA Publications, 2001.

McGonigal, Jane. *Reality Is Broken: Why Games Make Us Better and How They Can Change the World*. New York: Penguin, 2011.

McLuhan, Marshal. *Understanding Media*. Cambridge, MA: MIT Press, 1994.

Medina, Eden. *Cybernetic Revolutionaries: Technology and Politics in Allende's Chile*. Cambridge, MA: MIT Press, 2011.

Medosch, Armin. *New Tendencies: Art at the Threshold of the Information Revolution (1961–1978)*. Cambridge, MA: MIT Press, 2016.

Meigh-Andrews, Chris. *A History of Video Art*. New York: Bloomsbury, 2014.

Mesquita, André Luiz. *Mapas dissidentes: Proposições sobre um mundo em crise (1960–2010)*. São Paulo: Universidade de São Paulo, 2014. http://www.teses.usp.br/teses/disponiveis /8/8138/tde-15042014-100630/pt-br.php.

Michaels, Jennifer E. *Franz Jung: Expressionist, Dadaist, Revolutionary and Outsider*. New York: Peter Lang, 1989.

Mir, Rebecca, and Trevor Owens. "Modelling Indigenous Peoples: Unpacking Ideology in Sid Meyer's *Colonization*." In *Playing with the Past: Videogames and the Simulation of History*, edited by M. W. Kappell and A. B. R. Elliott, 91–106. London: Bloomsbury, 2013.

Mitnick, Kevin D., and William L. Simon. *The Art of Deception: Controlling the Human Element of Security*. Indianapolis, IN: Wiley, 2002.

Moles, Abraham A. *Information Theory and Esthetic Perception*. Translated by Joel E. Cohen. Urbana: University of Illinois Press, 1968.

Moylan, Tom. *Demand the Impossible: Science Fiction and the Utopian Imagination*. London: Methuen, 1986.

Muñoz, José Esteban. *Cruising Utopia: The Then and There of Queer Futurity*. New York: New York University Press, 2009.

Murray, Soraya. *On Video Games: The Visual Politics of Race, Gender, and Space*. London: L. B. Tauris, 2017.

Nakamura, Lisa. *Cybertypes: Race, Ethnicity, and Identity on the Internet*. London: Routledge, 2002.

Nelson, Ted. *Computer Lib: You Can and Must Understand Computers Now/Dream Machines: New Freedoms through Computer Screens—A Minority Report*. Self-Published, 1974.

New York Times. "Why German Reds Seized the Ship: Though Gift of 'Senator Schroeder' Would Make a Hit in Moscow." July 3, 1920. https://www.nytimes.com/1920/07/03 /archives/why-german-reds-seized-the-ship-thought-gift-of-senator-schroeder.html.

———. "Officials Reaffirm Red Piracy Theory." June 25, 1921. https://www.nytimes.com /1921/06/25/archives/officials-reaffirm-red-piracy-theory-belief-strengthened-by -report.html.

Nietzsche, Friedrich. *The Birth of Tragedy: Out of the Spirit of Music*. Translated by S. Whiteside. Edited by M. Tanner. London: Penguin, 1993.

Niewenhuis, Constant. "Another City for Another Life". *Internationale Situationniste* 2. December 1958. http://www.notbored.org/another-city.html.

———. "The Great Game to Come." *Potlach* 30. July 1959. https://stichtingconstant.nl/system /files/1959_the_great_game_to_come_0.pdf.

Niewenhuis, Constant, and Guy Debord. "La Déclaration d'Amsterdam." *Internationale situationniste* 2. December 1958. https://stichtingconstant.nl/system/files/1958_the _amsterdam_declaration_0.pdf.

Niewenhuis, Constant Anton. *Opstand van de Homo Ludens: Een Bundel Voordrachten en Artikelen*. Bussum: Paul Brand, 1969.

Obrist, Hans Ulrich. "Hans Ulrich Obrist in Conversation with Raoul Vaneigem." E-flux. May 2009. https://www.e-flux.com/journal/06/61400/in-conversation-with -raoul-vaneigem/.

Olea, Héctor. "Xul's Innermost Experience: The Vebivocovisual Presentiment." In *Inverted Utopias, Avant-Garde Art in Latin America*, edited by Mari Carmen Ramírez and Héctor Olea, 443–451. New Haven, CT: Yale University Press, 2004.

Oudenampsen, Meryn. "Aldo van Eyck and the City as Playground." In *Urbanacción 07/09*, edited by Ana Mendez de Andés, 25–39. Madrid: La Casa Encendida, 2010.

Papanikolas, Theresa. *Anarchism and the Advent of Paris Dada*. Surrey, England: Ashgate, 2010.

Pearce, Celia, Tracy Fullerton, and Jacki Morie. "Sustainable Play: Towards a New Games Movement for the Digital Age." *Games and Culture* 2, no. 3 (2007): 261–278.

Pederson, Claudia. "Gaming Empire: Play and Change in Latin America and Latina Diaspora." In "Mestizo Technologies: Art, Design, and Technoscience in Latin America." Special issue, *Media-N* 12, no. 1, November 2016, edited by Paula Gaetano Adi and Gustava Cembril. http://median.newmediacaucus.org /mestizo-technology-art-design-and-technoscience-in-latin-america/gaming-empire -play-and-change-in-latin-america-and-latina-diaspora/.

———. "Trauma and Agitation: Video Games in a Time of War." *Afterimage* 38, no. 2 (2010): 9–13.

Pederson, Claudia, and Nicholas Adrian Knouf. "Seized and Displayed: Seized." *Afterimage* 36, no. 2 (2008): 31–32.

Penix-Tadsen, Phillip. *Cultural Code: Video Games and Latin America*. Cambridge, MA: MIT Press, 2016.

Penny, Simon. "Virtual Reality as the End of the Enlightenment Project." In *Culture on the Brink: The Ideologies of Technology*, edited by Gretchen Bender and Timothy Druckrey, 231–249. Seattle: Bay, 1998.

Perkins, Stephen. "Utopian Networks and Correspondence Identities." In *Alternative Traditions in the Contemporary Arts: Subjugated Knowledges and the Balance of Power*, edited by Estera Milman. Iowa City: University of Iowa Museum of Art/University of Iowa Libraries, 2000. http://sdrc.lib.uiowa.edu/atca/subjugated/two_5.htm.

Pfeiffer, Ingrid, and Max Hollein, eds. *Surreal Objects*. Ostfildern, Germany: Hatje Cantz Verlag, 2011. Published in conjunction with the exhibition "Surreal Objects. Three-Dimensional Works from Dali to Man Ray" at the Schirn Kunsthalle Frankfurt, February 11–May 29, 2011.

Phadke, Shilpa, Shilpa Ranade, and Samira Khan, "Why Loiter? Radical Possibilities for Gendered Dissent." In *Dissent and Cultural Resistance in Asia's Cities*, edited by Melissa Butcher and Selvaraj Velayutham, 185–203. London: Routledge, 2009.

———. *Why Loiter: Women and Risk on Mumbai Streets*. New Delhi: Penguin Books India, 2011.

Philpot, Clive. "Fluxus: Magazines, Manifestos, Multum in Parvo." In *Fluxus: Selections from the Gilbert and Lila Silverman Collection*, edited by Clive Philpot and Jon Hendricks. New York: Museum of Modern Art New York, 1988. http://georgemaciunas.com/about /cv/manifesto-i/.

Phillips, Richard, and Waruna Alahakoon. "Hindu Chauvinists Block Filming of Deepa Mehta's Water." In *World Socialist Web Site*. February 12, 2000. https://www.wsws.org /en/articles/2000/02/film-f12.html.

Pilon, Mary. *The Monopolists: Obsession, Fury, and the Scandal behind the World's Favorite Game*. New York: Bloomsbury, 2015.

Plant, Sadie. *The Most Radical Gesture: The Situationist International in a Postmodern Age*. London: Routledge, 1992.

Poggioli, Renato. *The Theory of the Avant-Garde*. Translated by Gerald Fitzgerald. Cambridge, MA: Harvard University Press, 1968.

Popper, Frank. *Art-Action and Participation*. New York: New York University Press, 1975.

Prado, Gilbertto. *Arte Telemática: Dos Intercâmbios Pontuais aos Ambientes Virtuais Multiusuário*. São Paulo: Itaú Cultural, 2003.

Quinn, Zoë. "A Beginner's Guide to Making Your First Video Game." Kotaku. January 28, 2013. http://kotaku.com/5979539/a-beginners-guide-to-making-your-first-video-game.

———. *Crash Override: How Gamergate (Nearly) Destroyed My Life, and How We Can Win the Fight Against Online Hate*. New York: PublicAffairs, 2017.

Raabe, Paul, ed. *German Literary Expressionism Online*. Berlin: W. de Gruyter, 2008.

Ramos, Jeff. "Leaky World Creators Interview." La Molleindustria. January 24, 2011. http://www.molleindustria.org/node/327.

Rasmussen, Mikkel Bolt. "To Act in Culture While Being against All Culture: The Situationists and the 'Destruction of RSG-6.'" In *Expect Nothing Fear Nothing: The Situationist Movement in Scandinavia and Elsewhere*, edited by Mikkel Bolt Rasmussen and Jakob Jakobsen, 75–113. Copenhagen: Nebula/Autonomedia, 2011.

Rauschenberg, Robert. "Instructions for Participants in 'Open Score." In *9 Evenings Reconsidered: Art, Theatre, and Engineering, 1966*, edited by Catherine Morris, 36–37. Massachusetts Institute of Technology, MIT List Visual Arts Center, Cambridge, MA, May 4–July 9, 2006. Exhibition catalog.

Reichardt, Jasia, ed. *Play Orbit*. London: Studio International, 1969. Exhibition catalog.

Restany, Pierre. *60/90: Trente ans de Nouveau Réalisme* (Paris: La Différence, 1990).

Reyes, Juan Antonio Alvarez, ed. *Try Again*. Madrid/Gipuzkoa: La Casa Encendida/Koldo Mitxelena Kulturunea, 2008. La Casa Encendida, April 10, 2008; and Koldo Mitxelena Kulturunea, June 26–September 27, 2008. Exhibition catalog.

Rheingold, Howard. "Virtual Communities, Phony Civil Society?" Howard Rheingold.com. 1998. http://www.rheingold.com/texts/techpolitix/civil.html.

———. *The Virtual Community: Homesteading on the Electronic Frontier*. Howard Rheingold .com. 1993. http://www.rheingold.com/vc/book/2.html.

Richardson, Joanne. "The Language of Tactical Media." In *Anarchitexts: Voices from the Global Digital Resistance*, edited by Joanne Richardson, 123–128. New York: Autonomedia, 2003.

Richter, Hans, ed. *Dada: Art and Anti-Art*. Translated by David Britt. New York: Thames & Hudson, 1997.

———. *Dada 1916–1966: Documente der internationalen Dada-Bewegung*. Cologne: Verlagsgesellschaft Rudolf Muller, 1972.

———. *DADA-KUNST UND ANTIKUNST: DER BEITRAG DADAS ZUR KUNST DES 20 JAHRHUNDERTS*. Ostfildern: DuMont Reiseverlag, 1993.

Riley, Rita. *Tactical Media*. Minneapolis: University of Minnesota Press, 2008.

Robins, Kevin, and Frank Webster. "Cybernetic Capitalism: Information, Technology, Everyday Life." In *The Political Economy of Information*, edited by Vincent Mosko and Janet Wasko, 45–75. Madison: University of Wisconsin Press, 1988.

Robinson, Julia. "Scoring the Event." In *George Brecht Events: Eine Heterospektive/A Heterospective*, edited by Alfred M. Fischer, 28–33. Köln: Verlag der Buchhandlung Walther Konig, 2005.

Roditi, Edouard. "Hanna Höch Interview with Edouard Roditi." In *Dada*, edited by Rudolf Kuenzli, 231–233. London: Phaidon, 2006.

Rosemont, Penelope, ed. *Surrealist Women: An International Anthology*. Austin: University of Texas Press, 1998.

Rosen, Margit, ed. *A Little-Known Story about a Movement, a Magazine, and the Computer's Arrival in Art: New Tendencies and Bit International, 1961–1973.* Cambridge, MA: MIT Press, 2011.

Rosenzweig, Roy. *Clio Wired: The Future of the Past in the Digital Age.* New York: Colombia University Press, 2011.

Rumney, Ralph. "About the Historification of the Situationist International: Ralph Rumney in Conversation with Stewart Home, Paris 7 April 1989." Stewart Home Society. http://www.stewarthomesociety.org/interviews/rumney.htm.

———. *The Consul.* Translated by Malcolm Imrie. London: Verso, 2002.

Sadler, Simon. *The Situationist City.* Cambridge, MA: MIT Press, 1999.

Salen, Katie, and Eric Zimmerman. *Rules of Play: Game Design Fundamentals.* Cambridge, MA: The MIT Press, 2003.

Sandqvist, Tom. *Dada East: The Romanians of Cabaret Voltaire.* Cambridge, MA: MIT Press, 2006.

Sanquillet, Michel. *Dada in Paris.* Translated by Sharmila Ganguly. Cambridge, MA: MIT Press, 2009.

Sargisson, Lucy. *Contemporary Feminist Utopianism.* London: Routledge, 1996.

Sartre, Jean Paul. "For a Theater of Situations." In *The Writings of Jean-Paul Sartre.* Vol 2, *Selected Prose,* edited by Michel Rybalka, Michel Contat, and Richard McCleary, 185–186. Evanston, IL: Northwestern University Press, 1972.

Sassoon, Wilfred. "Popular 'America's Army' Video Game, Recruiting Tool Cancelled," *New York Times,* Special Edition, July 4, 2009, A8. http://www.nytimes-se.com/2009/07/04/recruiting-tool-cancelled.

Savio, Mario. "Mario Savio's Speech before the FSM Sit-In." Free Speech Movement Archives. December 3, 1964. http://www.fsm-a.org/stacks/mario/mario_speech.html.

Schaik, Martin van, and Otakar Máčel, eds. *Exit Utopia: Architectural Provocations 1956–76.* New York: Prestel Verlag, 2006.

Schank, Brian. *Avant-Garde Videogames: Playing with Technoculture.* Cambridge, MA: MIT Press, 2014.

Scheub, Ute. *Verrückt nach Leben: Berliner Szenen in den Zwanziger Jahren.* Hamburg: Rowohlt Taschenbuch Verlag, 2000.

Schleiner, Anne-Marie. "Dissolving the Magic Circle of Play: Lessons from Situationist Gaming." In *From Diversion to Subversion: Games, Play, and Twentieth-Century Art,* edited by David Getsy, 150–156. University Park: Pennsylvania State University Press, 2011.

———. "Does Lara Croft Wear Fake Polygons: Gender Analysis of the '1st Person Shooter/Adventure Game with Female Heroine' and Gender Role Subversion and Production in the Game Patch." In *Switch Journal* 9, June 14, 1998. http://switch.sjsu.edu/archive/nextswitch/switch_engine/front/front.php%3Fartc=222.html.

———. "Fluidities and Oppositions among Curators, Filter Feeders and Future Artists." *Intelligent Agent* 3, no. 1 (2003). http://www.intelligentagent.com/archive/Vol3_No1_curation_schleiner.html.

———. *The Player's Power to Change the Game: Ludic Mutation.* Amsterdam, NL: Amsterdam University Press, 2017.

———. "Velvet-Strike: War Times and Reality Games (War Times from a Gamer Perspective)." Velvet-Strike. Accessed May 5, 2020. http://www.opensorcery.net/velvet-strike/about.html.

Sedgewick, Peter. *Nietzsche: The Key Concepts.* London: Routledge, 2009.

Sengupta, Anuradha. "Tea and Selfies Driving a Revolution in Pakistan." Women's Media Center. May 31, 2016. http://www.womensmediacenter.com/news-features/tea -and-selfies-driving-a-revolution-in-pakistan.

Sezen, Tonguc. "'Huys'/'Hope'—Turkey's First Political Game." Georgia Tech News Games Blog. February 18, 2009.

Shanken, Edward. "From Cybernetics to Telematics." In Roy Ascott, *Telematic Embrace, Visionary Theories of Art, Technology, and Consciousness*, edited by Edward Shanken, 1–96. Berkeley: University of California Press, 2003.

Shaw, Adrienne, and Bonnie Ruberg, eds. *Queer Game Studies*. Minneapolis: University of Minnesota Press, 2017.

Sholette, Gregory. "Disciplining the Avant-Garde: The United States versus the Critical Art Ensemble." In *CIRCA: Contemporary Visual Culture in Ireland*, no. 112 (2005): 50–59.

Short, Emily. "Interview with Porpentine, Author of *Howling Dogs*." Emily Shot's Interactive Storytelling. November 23, 2012. https://emshort.blog/2012/11/23 /interview-with-porpentine-author-of-howling-dogs/. Accessed November 17, 2019.

SimEden.com. "An Interview with Jacques Servin: The SimCopter Scandal." Rhizome archive. http://archive.rhizome.org/artbase/1693/more/articles /simedensimcopterinterview.html.

Situationist International Online. "Unitary Urbanism at the End of the 1950s." In *Internationale Situationniste* 3, December 1959, translated by Paul Hammond. https:// www.cddc.vt.edu/sionline/si/unitary.html

Solar, Xul. "Pan-Ajedrez o Pan-Juego, o Ajedrez Criollo." In *Xul Solar: Entrevistas, artículos y textos inéditos*, edited by Patricia M. Artundo, 86–87. Buenos Aires, Argentina: Corregidor, 2006.

Spiteri, Raymond, and Donald LaCoss. *Surrealism, Politics and Culture*. Aldershot, Hants, England: Ashgate, 2003.

Stahl, Roger. *Militainment, Inc.: War, Media, and Popular Culture*. New York: Routledge, 2010.

Stalder, Felix. "30 Years of Tactical Media." In *Public Netbase: Non Stop Future: New Practices in Art and Media*, edited by Branka Curcic, Zoran Pantelic, Konrad Becker, Felix Stalder, and Martin Wassermair. Frankfurt am Main, Germany: Revolver-Archiv für aktuelle Kunst, 2008.

Stracey, Frances. "The Caves of Gallizio and Hirschorn: Excavation of the Present." *October* 116 (Spring 2006): 87–100.

———. "Destruktion RSG-6. towards a Situationist Avant-Garde Today." In *Avant Garde Critical Studies*. Vol. 20, *Neo-Avant-Garde*, edited by David Hopkins, 311–329. New York: Rodopi, 2006.

———. "Pinot-Gallizio's 'Industrial Painting': Towards a Surplus of Life." *Oxford Art Journal* 28, no. 3 (2005): 391–405.

Stryker, Susan. "My Words to Victor Frankenstein above the Village of Chamounix: Performing Transgender Rage." In *GLQ: A Journal of Lesbian and Gay Studies* no 1, vol. 3 (1994): 227–254.

Sudhalter, Adrian V. "Johannes Baader and the Demise of Wilhelmine Culture: Architecture, Dada, and Social Critique, 1975–1920." PhD diss., Institute of Fine Arts, New York University, 2005.

Sundaram, Ravi. *Pirate Modernity: New Delhi's Media Urbanism*. New York: Routledge, 2010.

The Tactical Media Files. 2008. Next 5 Minutes Festivals. http://www.tacticalmediafiles.net /n5m4/about.jsp.html.

Taylor, Seth. *Left-Wing Nietzscheans: The Politics of German Expressionism, 1910–1920*. Berlin: de Gruyter, 1990.

Tiampo, Ming. *Gutai: Decentering Modernism*. Chicago: University of Chicago Press, 2011.

Tu, Thuy Linh N., Alondra Nelson, and Alicia Hedlam Hines. *TechniColor: Race, Technology, and Everyday Life*. New York: New York University Press, 2001.

Turkle, Sherry. *Life on the Screen: Identity in the Age of the Internet*. New York: Touchstone, 1997.

Turner, Fred. *From Counterculture to Cyberculture: Stewart Brand, the Whole Earth Network, and the Rise of Digital Utopianism*. Chicago: University of Chicago Press, 2006.

———. "R. Buckminster Fuller: A Technocrat for the Counterculture." In *New Views on R. Buckminster Fuller*, edited by Hsiao-Yun Chu and Roberto G. Trujillo, 146–159. Stanford, CA: Stanford University Press, 2009.

Tzara, Tristan. *Seven Dada Manifestos and Lampisteries*. Translated by Barbara Wright. New York: New Calder Publications, 1981.

Tzara, Tristan, Franz Jung, George Grosz, Marcel Janco, Richard Huelsenbeck, Gerhard Preiss, Raoul Hausmann, et al. "Dadaist Manifest (Berlin 1920)." In *Dada 1916–1966: Documente der internationalen Dada-Bewegung*, edited by Hans Richter, 34–35. München: Goethe-Institut, 1966. Exhibition catalog.

Unattributed. "The Use of Free Time." In *Situationist International Anthology*, edited and translated by Ken Knabb, 74–75. Berkeley: Bureau of Public Secrets, 2016.

Unsigned. "Our Goals and Methods in the Strasbourg Scandal." In *Situationist International Anthology*, edited and translated by Ken Knabb, 263–273. Berkeley, CA: Bureau of Public Secrets, 2016.

Vaneigem, Raoul. *The Revolution of Everyday Life*. Translated by Donald Nicholson-Smith. London: Rebel, 2001.

Velvet Strike. http://www.opensorcery.net/velvet-strike/recipes.html.

Viénet, René. *Enragés and Situationists in the Occupation Movement: Paris, May, 1968*. New York: Autonomedia, 1993.

Virno, Paolo. "General Intellect." Generation Online. 2001. http://www.generation-online.org /p/fpvirno1.htm.

Von Neumann, John, and Oskar Morgenstern. *Theory of Games and Economic Behavior*. Princeton, NJ: Princeton University Press, 1953.

Waelder, Paul. "Interview with Natalie Bookchin." *A Minima*. January 2005. http:// newmediafix.net/aminima/bookchin.pdf.

Waldberg, Patrick. *Surrealism*. New York: Thames & Hudson, 1997.

Waldrop, M. Mitchell. *The Dream Machine: J. C. R. Licklider and the Revolution That Made Computing Personal*. New York: Penguin Books, 2001.

Wallis, Brian, Marianne Weems, and Philip Yenawine, eds. *Art Matters: How the Culture Wars Changed America*. New York: New York University Press, 1999.

Wolman, Gil G. "Address by the Lettrist International Delegate to the Alba Conference of September 1956." Translated by Reuben Keehan. https://www.cddc.vt.edu/sionline /presitu/wolman.html.

Wardrip-Fruin, Noah, and Nick Montfort, eds. *The New Media Reader*. Cambridge, MA: MIT Press, 2003.

Wardrip-Fruin, Noah. "The Pavilion." In *The New Media Reader*, edited by Noah Wardrip-Fruin and Nick Montfort, 211–212. Cambridge, MA: MIT Press, 2003.

Wark, McKenzie. *Gamer Theory*. Cambridge, MA: Harvard University Press, 2007.

———. "On the Tactic of Tactics." In *Anarchitexts: Voices from the Global Digital Resistance*, edited by Joanne Richardson, 138–140. New York: Autonomedia, 2003.

Wiener, Norbert. *The Human Use of Human Beings: Cybernetics and Society*. Boston: Houghton Mifflin, 1950.

Wilding, Faith. "Where's the Feminism in Cyberfeminism." OBN. 1998. http://www.obn.org/cfundef/faith_def.html.

Wilson, Peter Lamborn. *Escape from the Nineteenth Century and Other Essays*. New York: Autonomedia, 1998.

Winet, Jon. "In Conversation Fall 2003: An Interview with Joseph DeLappe." In *Videogames and Art*, edited by Andy Clarke and Grethe Mitchel, 94–106. Chicago: Intellect, 2007.

Wishart, Adam, and Regula Bochsler. *Leaving Reality Behind: Etoy vs eToys.com & Other Battles to Control Cyberspace*. New York: HarperCollins, 2003.

Wolf, Mark J. P., ed. *Video Games around the World*. Cambridge, MA: MIT Press, 2015.

Woodruff, Lily. "The Groupe de Reserche d'Art Visuel against the Technocrats." In *Art Journal* 73, no. 3 (2014): 18–37.

Wray, Stefan. "Rhizomes, Nomads, and Resistant Internet Use." Thing.net. July 7, 1998. http://www.thing.net/~rdom/ecd/RhizNom.html.

WTO News Releases. "The Simcopter Hack." 1996. Rhizome art base. http://archive.rhizome.org/artbase/1693/simcopter.html.

The Yes Men. Directed by Chris Smith, Dan Ollman, and Sarah Price. DVD. USA: MGM, 2005.

The Yes Men. *The Yes Men: The True Story of the End of the World Trade Organization*. New York: Disinformation, 2004.

Yoshimoto, Midori. *Into Performance: Japanese Women Artists in New York*. New Brunswick, NJ: Rutgers University Press, 2005.

Youngblood, Gene. "Bucky in the Universe." *Los Angeles Free Press*, June 5, 1970, 33, 39.

———. *Expanded Cinema*. New York: Dutton, 1970.

———. "World Game: Escape Velocity." *Los Angeles Free Press*, May 15, 1970, 24.

———. "World Game: Part Two: The Ecological Revolution." *Los Angeles Free Press*, April 10, 1970, 55, 58.

Yúdice, George. "Rethinking the Theory of the Avant-Garde from the Periphery." In *Modernism and Its Margins: Reinscribing Cultural Modernity from Spain and Latin America*, edited by Anthony L. Geist and Jose Monleon, 52–80. Minneapolis: University of Minnesota Press, 1999.

INDEX

Note: Page numbers in *italics* refer to figures.

Abstraction and Empathy (Worringer), 24
AIDS epidemic, 145, 209, 211
Albrecht, Bob, 131, 134
Albright, Thomas, 91
Allende, Salvador, 105
alternate reality game engine (SOAP), 207–8
America's Army (US Army and Ubisoft), 164–65, 166–67, 234
America's Diplomat (DeLappe), 164–65
Anthropy, Anna, 208, 216–17, 220, 223, 235; *Queers in Love at the End of the World*, 216–17, 220
anticolonial and decolonizing games and interventions: Monopoly games, 117; *Never Alone*, 16, 201, 204–7, *205*, 207, 226n52, 235; Saito and, 88; *Thunderbird Strike*, 206–7; *Tropical America*, 201–206, *202*, 235
anticolonialism: avant-garde and, 5, 20–21; cyborg theory and, 3; Dada and, 52; decolonization of education and, 191; in India, 140n81; soft technologies and, 140n81; surrealism and, 43, 52
antifascist movement and resistance, 32, 41–44, 118, 230–31
Anti-Material Cave (Pinot-Gallizio), 67, 93n33
Apollonian impulse, 24
Appel, Jan, 37
Arp, Jean, 21–22, 23, 25
Ascott, Roy, 12, 232; *La Plissure du Texte: A Planetary Fairy Tale*, 120–27, *121*
Ashby, W. Ross, 124
Association des Écrivains et Artistes Revolutionnaires (Association of Revolutionary Writers and Artists), 43
Auschwitz, 22. *See also* World War II

avant-garde, 1–2, 4–6, 10–15; anticolonialism and, 5, 20–21; Deleuze and Guattari on détournement and, 14; digital avant-garde, definition of, 11, 59; ludicism and, 6, 10–11, 14, 19–20, 24, 39, 41, 50, 231; tactical media and new avant-garde, 144–48. *See also* Dada; situationism; surrealism

Baader, Johannes, 26–27, 29, 31, 34, 36–38, 43; *Dadaisten gegen Weimar* ("Dadaists against Weimar"), 29; Huelsenbeck and, 36–37; *Jedermann sein eigner Fussball* ("Everyman His Own Football"), 29, *30*, 31; as "Oberdada," 36, 38; Plasto-Dio-Dada-Drama, 37
Bakhtin, Mikhail, 63, 92n4
Ball, Hugo, 21–26
Bannon, Steve, 219
BASIC (Beginner's All-purpose Symbolic Instruction Code), 135
Bataille, Georges, 43
Bateson, Gregory, 13, 140n80
Baudrillard, Jean, 34, 93n21, 111, 114, 138n29
Beer, Stafford, 105
Benjamin, Walter, 39; on profane illumination, 47, 56n103
Bernstein, Michele, 75–76, 94n34
Bey, Hakim (Peter Lamborn Wilson), 24, 147, 148, 150
Blank Noise, 176, *177*
Blauvelt, Andrew, 101
Bloch, Ernst, 2, 3, 188–89
Boal, Augusto, 15, 117, 191, 193, 196
Bogost, Ian, 15, 184, 185–90, 192, 195, 197, 199, 221
Bookchin, Natalie, 152–54, 233
Borges, Jorge Luis, 20, 49–51, 152, 153
Brand, Stewart, 12–13, 91, 101, 131–35, 232–33

CLAUDIA COSTA PEDERSON is Associate Professor of Art History at Wichita State University and Curator of New Media for the Finger Lakes Environmental Film Festival at Ithaca College. She has contributed to multiple journals and edited volumes on film and media.

Lightning Source UK Ltd.
Milton Keynes UK
UKHW041519090321
379824UK00019B/17